Launching Your Child In Show Biz

A COMPLETE STEP-BY-STEP GUIDE

DICK VAN PATTEN & PETER BERK

General Publishing Group
Los Angeles

Publisher: W. Quay Hays
Editorial Director: Peter L. Hoffman
Art Director: Susan Anson
Assistant Art Director: Maritta Tapanainen

For information:
General Publishing Group, Inc.
2701 Ocean Park Boulevard, Suite 140
Santa Monica, CA 90405

Library of Congress Cataloging-in-Publication Data

Van Patten, Dick.
    Launching your child in show biz : a complete step-by-step guide /
by Dick Van Patten and Peter Berk.
        p.   cm.
    Includes bibliographical references and index.
    ISBN 1-57544-013-X
    1. Performing arts—Vocational guidance—United States. 2. Child
    actors—United States.   I. Berk, Peter.   II. Title.
    PN1580.V36   1997
    792'.028'02373—dc21   96-51109
                                                            CIP

Printed in the USA by RR Donnelley & Sons Company
10 9 8 7 6 5 4 3 2 1

General Publishing Group
Los Angeles

To my sons, Nels, Jimmy and Vincent,
who followed in my footsteps as child actors,
and who I hope are having as much fun as I am.
—*Dick Van Patten*

To my wife, Diane; my sons, Jordan and Daniel;
and my parents, Howard and Lynn.
Thank you for starring in my life.
With all my love.
—*Peter Berk*

ACKNOWLEDGMENTS

The authors would like to thank the following people for their invaluable contributions to this book: Harris Sherline, Sheldon Marks, Natalia Clare, Don Grady, Mary Grady, Janice Fishman, and Marsha Hervey. We would also like to express our gratitude to General Publishing Group's Quay Hays and Peter Hoffman for their support and guidance, and to all of the performers, agents, managers, and casting directors who contributed their insights and suggestions. Finally, thanks to all child performers, not only past and present, but future—in fact, your parents may well be reading this now.

TABLE OF CONTENTS

PREFACE

This book has been written for all of you who have ever considered, even fleetingly, the possibility of launching a show business career for your child or children. Although other books have been written on this subject, we have tried to make this the most definitive and current book of its kind, one which we hope will be as entertaining as it is informative. After reading this book, we think you will see that an exciting, creative, and potentially lucrative new frontier has been opened up for your family, even if you don't happen to live anywhere near the soundstages of Hollywood or the theatrical stages of Broadway.

Although this book was a collaborative effort between two authors, *Launching Your Child in Show Biz* features recurring first-person recollections, anecdotes, and observations by Dick Van Patten. As a former child actor who not only made a silky-smooth transition to adulthood in the entertainment industry, but went on to work with a cast of children on the hit series *Eight Is Enough*, I can imagine no one more appropriate, qualified, and inspiring to help guide you and your child on what could well be one of the greatest and most rewarding adventures of your lives.

Peter Berk

FOREWORD

Having basically grown up in the entertainment industry, I've had the chance to observe the world of child actors from many different vantage points. I've seen aspiring actors who have the talent but not the personality to succeed. I've seen parents who don't know how to handle their children or how to handle themselves. I've seen kids who experience great success but can't cope with the sudden onslaught of fame. I've seen kids who feel helplessly adrift once that fame goes away.

Happily, I've also seen young performers who develop at an early age the kind of self-discipline that virtually ensures them success not only as kids, but as adults—whether in the entertainment industry or in a different line of work altogether. This self-discipline extends beyond just memorizing lines and showing up at the studio on time. It is, instead, a self-discipline based on careful preparation, a keen understanding of show business, and almost boundless perseverance.

As it happens, these are the very same qualities you will need as you guide your children toward a career in show business—qualities which this book can help you develop when you need them most: now. Needless to say, only you can ultimately forge your child's character in life, but this book can provide you with the skills, insights, and contacts to give you a competitive edge in today's increasingly competitive show business world, both professionally and personally.

These days, my career is focused on musical composition, not acting. But when I look back on my years in front of the camera, I feel especially grateful to have had supportive parents who took the time to understand the industry and who, most of all, knew that my needs as a son were far more important than my needs as a performer. By combining your own parental common sense with the information contained here, I'm confident that one day—regardless of what happens professionally—your child will be as grateful to his or her parents as I am to mine.

My best wishes,
Don Grady

INTRODUCTION

I was born in Queens, about twenty minutes from Manhattan. When I was two years old, my mother would wheel me around the neighborhood and people would stop her and say, "What a beautiful child. He should be in show business!" My mother loved the theater, and with all these people encouraging her, she took me up to John Robert Powers, then the biggest modeling agency in the world, and asked them if they would handle me. I was really very good looking, even though it's hard to believe now—pretty, curly blond hair and a cute face.

Sure enough, the agency did sign me, and by the age of three, I was starting to earn a "living" as a model. The fee was five dollars an hour and my mother would take me on the bus and subway every day to New York, some days for up to three modeling jobs. Until I was seven years old, this was my life.

One day, my mother's hairdresser said that his brother was a makeup man at MGM and that she should take me to Hollywood to try and get into films. The whole thing seemed like such a long shot, but at that point, nothing could stop my mother, not even the fact that she had no idea where the money for this cross-country trip would come from.

Ultimately, my mother—who was a physical training teacher—couldn't go, but she did wind up getting my grandmother not only to trek to California with me, but to help pay for the trip as well.

It would be nice to report that this trip launched my career in movies, but the reality was that my instincts—even at the age of seven—were right: traveling three thousand miles to see some beautician's brother was hardly a sound career move. Anyway, after three days of waiting in the MGM parking lot for a man who never even made it to the gate to meet us, the beautician's brother finally emerged and tried to "make up" for his indifference to us by keeping a picture of me—one I could, of course, have mailed to him from home.

Well, we never heard from the man again, and I sincerely hope my mother took her hairstyling business elsewhere.

Nevertheless, the one positive outcome of this ill-advised journey was the lesson I learned from my parents at the time: not to take rejection personally, and to keep persisting until someone, somehow, somewhere takes notice.

After this, I returned to modeling, meeting with agents after school and hoping against hope to make it to Broadway. My mother and I would walk up and down the streets of New York, banging on the doors of countless agents and producers, no matter how many of those doors were slammed right back in our faces. I learned something else during that period: that the parents of would-be child actors have to be even more persistent and resilient than their kids. Fortunately for me, my mother had a lot of courage, and my father—a furniture sales-man—also gave us his full support.

Finally, one agent told us he was looking for a young boy to play Melvyn Douglas's son in a play; best of all, they were looking for a *blond* young boy. Voilà! I had never acted, but I knew I literally had a "head" for the part and, indeed, I was asked to come back the next day to read for the role. Amazingly enough, I got it.

As it turned out, this was a major Broadway play, a dream come true for me, and a whopping salary (at least then) of thirty-five dollars a week. We rehearsed and rehearsed, I never worked harder, and the play closed four weeks later!

Still, I now had a credit and some credibility, both of which helped me to start landing a series of other plays, some of which happily ran a lot longer than a month. It seems I was something of a natural, and I do remember always trying to lis-ten, cooperate, and be as mature as someone under ten years old can possible be.

One of these plays wound up running a year, during which time I not only worked nights, but had to show up in school still in full body makeup the next day because it would take too long to remove after each performance at night. For the kids at my school, who could barely comprehend what my night life was all about, the sight of me looking like something out of a B movie each morning provoked more than a bit of daily snick-ering. Good thing it was worth it!

As I went from play to play, working with top directors such as Josh Logan and Max Reinhardt, and with many of the era's leading actors and actresses, the demands on my time got greater and greater, but the work itself became easier and easier. I knew I had found my niche, and I truly was enjoying what I was doing, especially when there were other kids in the cast. I didn't know any other life.

During these years, which entailed almost thirty plays in a row, I also learned that kid actors are sometimes treated strangely, like second-class citizens, and the same is true of their mothers. The key to overcoming that, then and now, is professionalism: being on time, knowing your lines, thinking about your fellow actors, and not imagining for a second that without you the show won't go on. Most of all, I learned that life as a child actor was an invaluable education. I don't agree with people who say you lose a lot of your childhood when you're in show business. It provides great discipline and, I believe, a great advantage, even when you experience rejection.

After all, you're going to be rejected in life when you grow up anyway; it's not advisable to grow up thinking life is always going to be smooth sailing. If so, you're in for a tremendous shock. Yes, there were times when I was dejected, but my parents were always loving and encouraging (a must in this business, without question). Because of learning all of this as a child, life has been a breeze for me ever since. I was used to these ups and downs and prepared for them.

Don't misunderstand, though: if a child doesn't want a show business career, then it's absolutely wrong to push him or her into one. Not only will pushing kids affect them emotionally, but chances are they will be completely unnatural as performers and put themselves right out of the competition before even getting started. On the other hand, if a child is so inclined, I feel very strongly that he or she can derive fabulous benefits from growing up as an actor, as have people such as Ron Howard and Richard Crenna, who are wonderfully well-adjusted and even more successful as adults than they were as children.

Over the years, as I grew into a teenager and older, I continued on the stage and ended up at one juncture on two separate radio soap operas: one live at 10 o'clock in the morning, and the other live at 3:45 in the afternoon. As a result, I had to leave public school and enroll in a professional children's school for young actors (more on this in Chapter Twelve) in New York where people such as Milton Berle and the director Sidney Lumet went. Best of all, that's also where my future wife, Pat, was going to school while launching her own career as a dancer. A highlight of this period was appearing in the play *O Mistress Mine* starring the legendary Alfred Lunt and Lynn Fontanne. As an aside, I recall being one of some three hundred kids who tested for this rather sizable part and that the young actor who auditioned right before me was quickly dismissed. His name? Marlon Brando.

Because this was easily the best young actor's part on Broadway (and we eventually took the show on the proverbial road), I was almost immediately offered a seven-year contract at—where else?—MGM. The beautician's brother incident had nothing to do with why I turned the offer down, though. Instead, it was on the advice of Lynn Fontanne, who dogmatically put forth what was then a very common point of view; namely, that being in the movies had nothing to do with acting, and that only the stage could be home to a "real" performer. So I stayed with the show for four more years, and I can't say I was sorry—there was virtually never an empty seat in the house during the entire run.

By the time I was approaching twenty, television was emerging and—Ms. Fontanne's advice notwithstanding—I wanted to be a part of it. Determined as ever, therefore, I auditioned for the role of Nels in a new series starring Peggy Wood called *I Remember Mama*. I found out later that another boy had actually got the part, but was promptly fired. No, it wasn't Marlon Brando again, although three of the boys who ended up playing my best friends on the show did go on to some success themselves: James Dean, Paul Newman, and Jack Lemmon. How's that for a sitcom cast?

Even though I knew television was appealing to an actor, I was still unprepared for its impact. Suddenly, it caught everybody by surprise and developed very quickly. Although I went on to play Nels—a name I gave one of my own sons, incidentally—for eight years, it only took the first three weeks of being on the air for people to stop me on the streets, sometimes screaming with excitement. I began to see just how powerful this new medium was when I realized that I was being recognized by more people from my three weeks in television than from my fifteen years in theater.

During the run of *I Remember Mama*, which was shot live, I was lucky enough to get my biggest show business break to date: the role of Ensign Pulver in the brilliant *Mister Roberts,* starring Henry Fonda. We would air *Mama* live on Friday nights from 8:00 to 8:30, and then I'd run downstairs, get in a waiting cab, change right in the taxi, and rush to the theater. Crazy but fun!

As it happened, I would later appreciate the importance of television in my life once again with the role of Tom Bradford in *Eight Is Enough.* Of course, I had been fortunate enough to appear in dozens of TV shows and feature films during the '60s and '70s, but this series not only became a public favorite, it also gave me the chance to—fittingly enough—work with a houseful of kids.

My road to *Eight Is Enough* in a way began when I did a Mel Brooks TV series in 1975 called *When Things Were Rotten,* a satire on Robin Hood. One day several months earlier while we were playing tennis at my house, Mel had come up to me and said, out of nowhere, "I know you're not a fat guy, but you have a fat man's face, a round face. I'd like you to play Friar Tuck in this series I'm doing, and we'll pad you to make you look fat." Sounded good to me.

Anyway, we went on the air and did thirteen shows we all thought were very funny, but then ABC promptly canceled the series—believing, I guess, that what was rotten was the show itself. Mel was very upset, and rightfully so, saying, "What is this? They're standing in line to see my movies, and I give them free Mel Brooks on TV and they cancel it?"

As luck would have it, though, when they canceled *When Things Were Rotten,* Fred Silverman, the head of ABC, put me under exclusive contract to the network, and I was thrilled—especially since I got paid whether I worked or not.

Soon after, in April of 1976, Fred put me in two pilots, one called *The Love Boat,* and the other, *Eight Is Enough.* In *The Love Boat,* I played the doctor, later played by Bernie Kopell (another *When Things Were Rotten* alumnus). Both pilots sold, and I was obviously very happy, not even caring which show would ultimately cast me.

Of course, it was decided that I be in *Eight Is Enough,* and I'm sure glad I was, especially since it allowed me to work with a lot of young actors with whom I became very close over the years. Adam Rich, for example, was seven years old at the time, the same age I had been when I did my first stage play. What's more, another cast member, Willie Aames, was sixteen, the same age I had been when I did *I Remember Mama*. Thanks especially to the talent of the kids on the show, the pilot went well and the series got off to a solid start.

From the beginning, I was extremely impressed with how disciplined and professional all of the young actors on the show were, always knowing their lines, always well behaved, and always a pleasure to work with. Quite simply, they were great, and the reason they were great is that each of those kids had auditioned against two or three hundred other kids for the part. Naturally, the ones that got it were the best.

I can't tell you how nice those five years were on *Eight Is Enough*. All of those young actors became like extended family members to me, and I think I was able to help them along the way by recounting my own experiences growing up in the business. I'm happy to say that we have stayed close since then and that all eight of them seem to look back on those years with very fond memories.

If you get the sense that I'm grateful for starting my career in show business at the ripe old age of three, then you are absolutely right. That's why I encouraged my own sons to also enter the business at a young age, and that's why I was so pleased to collaborate on this book.

I have a lot of respect for child actors, and I know that if they want to do it and they're good at it, they can continue in the industry and make the transition to adulthood. Most of all, they can have a great life full of fun, surprises, and recognition that no other work I know of can provide.

Certainly, there are no guarantees and there may be untold obstacles ahead, but as far as I'm concerned, if you have a shot at the wonderfully fulfilling kind of career I have been so lucky to have, the risk is more than worth it.

Enough about me, then. Let's now turn the spotlight on you—and your child.

CHAPTER
ONE

NOTHING'S IMPOSSIBLE

He was born in Canada, and like most other Canadian boys, he hoped one day to become a professional hockey player. Unfortunately, he took after his 5'6" father and 5' mother and stopped growing around the age of fourteen, which left him no alternative but to turn his career ambitions in an entirely new direction (maybe a blessing in disguise, considering the dozens of facial stitches his face had acquired along the way!).

The new direction was music, and so he played guitar and earned a few dollars with a local band named Helix. But soon he had to admit he was on thin ice in that field as well.

His mother says the first time he brought up the idea of acting was when he announced plans to join a high school drama group in order to meet girls. Ironically, he was convinced that the only roles he would ever get would be as the proverbial Best Friend, "the guy who *never* gets the girl." Perhaps even more ironically, his own parents—loving and supportive as they were—had trouble taking his interest in an acting career seriously.

Nevertheless, *he* did, eventually moving to Los Angeles and exploring virtually any opportunity available to him. Then, at last, his hard work and endless determination paid off with the big break that would turn him into a star: a regular role on a new family sitcom for NBC.

Big break and all, however, he was still sharing a one-room apartment, couldn't afford a car of his own, and had to be picked up most mornings by one of the stars of the show. When *People* interviewed him for a cover story in 1987, he said, "My roommate saw this beautiful blonde in a Mercedes with a sunroof picking me up every day and figured I had it made."

Well, as it happened, he and the beautiful blonde were just friends, but his roommate was right about one thing: He *did* have it made. In fact, not only did he become the Emmy-winning costar of one of the decade's most popular and acclaimed shows, but he also wound up as the motion picture leading man he had been sure he'd never be.

The point in relating this one actor's story is to show you that most of today's young stars started off much like your child is today. With only a few exceptions, these kids had no special advantage of which to speak. No millionaires bankrolling them. No relatives in the business hiring them. What they *did* have in common was just a great deal of determination, patience, professionalism, and luck (which at the beginning sometimes plays the biggest "role" of all!).

Chances are you already have the right amount of determination on behalf of your child, and hopefully you'll have the necessary patience and luck as well. The only missing ingredient in your recipe for success, then, is professionalism. Quite simply, you need to know the ins and outs of this highly complex business.

There are no shortcuts. Every bit of knowledge you acquire will become a factor in giving you an edge over the competition, and arming you with that knowledge is what this book is all about. Here, you'll learn in detail what to do and, of equal importance, what not to do. You'll be exposed to the hard facts and be given the advice of leading experts in the industry, while also being entertained and enlightened by child stars of the past and present. Moreover, you'll be provided with essential in-depth lists of everything from top agents to vital show business publications and other important tools to ensure that you always know just where to turn every step of the way.

Before moving forward, however, maybe a few words of encouragement from Marcie Leeds will offer the proper inspiration. The young actress who played the Barbara Hershey character as a child in *Beaches*, Marcie says, "What counts most is having hope. You can never quit. You must keep going if this is what you want. If you stop, you'll never get to the finish line. But take it at your own pace and don't be worried about how long it takes. Nobody can fit every role. Just keep looking ahead and let it come naturally. All I know is that it worked for me."

The young man from Canada might well have said the very same thing. As you may have guessed, the series he costarred in was *Family Ties*, the blond driver of the Mercedes was Meredith Baxter, his movies have included *Back to the Future* (and its two sequels) and the appropriately titled *Secret of My Success*, and his latest TV series is *Spin City*.

As if you didn't know, his name is Michael J. Fox.

RECOGNIZING TALENT IN YOUR CHILD

AND "ACTING" ON IT

Has it ever occurred to you that your own child could be a star someday? Actually, it occurs to millions of parents around the country every year. After all, what parents wouldn't want their child to enjoy that kind of fame, respect, wealth, and creative freedom?

The problem is that most parents casually write off the whole idea as nothing more than a pipe dream. Something only *other* people's kids will ever have. Something that's a lot of fun to talk about, yet could never really happen to them.

Nevertheless, you're reading this book because you want to do more than just fantasize about your child making it to the top in show business. You want to find out how to turn your words into action. And the first two steps in that process are this: pinpointing your kid's talents and making them work in your favor, and making sure you and your child are emotionally prepared for what's ahead.

YOUR CHILD: FROM PLAY ACTING TO REAL ACTING

As eager as you are to get going, remember it's not enough for *you* to want your child to succeed as a performer. Your child must want it as much, if not more: *He's* the one who's going to have to take those lessons and give those readings; *she's* the one who will need to invest a great deal of free time today to achieve a show business career tomorrow. I vividly remember, for example, planning to go on a sleigh ride one afternoon as a child, and having to give it up to go on an audition. I wasn't happy at the time, but now, of course, I'm very happy I went because I'll venture that my life has turned out better than the lives of the kids who played in the snow that day.

Definitely remember, then, that regardless of how you feel about it, *developing the necessary drive and determination will ultimately be up to your child.*

Before the two of you even discuss a show business career, though, there are definite signs to look for—signs that indicate this is a child who will keep trying until he or she makes it.

- Does your child enjoy attention?
- Is your child energetic (rarely a problem)?
- Is he or she a born ham? (If not, don't worry—I was a shy child but became so enveloped in the characters that I would overcome that shyness when performing.)
- Does your child see professional kids performing and say, "I could be just as good as they are"?
- Does your child show a strong interest in entertainment and entertainers?
- Does your child ever talk about being an actor when he or she grows up?
- Is the child creative, displaying an active imagination?
- Does your child usually finish what he or she starts?

If your child passes this "test," you'll be starting out in good shape. If not, you can still look for hidden qualities. For example, ask if he or she is willing to give performing a try. Chances are your child will be interested if not excited by the whole idea. Whatever you do, however, be positive and upbeat. Treat the idea as a chance to share some very enjoyable times, because that's exactly what will happen.

After a few interviews, auditions, and then jobs, your child will probably be so motivated that you can't keep up. But if you still have the strength, pat yourself on the back. The main hurdle will have been crossed. You and your child will be sharing a rare and thrilling adventure. You'll be closer than ever before. You'll be a team.

You bet. Unfortunately, some parents miss out because they fail to recognize that fact. In reality, every child is talented in some way or another. Sure, some kids are already mini-Pacinos or Streisands at seven, but that doesn't mean they'll get all the jobs. *In most cases, what agents look for isn't the traditional kind of talent at all.* It's a knack for coming across relaxed and natural. For expressing oneself honestly. For listening and interacting with others. For memorizing lines and interpreting characters. For showing enthusiasm and a willingness to work hard. For caring about doing the best job possible. Without all that, even the most gifted prodigy in the world will be in for a tough time in the job market.

Of course, even though today's successful young actor must first and foremost seem just like the kid next door, special skills are sometimes still essential. By all means, then, encourage your child to take singing and dancing lessons (particularly if he or she is intrigued by the musical theater). And keep in mind that even seemingly unrelated skills, ranging from baton twirling to roller skating to baseball, will probably also come in handy someday. In short, every talent your child masters will contribute to greater well-roundedness as a performer *and* a person.

"There's no way a parent can know which artistic area a child will excel in," says director Bob Williams, whose son, R.J., has been acting since he was three, has appeared in dozens of television shows and commercials, and a few years ago landed the starring role in the weekday morning children's show *Wake, Rattle & Roll.*

"You have to open up the creative horizons of children however you can and then let them find their own way. They don't start off by saying, 'Here I am, I'm a star!' They find their own niche, move at their own pace, and develop their own potential."

Another expert on this subject, along with countless others who have gone through the same experience, is Andrea Pruett, whose son, Harold, already has had a long career in film. A few years back, he secured a plum weekly role on Fox Television's *Outsiders.*

Andrea feels her son's multifaceted schooling was beneficial to his career from the very outset. In fact, his training as a singer and dancer secured him a regular spot on *The Tim Conway Show*, while his talents as an actor led him to roles in everything from *Sybil* to *Wonder Woman*. Not surprisingly, Harold earned a reputation around Hollywood as a jack-of-all-trades.

Says Andrea, a Georgia native who essentially has served as her son's personal manager for most of his career, "You must keep in mind that every ability your child has will only put him or her at an advantage in this very competitive business. The more a child understands what it means to be professionally trained along the way, the more that child will mature as a performer. After all, as kids grow in this business, some of the things that were once cute and natural suddenly seem awkward and forced. That's why they're so much better off if they can do a variety of things well and really begin to understand what performing is all about."

Therefore, *develop any and all talents you can in your child, but not at the expense of his or her own identity and personality.*

Help kids find their way. Don't attempt to turn them into someone they're not, because—and this can't be stressed enough—no casting director responds to an overly "mannered" or overtrained child. Even adult actors are often at risk of losing their innate naturalism if they opt for too much, or *any,* professional training. Once, on the set of a movie, I saw this for myself when two well-known actors—one a longtime, highly trained, and internationally famous actor and the other a comedian trying to venture into dramatic acting—had a scene together, and it was the comedian who by far turned in the more convincing performance. The reason is simple: He was working from pure instinct instead of from careful planning, and the result was an element of believability and easy naturalness that brought the scene to life.

Ideally, however, your child will be learning the skills and disciplines of an adult, while still boasting the naturalness of a child. Among casting agents, that's known as the best of both worlds.

LOOKING GOOD

You probably grew up hearing the cliché, "Don't judge a book by its cover." In show business, however, the unfortunate truth is that *your child's workload will often depend more on looks than on talent.* For television and print ads, especially, casting directors want kids who project a certain image for the product. In their minds, a child doesn't have to be a brilliant actor as long as he or she has the "right" look.

And what is the "right" look? Happily, there is no easy answer to that, because the industry is more open to different types now than at any time in its history. Just check out a recent sampling of TV shows, commercials, films, and print ads. You'll immediately see that the so-called "character" child is all the rage.

Put another way, *there's more hope than ever for ALL aspiring young actors.* Tall, short, fat, thin, handsome, homely, tough, soft, Caucasian, African-American, Hispanic, Asian. These days, everyone has a shot. The casting system in the entertainment business is still far from perfect. But it's improving every day. Though comparable figures aren't available for young people, recent Screen Actors Guild reports showed that acting opportunities for adult minority members, especially African-Americans, have shown a marked increase since 1990. These reports, spanning the realms of feature films, television, and commercials, suggest not only that the industry is at last opening its doors to talented people of *all* ethnicities, but that audiences are more and more willing to embrace actors and commercial spokespeople of all ethnic backgrounds as well. High time, needless to say.

When you consider the career stature of a Dustin Hoffman or a Dudley Moore—people who don't boast much in the way of *physical* stature—it's also clear that audiences today enjoy watching "real" people on the screen. This applies to children, too. For that reason, you can't dismiss your child's chances simply because he or she could drop a few pounds, is exotic looking, or is a member of a minority. If anything, the less the child looks like a "movie star," the better off he or she may be.

There are, however, a few unwritten rules within the industry. For example, casting directors try to find kids who resemble the actors playing their parents and siblings, who can listen to instructions, and who aren't shy or too soft-spoken. In addition, they prefer hiring kids who are a bit small for their age and can play younger characters since there are fewer labor regulations governing the employment of older children.

Whatever the age, sex, or background of the child, casting directors mainly look for what most of them can only describe as "something special." Their job is to find the future Jonathan Taylor Thomas (*Home Improvement, Man of the House*) or Olsen twins. Maybe it will be your child's sweet smile that will win them over. Or that freckly face. Or possibly the way his hair covers his eyes. You can't know. There's no book you or a casting director could read that defines exactly what it takes when it comes to a child's looks. Even within the entertainment business, there's no one set rule on the subject. It's all subjective and it's always changing.

So *don't concern yourself with wondering whether your child's looks meet some imaginary standard you have in mind.* Diversity is in. Any child has a chance to charm a casting director. If you're worried that your child's looks aren't "trendy" (whatever that means), forget it. Maybe someday he or she will be the one whose looks set trends.

PARENTS: GETTING MOTIVATED

Chances are you're tired of watching someone else's child peddling that brand of cereal or starring in a weekly sitcom. After all, your kid is just as cute and smart as any working young actor around. In other words, you're not only motivated, you're downright teed off!

Good—because you have a fight ahead. This is a tough, competitive business, and you can't let anyone or anything discourage you from fulfilling your goals. Not other parents, not agents or directors, and—most of all—not yourself. You won't have the luxury of waiting for things to happen. You're going to have to *make* them happen. And to do that, you must first get motivated.

As part of getting motivated, you will need to make a very big commitment to your child's new career. A commitment to stay on top of all casting opportunities, whether you have an agent or not. To have the right materials (photos, résumés) ready, day and night. To always keep one or two complete outfits for your child nearby and ready to wear in case a last-minute audition comes up. To learn at least something about how to read contracts and manage money. To build up your child's confidence constantly. To help him or her understand roles and memorize lines. To spend a sizable chunk of your week making calls, reading industry publications, sending out materials, and sitting behind the wheel of your car. Essentially, to give up a part of your life to alter the course of your child's life.

A key point: It's entirely possible to be both an ambitious parent and a nice person. Balance friendliness with determination and you'll be every agent's and director's dream come true. Don't forget: A child is judged in part by his parents. *Pushy parents can kill a child's career even before it's started.* The better impression you make, the better the chances of success will be down the line.

Andrea Pruett admits there are a few stereotypical "stage mothers" out there (a few fathers, too), but is proud to say that when it comes down to it, she is more stage mother than personal manager. "I think stage mothers have basically gotten a bad rap," she notes, and I couldn't agree more. After all, when a mother wants her son or daughter to become a doctor or lawyer, everyone admires her pride and determination, but when she is thinking show business, everyone cries "Stage Mother!" as if they're dirty words.

As Andrea also notes, "There are a lot of very good parents out there who've learned how to be competitive without being overly pushy, demanding, or obnoxious. These are mothers and fathers who are willing to put in fourteen-hour days to get their children's careers off the ground, but are smart enough not to alienate other actors, other parents, or the children themselves in the process. If *that's* the definition of what a stage mother is, I plead guilty!"

ENCOURAGING YOUR CHILD

As you work more and more closely to prepare for this exciting new phase of your child's life, remember that you are a chief inspiration and source of strength. Encourage your child every step of the way. Say how proud you are. Reward him or her emotionally for each new accomplishment. *Set the right example by being patient, confident, and supportive.* After all, it could end someday, so make sure your relationship will stay firmly in place no matter what happens.

As much as your child wants to embark on this new career, he or she is bound to feel a little uncertain here and there. So keep expressing how much you love and believe in your child until those uncertainties disappear. The secret is to work *with* the child, not *on* the child. To act like a parent, not like an agent.

IN REVIEW
----

1. *Don't assume your children aren't qualified for show business.*
2. *You may entice them, but wanting a show business career must ultimately be their choice.*
3. *They must be ready to accept the hard work ahead.*
4. *It's a good sign if they are energetic, communicative, creative, imaginative, and receptive to attention.*
5. *Any and all looks are acceptable in today's market.*
6. *Don't think children won't make it because they don't look like a "movie star," have unusual features, or are members of a minority.*
7. *Casting agents prefer hiring kids who are a bit small for their age, so they can play younger roles.*
8. *Good looks aren't important today, but agents look for kids who are expressive and have charisma.*
9. *Develop any and all talents possible in your children.*
10. *Remember that being natural is the greatest talent a young actor can have.*
11. *Don't wait for things to happen.* Make *them happen!*
12. *Be prepared for the long hours and constant demands ahead.*
13. *Becoming overly aggressive may alienate the agents, producers, and directors you meet.*
14. *Support your kids by showing patience, love, and pride in their accomplishments.*

CHAPTER
TWO

WHAT ARE THE TARGETS?

A wide variety of careers fall under the general heading of show business. As confusing as it can sometimes be to find which one is best suited to your child, *you'll need to understand the full range of options available before you get started.* You'll want to know what's out there, and how to attain it. You'll need to understand the *business* of show business.

First, assuming he or she is old enough, discuss with your child what area of entertainment is most appealing. Would he or she like to be in movies? In commercials? In a TV series? On the stage? What about becoming a model? Or a singer? Or maybe a voice-over performer for cartoons? The reality is that, at least in the early stages of a career, your child will not have the luxury of choosing the precise nature of the jobs being offered, but will rather be glad to accept almost anything he or she is offered. On the other hand, by keeping some ultimate show business targets in mind along the way, you and your child can better direct the course of a career once your child does have more choice in the matter.

With this in mind, let's review all of the opportunities out there.

FILMS

As I mentioned earlier, film was looked down upon as an industry stepchild when I was a young actor, just as television was first looked down upon by film actors in the early '50s. Today, of course, for many parents and children alike, there's no more compelling fantasy than that of becoming a movie star.

The benefits are clear enough. High visibility. Exciting locales. Good money. Creative versatility. But keep in mind that working in movies involves a rather lengthy commitment of time. Time that might deliver even wider exposure and larger paychecks, even though money *isn't* the main objective. In addition, film assignments may well require your child to pull out of school for a bit and perhaps even live away from home. A small price to pay for such tremendous rewards, but worth considering nonetheless.

TV

From the point of view of job and financial security, almost nothing can beat a regular role in a TV series. From the Brady Bunch to the Cosby kids, young performers on hit series have become like old friends. These kids aren't just actors playing a role. They're more like family members who step into our living rooms every week.

Although series are usually cast in New York and Los Angeles, the majority of them are filmed or taped on the West Coast. Before the show becomes a series, however, it is presented to commercial networks, cable networks, and syndication companies as a pilot, and then tested for audience response. Pilots take from one to three weeks to film, depending on whether the projected series is in half-hour or hour-long episodes. Like series, most pilots are shot in and around Hollywood. So be ready for an extended visit out there once your child is cast.

For each TV series that has made it on the air, hundreds of pilots have failed to make the grade. After all, how many cop shows or family sitcoms can there be? But don't let that discourage you. If a child actor is lucky enough to be cast in a pilot, that alone reflects a considerable vote of confidence in him or her. It means the casting agent and producer thought the child had the right stuff to appear each and every week. So even if your child does do a couple of pilots that are clunkers, it's a big step in the right direction. Your child still has impressive new credits and excellent footage to show casting personnel. With that going for an actor, someday there will likely come a pilot that does get off the ground.

COMMERCIALS

Commercials frequently offer the ideal training and proving ground for up-and-coming actors. Over the years, they have helped launch the careers of so many top actors that they must be considered seriously as a viable starting point. In fact, commercials often represent a tremendous challenge to the ability of a performer. Remember, an entire idea or message must be delivered convincingly in less than a minute!

Happily, the commercial world is open to children and teenagers (as well as adults) of all physical types. At long last, the advertising executives who often determine casting know that commercials must reflect the variety found in real life. This means employing actors who run the physical gamut from A to Z.

Flip the channels and you'll understand why commercials are actually considered by many to be typical of this country— a kind of "melting pot." Largely because of this, commercials offer the greatest range of opportunities for the greatest variety of performers.

Keep in mind one bit of reality, however: Shooting commercials can be among the most grinding and boring work available to a child, especially when you consider the number of takes and level of pressure generally involved. I still remember my son Vincent doing an all-day shoot for Colgate when he was four and having to wear an Eskimo suit, no less, with fake snowflakes getting in his eyes all day and with a decidedly unglamorous "spit bucket" located just off-camera for the actors to remove evidence of previous takes. Nevertheless, Vince never complained and earned more than enough to compensate for that one day of spitting, sweating, *and* snowflakes.

Commercials, then, could easily be your child's passport to success. They might not be one's lifework, but they just might lead to a lifetime *of* work in show business.

STAGE

Once again, this is an area that involves hard work but offers endless reward for those who are willing to invest the time and effort. Be it in a drama, comedy, or musical, your child will know what it's like to be applauded by an audience after every single performance. Actors probably never experience a better feeling of fulfillment than that which comes from direct contact with a live audience. Having been in countless stage productions over the years, including a Chicago production of *Showboat* produced by Harold Prince from late 1996 through early 1997, I can certainly tell you from personal experience just how thrilling performing in front of a live audience can be.

The stage is also a perfect training ground for most actors, young and old. Over the years it has produced many of our finest performers in all media. The song "There's No Business Like Show Business" expresses the magic of live theater that captures the heart and mind of any born actor, child or veteran. The stage provides the wonderful direct audience connection that many performers feel acting is all about. And by allowing young actors to develop that kind of give-and-take with an audience, the theater teaches them how to relate better to other people, not only as a performer, but long after the curtain has come down as well.

Switching to the stage, though, is sometimes a difficult transition for an actor accustomed to working before the camera. Playing before a live audience is a very different experience, and for some it's unnerving, or perhaps boring because of the repetition involved. Two years into the play *The Skin of Our Teeth*, for example, I had grown so weary of having to repeat the same lines every night that I actually started forgetting them on stage until Tallulah Bankhead reminded me that the lines were *new* to each night's audience.

Fortunately, many other young actors adjust quickly and even thrive on the stage. A case in point is Ron Howard, who started as a very young film actor. One of his earliest roles was with Robert Preston in *The Music Man*, and later he played Opie Taylor in the long-running *Andy Griffith Show* on television. Still later, when he turned eighteen, Ron made yet another adjustment by performing every week in front of a live studio audience in *Happy Days*, and it was clear that he made that adjustment beautifully. Not only as an actor, I should add, but as a person, as reflected in the fact that he never once let his ego become bruised when one of the show's costars, Henry Winkler, started getting the majority of the attention from the public and the majority of the applause during live tapings.

In fact, Ron is an ideal illustration of a child actor who branched out successfully into many areas of the business over time. Always an avid student of filmmaking, he started directing many years back and since then has created such hits as *Splash*, *Cocoon*, *Parenthood*, *Apollo 13*, and *Ransom*. What's more, Ron is also one of the corporate heads of Imagine Films, where he is able to combine his creative instincts as an actor and director with good business sense on an everyday basis. With a multifaceted success story such as Ron Howard's in mind, kids are well-advised to use free time on the set to learn whatever they can about the process as a whole (without getting in the way), just in case they someday think of stepping behind the camera themselves.

PHOTO MODELING

Tom Selleck. Cybill Shepherd. Brooke Shields. When you hear these names, you think movie or TV star, not model. Yet all of these celebrities, and many others like them, owe their present success to their past experience as photo models. The lesson is clear. Holding up a bottle of cologne in a magazine layout today could lead to being on the cover of that same magazine tomorrow.

Every job leads to another. So even if your child doesn't see modeling as a career choice now, it shouldn't be dismissed. Not by a long shot. On the line are more credits, more contacts, more visibility, and more dollars. All of which could lead your child straight to where he or she wants to be, whether that's in front of a movie or TV camera or in front of a live audience. Also, make it clear to your child that modeling doesn't always have to do with fashions or products found in magazines such as *Cosmopolitan* or *GQ*. You're also talking about print ads for everything from spaghetti sauce to household appliances. That's why being tall, thin, and "good-looking" are only assets, not guarantees of fame and fortune.

In the other extreme, yours may be a child who is interested
only in modeling. Great! Anyone hear Cheryl Tiegs or Christie
Brinkley complaining? A career in modeling offers boundless
opportunities for excitement and achievement. If that's what
your child wants now, or decides he or she wants later, offer
support all the way.

IN THE MEANTIME, IN-BETWEEN TIME
(OTHER JOBS TO CONSIDER)

"Oh, what a cute daughter you have. So, when do those braces
come off?" "I guess zits run in your family." Sound familiar?
Well, it's true that even kids facing such normal youthful
unpleasantness can still get top jobs in film, on TV, and on the
stage. But just in case your child *is* in this "twilight-zone" phase
of growing up and you're concerned about marketability, why
not consider a few alternate forms of work?

For example, there is a good living to be made in voice-
over work. This can entail anything from doing TV and radio
commercials to narrating documentaries or recording books
on tape. As you might imagine, your child's chances will be
substantially increased if he speaks clearly and confidently. Just
tell him to think about another kind of M.O.M., as in
*M*inimum *O*f *M*umbling.

Check out five TV spots featuring kids and at least one of
the voices you're hearing probably doesn't belong to the child
you're seeing. It actually belongs to a professional voice-over
actor. The youngster on the screen was apparently pleasing to
the eye, but not to the ear. And because of that, another child
got a job recording a voice-over.

There are numerous other ways a voice-over actor can apply
that craft. Be it on Saturday morning cartoons or Christmas
recordings, the work is there.

Other types of jobs to think about for your child include
work as an "extra" (there's a special guild for this, discussed
in Chapter Thirteen); educational and industrial shows ranging from filmed corporate pieces on the wonders of car tires
to live productions at trade conventions; or performing in the
innumerable children's videos made every year. There is even
quite a demand for modeling select parts of the body. Just

think how many ads show close-ups of products being held by hands, rubbed on elbows, sprayed on hair, inhaled by noses, or applied to feet.

Don't let pride get in your way. There's absolutely nothing wrong with any of these fields, especially on a temporary basis. The idea is to get work and get established in the industry. You know your child has more to look forward to than holding up a candy bar in a commercial. But patience is the name of the game here. Let your child make a few dollars as a hand model now. Hopefully, the rest of the body will soon follow.

IN REVIEW
----

1. *Try to have definite goals in mind.*
2. *Film may be the ultimate target career, but involves a big commitment of time—possibly away from home.*
3. *Landing a regular role on a TV series isn't easy, but can lead to tremendous creative and economic rewards.*
4. *Many consider commercials to be the best showcase for young actors.*
5. *Working on the stage teaches kids about acting and about interacting with others in real life.*
6. *Stars such as Tom Selleck, Cybill Shepherd, and Brooke Shields all got their starts as models.*
7. *Don't forget other possibilities such as voice-over acting, working as an extra, or specialized modeling.*

CHAPTER
THREE

WHERE ARE WE GOING?

Once you and your child have made the decision to move forward and have at least some idea of the field on which to concentrate, sit down and map out a definite course of action. There's a big difference between *feeling* ready to get started and actually being ready to get started. And the first step toward *being* ready is to...

BE AWARE!

To really compete in today's marketplace, you must do everything in your power to understand that marketplace. Be aware! The information and insight you need are available with a minimum of difficulty or money.

To begin with, you and your child should *watch the kids who are already working* in show business. Analyze what you see and try to figure out what it is they have in common. Try to determine what makes for success today. Let simple observation of kids on screen, on stage, and as models tell you who's hot and who isn't (even though you're not out to "clone" someone else). Once again, be aware.

One of the best ways to find out what's going on in show business is to subscribe to the various industry magazines (referred to as the "trades"). These are invaluable not only for the news stories and feature articles they contain, but for their extensive lists of agencies, casting opportunities, and current productions, as well as ads offering everything from top photo reproduction services to quality printers. For your purposes, the most important of these magazines are

Variety. Published weekly in New York and daily in Hollywood, it is considered the bible of the entertainment business. Receiving the daily version will keep you fully up to date on all film and TV projects now shooting or scheduled for the near future (complete TV lists are published every Thursday, film lists every Friday). Weekly *Variety* provides the added bonus of national casting information.

Hollywood Reporter. A companion to daily *Variety* and required reading by most people who follow show business, the *Reporter* similarly combines hard news stories with lighter features and interviews. Although casting information is offered, it tends to cover only the Hollywood market. Complete listings of all film productions are included every Tuesday; TV productions are listed the first and third Tuesday of each month.

Drama-Logue. Published every Thursday, this weekly offers a comprehensive listing of union and nonunion film, TV, and stage productions, in addition to extensive casting news (although it is geared toward the Hollywood area).

Back Stage. A New York version of *Drama-Logue*, it contains substantial casting information for the East Coast area.

Show Business. Also published in New York, it includes highly useful lists of agents, managers, casting directors, advertising agencies, and casting opportunities.

Dance Magazine. A New York–based monthly featuring news and stories covering all areas of the dance world.

You'll find subscription information on these publications in the back section of this book.

Depending on the state in which you reside, there may be numerous other ways to find out what is going on in show business in your area. In the back of this book, you'll also find regional information concerning, among other things, casting offices and modeling and talent agencies. You'll notice that in certain states no such offices are listed, but in every case you'll find a film commission or a government office that is aware of productions planned in the vicinity and can direct producers and casting people to talent sources. A nearby SAG, AFTRA, or

ACTRA office may be helpful, too. If all these places are of no help, get in touch with the Theater Arts department at your nearest college or university. Producers and casting directors frequently turn to them for actors and extras.

In certain states, casting offices and modeling and talent agencies are one and the same. When you call them, try to find out as much as you can about their specializations. Kids? Extras? TV? Movies? Commercials? Modeling? That way, when you do get an interview for your child, you'll be armed with all the information you need.

It's not unusual for casting offices or casting directors to give classes in acting and "cold" readings for commercials, scene study classes, and commercial workshops. If there are no acting coaches in your vicinity, this kind of training can be invaluable. And since these individuals interface regularly with the production community, there is an added advantage in training with them.

GOING PUBLIC

As your own awareness of the business broadens, make certain your child is broadening his or her experience, too. School plays, talent contests, community theater, singing in a choir— these are all means of cultivating one's confidence as a performer. Along those same lines, *encourage your child to enroll in any type of class or program that will offer experience in front of the public*, even if it seems to have no direct bearing on a show business career.

Most children, unless they are born hams, may be reluctant at first to face an audience, even one made up of immediate family members. For that reason, don't make the mistake of turning every social occasion into showtime. Like everything you'll be doing, this should be a gradual process, not a crash course. Pace yourself and your child. Let your child get to the point where he or she *wants* to entertain in front of company or among friends. It's only when that seed is planted that success is able to grow.

CLASS ENCOUNTERS

Just how much training does your child need? Are acting, singing, or dancing classes required, or does natural talent suffice?

The answer in great part depends on your child. In my son Vincent's case, he was virtually never out of work and starred in three TV series as a child and young man, but never had a day's worth of formal training.

Certainly, though, a young performer anxious to work on the musical stage will need professional instruction in singing, dancing, or both. On the other hand, a dramatic actor might cruise along on natural talent alone, at least in the beginning.

The best rule of thumb is to develop every talent your child exhibits, time and money permitting. Obviously, no child should be expected to juggle too many show business classes at the same time. But by examining what natural talents your child has, what target career you both have in mind, and what amount of training your budget will allow, you will reach the right course of action. Each talent you foster may prove very useful someday.

The next crucial consideration, then, is the age at which you should start your child's training. Although it ultimately depends on the type of training involved, most teachers and agents agree that *there is such a thing as starting a child's show business training TOO early.*

ACTING

Although some pros feel differently, the general consensus in the business is that formal acting training should begin no earlier than at eight years old. The thinking is that children are better off just being their natural selves during those early formative years rather than learning someone else's method of acting.

Bob Williams is one expert who's clearly opposed to sending very young children to acting classes. "Even though I'm a director myself," he says, "I never wanted to give my son line readings or tell him how to act, because it could turn out that the director he's working for is after an entirely different interpretation. Also, a lot of drama coaches have never worked in the business and don't really understand how it all works. As far as I'm concerned, if you take thirty people in a class and teach them all the same thing, you're stamping everyone out of a mold and neglecting each child's individuality."

Judy Savage launched her own talent agency several years ago in Los Angeles and has represented such young actors as Chad Allen (*St. Elsewhere*) and Brice Beckham (*Mr. Belvedere*) along the way. She agrees that children up to six or seven years old have a special brand of naturalness that should be left alone. At the same time, however, she makes an exception when it comes to kids taking commercial workshops, where they can learn how to do commercials and get a feel for the lingo of the business (these workshops are often advertised in the trades).

According to Judy, "When kids turn ten or eleven, they might *then* need to start studying acting more formally. Something happens to their natural, outgoing personalities and they start getting more self-conscious and less open. A good acting class can help open them up again. But kids younger than that should just be allowed to be themselves."

Diane Hardin and Nora Eckstein formed the Young Actors Space, a highly regarded acting workshop in Los Angeles. Diane set out to be an actress herself, and in fact spent the '50s, '60s, and '70s working mainly on stage, but also in films and in TV commercials (for Hills Bros. coffee and Cheers detergent, among other products). Her work as a teacher began in the mid-'70s, thanks to a situation that sounds like something from a movie itself.

Living in Santa Monica, California, at the time, Diane went to her kids' PTA meeting one night and heard the school principal tell everyone about nine somewhat delinquent boys who were causing problems for the other students. As someone who knew firsthand how enjoyable and gratifying improvisation can be, Diane decided to offer to coach this emotionally unstable group. And as it turned out, she wound up not only helping all nine kids, but having one of the most fulfilling professional experiences of her life, one which led to a highly successful career teaching young performers.

Nora's a show business child through and through. Her mother is Ann Guilbert, best known as Millie Helper on the classic *Dick Van Dyke Show*. Her father is George Eckstein, an accomplished producer who worked on such series as *The Untouchables* and *The Fugitive*, and produced the classic TV movie *Duel*, which gave a first big break to a hardworking young television director by the name of Steven Spielberg.

Nora likewise put in her time as an actress, but found during and after college that working with children was what she really wanted. Fate led her to Diane, and the two became both close friends and coworkers, running Young Actors Space and managing several young performers as well.

Diane, for one, sees the issue of acting lessons for children somewhat differently from many other experts in the field. "When these children come out of a school like Young Actors Space, it's no accident they give such good readings at auditions," she says. "Regardless of their age, they have acquired an invaluable skill and they know what they're doing."

In favor of early training or not, *all* experts suggest parents check out performing arts schools very carefully up front. Meet the teachers. Attend the classes. Speak to other parents. Most of all, watch the students themselves to see whether they seem to be learning or just playing. An acting class must be more than another version of day care. *Make sure this is the right school and right teacher for your child.*

What is it you should be looking for in an acting teacher? Nora recommends only those who are going to build a child's confidence, not undermine it. "There are teachers who are extremely rude and obnoxious to their students," she says. "I think children should walk out of an acting class feeling better about themselves—not terrified of the next class!"

While different people have different theories as to when (or if) kids should start acting lessons, most agree that *one acting class a week is enough.* Too many lessons of any kind will only cause a child to grow tired and disinterested. However professional that child is or wants to be, he or she must have time to have fun, be with friends, and relax.

PREPARING FOR THE MUSICAL THEATER:
DANCING SCHOOLS AND SINGING LESSONS

Many local schools are designed mainly for people who want to look decent at the next school prom or be able to sing "Happy Birthday" relatively on key at a friend's party. The last thing most of the students are thinking about is a career in show business. Your situation is entirely different and requires a more serious approach to the choice of teacher and school.

Depending on where you live, you may have to look beyond your hometown to find a suitable dance or vocal coach. This doesn't mean you'll be expected to drive seven hours so your child can take a one-hour lesson. But you will have to research where the best *and* closest schools or coaches are.

Until your child has an agent or manager to help you, your best chance of finding proper dance training is to pore over *Dance Magazine*, or call a dance coach at a nearby university for advice. For suitable vocal instruction, contact the National Association of Teachers of Singing (NATS), based in New York, or try the music department of a local university. Finally, it's worth a try to ask the agents or managers in your area for recommendations. And while you've got them on the phone, let them know you'll soon be sending in a photo and résumé of your child for their consideration. That process will be covered in Chapter Five.

Obviously, you want your child's dance training to get off on the right foot. Nevertheless, not every young performer is blessed with such grace at first, and some never are. That doesn't spell the end of a child's musical career, however, because even if he or she does have two left feet, your child can still have all the right stuff as far as casting directors are concerned.

Without question, *one's physical well-being will be a key factor in one's training as a dancer.* If your child can stay in shape—through correct diet and exercise—he or she can flourish as a dance student. It's not enough to practice twenty turns or thirty leg lifts every day. Young dancers need athletic balance in their lives. Fortunately, convincing your endlessly active child to run around, play ball, or ride a bike will hardly be your most difficult challenge.

Can your child sing? Of course! But does your child sing *well* or sound like a raptor from *Jurassic Park*? Why not find out? In my case, the answer was a resounding "No," and I had to give up many a good part because of it. But you should certainly investigate because it may give your child one more important talent to add to that résumé. At the very least, singing lessons will provide another form of self-discipline that is certain to be valuable down the line.

Your first decision will be whether to enroll your child with a vocal instructor or a vocal coach. Many singing teachers offer the benefit of both forms of training. Basically, an instructor is more nuts-and-bolts oriented, emphasizing breathing techniques and control. A coach is more concerned with building up a student's personal repertoire and helping him or her present each song with the appropriate confidence and emotional sincerity. Each has its place. It all depends on what your ultimate target is.

All instructors and coaches appear to agree on one point: It can be dangerous to overtrain a child's voice, especially before that child has reached puberty, because one's vocal cords must be allowed to develop normally without any undue strain.

Vocal instructor/coach Paul French says that he goes by a very simple rule. "If it literally begins to hurt a student to sing, it's time to back off. Therefore, if I'm working with, say, an eight-year-old child, I always have a strict limit as to how much vocal technique we'll deal with. Instead, I'll work for half a lesson on ear training and singing songs."

Leona Roberts taught in Los Angeles for many years and, like Paul, became a member of NATS. She agrees with her colleague. "Lots of parents try to exert pressure on their kids, but I wouldn't let them," she says. "I wouldn't want my young pupils looking at me with an expression that says, 'Can't you save me from this?' I would want them to enjoy themselves while they're learning."

Leona encourages her students to study all kinds of music, particularly those in which they're most interested. If they're preoccupied with pop music, she urges them to take only one lesson a week. "After all," she asks half-jokingly, "why should they strain themselves when they'll probably end up using a million dollars' worth of studio equipment to augment their voices?!"

Another common note among vocal instructors and coaches is their advice for the student to study an instrument in addition to voice—preferably the piano. Their thinking is that instrumental study will provide a greater understanding and appreciation of music as an art form. Paul French points out that many rock performers never bothered to learn piano or how to read music, and that some of them have paid the price. So whether a child is looking to become a professional musician or just to have one extra skill as a performer, it makes sense to do it properly from the start.

Ken Kendall, also a Los Angeles–based member of NATS who has taught and coached numerous kids along the way, stresses the importance of getting his younger students not simply to go through the mechanics of singing, but to use their imaginations as well. Toward that end, he encourages them to explore classical and contemporary material that provides rich visual images. The result is that the child is more apt to convey what the music is about, have fun performing, and gain confidence in front of audiences.

"Of course, that can be taken *too* far," Ken laughingly admits. "I can remember as a four-year-old singing a song about Santa Claus with a bunch of other kids. As it happened, we were all standing in front of a fireplace. I got so carried away with what the song was about that I became convinced Santa was about to come crashing down our chimney any second. All I could do was scream and run away in terror!"

Training of itself is no surefire ticket to success, so don't go deeply into debt for these or any lessons. Set up a schedule of classes that's emotionally comfortable and financially manageable. Put aside whatever money you can, and make the most of it. Remember: *You don't have to be rich to get your child into show business.* Your child's best qualities have to do with talent, ability, and personality—not just how extensively he or she has trained.

Like everything else in life, nothing in show business is written in stone. There are no cardinal rules or standard procedures, no easy solutions or pat answers. Choosing the right training for your child is a case in point.

It's entirely possible that you don't know the first thing about acting, singing, or dancing. In this case, *rely on your instincts.* More often than not, it will be your own intuition that will help you guide your child's overall career. Granted, the decisions will still be tough ones, and, on occasion, you may later change your mind entirely. But there's nothing wrong with falling back on common sense and gut reaction when you reach those proverbial forks in the road.

Use the same solid instincts you use every day as a parent to help determine which schools are best for your child. Moreover, make certain he or she also reacts positively to these schools and their staffs. After all, you may be footing the bill, but your child is the one who is going to pay the price down the line if he or she is unhappy now.

IN REVIEW
----

1. *Be aware. Observe working children and read the trades.*
2. *Encourage your child to accept every opportunity to perform in public.*
3. *If time and money allow, develop all of your child's talents with proper training.*
4. *Bear in mind that most experts warn against overtraining kids or starting them too early.*
5. *Check out all teachers and schools.*
6. *Use your parental instincts where there are no clear-cut answers.*

Don Grady

Like Ron Howard, who parlayed his success as a young actor into a thriving career as a director, Don Grady represents another former child star who has risen to prominence in an entirely different, yet equally creative, facet of show business over recent years. Though millions know Don for his long-standing leading role of Rob Douglas in the classic TV series *My Three Sons*, as well as for his year on Disney's *Mickey Mouse Club* and for his impressive array of dramatic television roles, he owes his current success not to a television studio but to a recording studio, as a highly respected film, television, and theatrical composer whose credits run the gamut from the *Kennedy Center's 25th Anniversary* to *EFX* (the heralded Michael Crawford production in Las Vegas) to the theme of *Donahue*.

Indeed, so accomplished has Don become in the realm of music that his entertainment industry achievements would be noteworthy even if had never stepped in front of a camera in his life.

The son of Mary Grady, the industry's preeminent agent for young performers, and the brother of my talented *Eight Is Enough* "daughter," Lani O'Grady, Don should stand as an ideal illustration of how to handle sudden fame and how to move forward when that fame invariably quiets down. While many young performers have faced career uncertainties after the run of a hit show, Don knew that the spotlight of *My Three Sons*—despite its remarkable twelve-year run—couldn't shine forever. Wisely, therefore, he became a serious and disciplined musician—having always loved music from his earliest childhood—and was able to pursue his love for composition on a professional level even while *My Three Sons* was still on the air. The result: a second career that has become no less rewarding than his first.

In a recent interview, Don Grady discussed his work—then

and now—and offered some well-informed advice to parents and young performers alike.

Q: *How was your career as an actor launched?*

A: My mom and dad played accordion. When I was three years old, they gave me a drum set and I joined them to make up a trio. Over the years, we would go and play in different clubs and community events throughout the Oakland area. As a result, I grew up doing this amateur performing. When I became professional at the age of twelve—Disney was looking for a new Mouseketeer at the time—I was playing eight or nine different musical instruments. Once I was fortunate enough to get the Disney job, the whole family moved down to L.A. to help give me a chance. After my stint as a Mouseketeer my mom would take me on different interviews and to auditions and she'd look around the room and immediately know which child was right for a given part. So she got interested in agenting and started her own talent agency in 1964. My father stayed in the salami business. His father had come over from Italy and started the business; my father took over and I would probably have taken it over from him if it wasn't for this drum set they bought me.

Q: *What was your reaction to joining the Mouseketeers?*

A: It was a huge rush. The show was very big when I was a kid. It was so exciting. Actually, during the audition, we didn't think we had gotten it, because Disney at the time focused his attention on the other boy up for the one spot that was open. In fact, even when they put us on the plane after the audition, they were congratulating this other boy, and not even looking at me or my mother. Later, we found out that they were deliberately doing that because they knew they wanted me, but also knew I'd be coming into a situation where there would be a lot of attention given to the other kids in the cast. They were screening me to see how I handled being second fiddle, so to speak. Which was remarkably sophisticated and thoughtful psychologically, considering what I was about to go through. I credit Disney for doing that—seeing in advance how kids can handle competition. If I had broken down or acted really glum, I probably wouldn't have gotten the job. When they called, we were living in Lafayette, California. My mother picked up the phone and the casting agent said, "Congratulations, Mouseketeer mother!" She turned to me and said, "You got it!" It was incredible. Even at the age of twelve, I knew instinctively that something had happened that was going to change my life forever.

Q: *How did you land the role on* My Three Sons?

A: I had done a year of *The Mickey Mouse Club*. This was the show's last season. Amazingly, they were only on for three years. After the show ended, I started doing all these Westerns, including *Have Gun, Will Travel, The Rifleman, Wagon Train,* and *Colt 45,* among others. I had gotten a reputation as a dramatic young actor. When *My Three Sons* came up, it was obviously a departure, a sitcom. But they were desperate, because the original Rob who had filmed the pilot wasn't working out. I remember getting called in for an emergency interview. They actually had to get me out of school to go down to the studio. I did the interview, and by the time I got home from school that day, I found out I had gotten the part. I had actually been hoping to land a role on a new Western series starring Robert Fuller, but I didn't get it. I remember hearing I had gotten this series with Fred MacMurray and I again had that feeling that this would be another life-changing experience. I also remember a moment at the end of shooting the first season of *My Three Sons* when I realized we were all going to be famous. The show was starting to look like it might be a hit. The ratings weren't that great yet, but I had a real good feeling about the show. Sure enough, by the beginning of the third season, we were in the Top 10. Most of the run, except for the last few years, we stayed up there pretty high in the Top 10.

Q: *How did you adjust to the sudden fame?*

A: I actually found out fairly quickly that I really wanted some kind of anonymity and I felt that I needed a degree of privacy in order to maintain my integrity as a person and as an actor. I think it was the third or fourth season of the show when I disguised myself, put on a red beard, and went and got a job in Vail as a busboy and a bellboy at a hotel. I worked that job during our off-season for about three months. Nobody knew who I was until a group of girls came in from Chicago and they recognized my voice. That night, when I was busing at the restaurant, a very fancy restaurant at Vail Lodge, these high school girls stormed the restaurant with my picture, asking for autographs. The manager fired me on the spot. That story is just to say that I really didn't do that well with fame. I found that I wasn't really the kind of person who ate it up or craved it. I liked the work but I enjoyed my privacy, too. You don't have to love fame to be in the entertainment business, of course. There are many actors who are terrific performers but aren't comfortable with their celebrity status. Other people seem to need and want that, and that's fine too. The bottom line about me is that I'm a musician and a composer first; I had been since I was a kid. Some people could only think of me as an actor, but the truth is that I've always been happier as a composer.

Q: *How did you handle the considerable responsibility of keeping* My Three Sons *so popular over the years?*

A: I did shoulder a lot of the responsibility on the show. Years later, the production manager, John Stephens, told me they had been amazed that I was handling it all. But the producers could work me more than the other kids in the cast, because I was older and didn't have to contend with the same kind of school hours. How you handle something like this depends to a huge extent on what kind of life you have at home. If you're fifteen or sixteen and when you get home, your parents tell you to take out the trash, mow the lawn, and clean your room, it forces you to keep a good perspective on who you are. You've got this life at work where you're a star when you get there—people are waiting on you in essence, and you're holding court. You've got people making you up and dressing you and making sure everything is right for you. Then you get home, and you go from the prince to the pauper; you're right back in the middle of reality. I had a good family upbringing that way. Both my parents have a work ethic about them, and it gave me the stability I needed to get through that. I know people reading this might be thinking, *What's there to get through?* but where you really need this kind of stability is not only when you're enjoying big success, but when the success isn't there anymore. If you have a good work ethic, you can do your job professionally and maintain a level head whether or not you're working in the business anymore. Because when that hit is over or that series is done, what you do with your life is really critical. That's why a lot of kids coming out of the industry have a rough time. Their days of holding court are over and there's no longer a flurry of people around them boosting their ego every day. I had a hard time with it; every kid has a hard time with it. There's no escaping the sensation that something's gone away. It's difficult to deal with, especially if you're committed to trying to get back in the limelight again. In fact, if there's any one warning I would give to parents of kids going into the business, it's just *that*—you don't know what's going to happen after the hit series or big success is over.

The best kind of personality for a kid in the business, then, is the kind that bounces back easily and moves on to new challenges, rather than looking to the past and always trying to recapture something they may not be able to recapture. The ones with a buoyant kind of resilience will always be the ones who do the best. Let me draw an analogy that might help. We don't think anything of training kids to be potential Olympic stars, although it's comparable to show business in that the kids start at around five or six years old. Some of these athletes become very big stars. The difference is that what the kid training for the Olympics is getting is an amazing sense of self-discipline which can then be applied to any area he or she wants to focus on, in or out of athletics. That child has learned that if one focuses one's attention on being the best, being professional, and getting the job done right, one has then acquired a wonderful kind of discipline that's invaluable at any age, but especially at eighteen or nineteen, right on the brink of adulthood. I felt I had that in the training that I got— tap dancing and learning to play instruments. Discipline was the key for me when it came time to change gears from acting to music. If you're a young adult and have had huge success but don't really have any self-discipline, it's going to be extremely hard to attain that kind of success again. It really makes all the difference in the world.

Q: *Do you wish there was still room for a values-oriented, so-called innocent show like* My Three Sons *on television today?*

A: You couldn't bring back the show verbatim, but wouldn't it be nice to have a sitcom where parents, in this day and age, were trying to keep their kids from getting into drugs or hanging with the wrong kids? So many problems have come up in contemporary life, and there's often humor in that; a few shows, such as *Cosby*, have handled it well. But it just seems as if most shows are just trying to outdo each other in regard to sensationalism.

Q: *Any favorite* My Three Sons *anecdotes?*

A: Two quick ones: The first one that comes to mind is when Tim Considine was on the show [playing the oldest Douglas son, Mike, early in the show's run]. I really loved Tim, but once in a while, we wouldn't get along. I should add that later in the run of the show, the writers would hang around the kids in the cast to get ideas from us, thinking we had basically "become" our characters. Anyway, Tim and I once got into a real off-camera fight in the back of the Douglas station wagon, and they had to pull us out of there. We were swinging at each other. I don't even remember what it was about, but two weeks later, we were fighting in a scene for the show. The writers had seen us fighting and realized, "Hey, we haven't thought of that. They're boys—of course they're going to fight." We later did an episode in which Chip discovers a lion in the attic that had escaped from the zoo. At one point, the lion got loose on the set and we all had to freeze. This lion was on the loose for something like an hour. Every time the trainer tried to get him, he would go somewhere else. Finally, they got the lion to move away from most of us and it was moving down a back alley toward where the dressing rooms were. Just then, we heard a door open and remembered that [costar]

William Frawley was coming back. So he's walking down this alley, looks up, and finds himself face-to-face with a lion. You could hear the scream halfway across the studio!

Q: *After the series, how did you develop your career as a composer and musician?*

A: It took years for me to really make a serious living in music, but I was determined and patient. The hardest part, of course, was overcoming my background as an actor. It's a double-edged sword—it gets you attention, but it makes it hard for some people to take you seriously at first. It took a long time, but I wouldn't give up; I applied myself diligently and kept writing. Ironically, it was Disney that gave me my first break. Barbara Epstein was producing *The New Mickey Mouse Club* for the Disney Channel, and she asked me to compose some music for the show. Also, Disney "provided" me with my wife, Ginny. We met during the years when I was still trying to get off the ground in music, when I did a Disney reunion of *Mouseketeers* and she was a dancer on the show. Anyway, that transition from acting to music was very difficult, but it goes back to what I was saying before about perseverance and discipline and believing in yourself. Then, after I got that break, I found that it just kept building from there. Since about '88 or '89, I've been fortunate enough to write scores for a lot of exciting projects, including *Donahue*, a two-hour George Lucas live arena special, *EFX*, *The Revolutionary War* [a Cable ACE Award winner], special material for the 1992 Democratic Convention, several two-hour movies and specials, and a number of live shows for Universal Studios Hollywood and Florida. My preference is dramatic underscoring, so these projects have been highly rewarding for me, as was having the opportunity to conduct the London Symphony for a *George Lucas Live* special. I must say I don't miss acting. It was fun, but the truth is—this is what I want to be doing now.

CHAPTER

FOUR

AGENTS AND MANAGERS:

WHAT THEY DO AND HOW THEY DIFFER

Soon your child will be receiving the proper training, and you'll be receiving the proper publications. You'll both be aware of what's going on and you'll probably share a good idea of what kind of career to pursue. The next important step will be to find representation. You know there are distinctions between agents and managers, but you're not exactly sure what they are. You know you'll need to get one or the other, but you're not exactly sure how.

Fundamentally, the difference between the two is simple. Talent or theatrical agents representing a performer must
- be licensed by the state;
- be responsible for getting their clients interviews and auditions; and
- never take any money in advance, although 10 percent is earned once a job has been completed.

A personal manager is exactly what the name suggests. It is someone who
- works with clients on a more personal level;
- serves in part as a career counselor;
- maximizes his or her clients' strengths and minimizes their weaknesses; and

- works closely with clients in choosing jobs and determining overall career direction.

Although managers do not get involved with arranging interviews, the experienced ones are usually well-connected with agents who handle child performers and work *with* those agents toward the obvious common goal: success. The price of that success, however, has just more than doubled. A manager usually collects an additional 15 percent of a client's professional income.

The best time to see a manager's expertise in full force will be when you have an important and difficult decision to make about your child's future. Should your child go to New York to take those lessons? Is this really the right hair and best clothing style? Should we accept the regional theater offer or keep trying to land a national TV commercial? Tough dilemmas, each of them. That's why you'll be delighted to get feedback from someone who knows the business *and* cares about your child.

Managers are also exceptionally valuable in reminding agents to send their jointly shared clients for interviews. Even more significantly, they almost always have far fewer clients at any given time. This will represent a wonderful form of comfort and security for *you*. Here will be both a professional who can explain the ins and outs of the industry and (assuming he or she has been well-chosen) a friend who is available day and night for support. That's why it's not uncommon for managers and their clients to share the closeness of family members.

According to Nora Eckstein, one of a manager's primary goals is to give young performers a shot of confidence. "When children go out on auditions," she says, "we are coaching them right up to the second they walk in the door. We want them to feel really great about themselves."

Judy Savage agrees. "For working mothers with no place else to turn, a manager is essential in helping steer a child in the right direction. Managers have fewer clients, so they can spend more time with clients than agents do. There are some managers who also teach acting classes [such as Nora and Diane Hardin], take clients on interviews, and coach them. Managers like these are most desirable, because they just about ensure that 'their' kids will get jobs."

Not all kids need to be signed by a manager. Some parents are educated enough about the business to act as their child's own manager. Parents in this situation might even take a manager's percentage.

The big question, then, is this: agent, manager, or both? Volunteering to hand over a full quarter of your child's earnings won't be an easy move to make. Still, it will all come down to the very reason most experts recommend signing with each: Without agents and managers, your child might not generate any income whatsoever.

For that reason, unless you are clearly qualified to manage the career, you'll be best off getting your child an agent *and* a manager. Hopefully, you'll wind up having one who handles the day-to-day necessities (i.e., auditions, casting calls, interviews) and another who primarily considers the long-range picture (where your child's career is headed, how to best showcase his or her talents). That's known as covering all the bases.

Finally, it should go without saying that trust is a key element here. *Check out each agent and manager thoroughly up front.* Do this by speaking to any friends or contacts you have in the industry. By visiting the agent's and manager's offices to see how busy and professional the operation is. By checking out their other clients. And, most of all, by talking to them personally.

GETTING AN AGENT AND/OR MANAGER

Whether you go with a talent agent or a personal manager (or both), you'll have to follow the same basic course of action. To start, get a list of the agents and managers you'd like to target. If your child is still a bit iffy as a performer, you may want to concentrate on those in the local area, unless you live in a remote part of the country. On the other hand, if your child and your budget are ready, by all means think in terms of a big-city agent or manager.

Your initial contact will generally be through the mail. Simply send one or two black-and-white or color photographs, preferably one head shot and one full-length shot. *The photos you send should not be professionally done.* It's unnecessary and won't score you any extra points. Instead, just make sure you capture the essence of your child's looks and personality. That's all anyone will be looking for. And don't be afraid of simplicity. A lack of pretension will actually work in your favor. Few agents or managers want an overly primped, overly posed child as a client anyway.

On the back of the photo, staple a list consisting of your child's name, vital statistics (including coloring, age, height, weight, and the like), address, phone number, and any experience he or she has had in the business (even include school plays).

Finally, include a brief note to the agent or manager explaining that you are seeking representation for your child. Enclose a self-addressed, stamped envelope large enough to hold the pictures if you want them returned.

The typical response can take up to several weeks. If an agent or manager senses something special in the photos, you will then be contacted so that an appointment can be made. This will be an opportunity to demonstrate that your child has as much charm and charisma in person as in photographs.

During that all-important first meeting, your child may be asked to sing or dance (if he or she does either), or, if the goal is acting, to deliver a monologue or scene to demonstrate his or her abilities. Any young actor would do well to memorize and be ready to perform any one of several monologues ranging from the humorous to the more serious. He or she will repeatedly use them throughout the early part of a career.

Your child might also be asked to read from a script—one he or she has never seen before. This is called a "cold reading," and it strikes terror even in the hearts of seasoned, older actors. It can be a truly difficult experience for a child with reading problems, and an unnerving one for the competent reader, too. Therefore, it is by no means a waste of time to practice reading cold at home, just as an exercise. It will give you a chance to help the problem reader improve those skills, and the more competent reader to be that much better prepared for the unexpected.

In the long run, your child's personality and looks are going to be of the greatest interest to the typical agent or manager. Is your child at ease around new people? Does he or she show a strong interest in a show business career? Does your child exude confidence (not to be confused with cockiness)? Is your child good-looking or in possession of interesting "character" features? It may well be that much of your child's first meeting with an agent or manager will be more like a casual conversation than a formal interview. But don't forget for a second that you *both* will be under intense scrutiny at all times (although you will not be in the room during the actual interview).

These pros can easily tell when a parent wants a career for a child more than the child does. When that happens, agents and managers can quickly sense that the child shouldn't be doing this at all. Also, children looking for representation must be at a stage where they are not afraid to leave their parent. Occasionally, there are children who convey a great look in their photograph, but at interview time hide behind their mother's skirt and don't want to leave her. Such a mother would almost certainly be wasting her time taking the child to an interview. Fortunately, there are also those children who have a good look *and* are naturally outgoing and adaptable from the moment they walk in. *These* are the children all agents and managers hope to discover.

Nora Eckstein points out that children looking for an agent or manager must be bright and alert. They simply don't survive very long in this business if they aren't. "They have to pick up on so much new information so quickly," she says, "which means they have to have very good concentration. When you're filming, there are so many things going on all at once besides acting. Children also have to *want* a career in show business. They have to want it desperately, though I don't mean 'desperate' in a negative way. They just need to have a lot of personal drive, because it's a competitive field that will demand a lot of their time and energy."

By this point, hopefully you will have encouraged the kind of self-assurance that will permit your child to relax and be him- or herself in any situation. Nonetheless, at an interview with a prospective agent or manager, your normally assertive kid may suddenly exude all the zest of a mailbox. Since you'll essentially be asking the kid to go off with a stranger—exactly the opposite of what you normally teach—it will be perfectly understandable if he or she goes in a bit scared. Therefore, if the interview is less than a smashing success, don't scold your child or show disappointment. There will be other opportunities ahead.

If your child isn't accepted right away by an agent or manager, whether through the mail or after an interview, don't take it personally. Your child may not be the right physical type, or possibly looks older in person than in a photograph. Perhaps your child resembles another client too closely. Whatever the reason, it won't be your cue to throw in the towel.

MODELING AGENTS

As a rule, modeling agents don't see anyone without an appointment. Your first contact will be through the mail. Send a note to each that includes your name, address, telephone number, and a line or two explaining that you're interested in having your child signed up. If you don't live in a city where an agency is located but are willing to commute or move there if your child is accepted, mention that as well. List the dates you can conveniently visit the area so an interview can be arranged.

Once again, your best shot at getting that interview will be just that: a photograph (or two) of your child, either black-and-white or color pictures—preferably, a full-length shot and a close-up. The same rules apply here as in the case of attracting a theatrical agent or manager: There's no need for professional photos, as long as the pictures are clear and flattering.

On the back corner of a photo, *lightly* write in pen your child's name, address, phone number, age, weight, height, hair and eye color, and clothing size. If you want your photos back, include a self-addressed, stamped envelope big enough to fit them in, with sufficient postage.

The waiting game will then begin.

Several weeks later, your child's photos may be returned with a polite thank-you and little or nothing more. If so, don't expect to be told why he or she wasn't accepted. Just keep trying elsewhere. If you don't hear back at all from an agency after six weeks or so, it won't hurt to call and politely ask why. Expect the conversation to be curt and to the point. Simply say that you haven't heard back yet and want to make sure the materials arrived. Hopefully, they will have arrived at the agency but, as with any mail-related venture, it's wise to double-check.

In the best of all worlds, the agency will spot something appealing about your child and you'll get a note (maybe a call) specifying an appointment time for a personal interview. Actually, each modeling agency handles appointment-making in a different manner. Some tell you the exact day and time. Others just give the days of the week and blocks of time during which prospective new clients are interviewed. In the second situation, you'll basically be given an open invitation such as, "Come any Thursday between 2:00 and 5:00 p.m." When that happens, try to make it the *first* Thursday (or whatever day it is) that you can. There's no reason to stall. If the agency is interested enough in your child to respond, why hesitate for a second?

For the interview itself, don't overdress your child—just have him or her neatly attired and groomed. Beyond that, though, go with whatever look sold the agency in the first place. Just because this is a modeling agency doesn't mean it won't still be looking for a natural, unpretentious child who dresses the way all kids do at that age.

When you arrive at the agency, have on hand an extra copy of the photos and written information you first sent. The interview may be quite short, but don't let that discourage you. These people have a keen eye and will probably know pretty quickly if your child has what they're looking for.

There is also a possibility that the agency will be impressed, but will tell you that representation will have to wait until your child grows into a new clothing size or has straighter teeth. Don't head home to wait it out or head to the dentist to straighten those teeth. Try another agency. The next one may want to sign the kid on the spot. This is why you're well-advised to *write to several agencies in the beginning*—modeling *and* theatrical. If one falls through, you'll still have lots of other prospects in the wings.

A given agent may tell you your child's chances would be improved if those teeth were fixed, or that hairstyle changed, or the diet altered. But that's just one person's opinion. Keep making the rounds. If the same advice is given everywhere you go, only *then* should you consider a minor alteration or two. Taking a single agent's judgment as gospel can be emotionally, physically, and financially dangerous.

Many agencies will send children out on a few auditions

(also known as tryouts or calls) before signing them up. This is a perfectly reasonable request. It is the agent's right to check out a client's potential before committing to a contract. As nerve-racking as this extra waiting period may be, it will be in your best interests to comply. Especially since you'll establish a good working relationship with the agent by being cooperative.

No legitimate agency will ask for money in advance. When your child has completed an assignment, the check will go to the agency, which will then deduct its percentage and send the balance to you. An exception to the don't-pay-up-front rule will be if you're asked to foot the bill to place your child's photo in the agency's book of head sheets. This fee shouldn't exceed $100 or so, and it will be money well spent. Head sheets feature clients' photos along with their vital statistics in a booklet or poster and are shown to casting agents and photographers, among others.

PLEASE SIGN HERE

The first big break you'll enjoy is winning over that agent or manager of your choice and being asked to sign a contract. This will be a definite milestone and proof positive that a professional sees the same potential in your child that you do. It will also be a time when your emotions may try to take over. You may even hear a small voice telling you over and over, "Dummy, don't blow it. This is what all those lessons, hours, and expenses were for. Sign it! Sign it! *Sign it!!*"

But take the time to ask a few vital questions: Does this person have integrity? Does he or she seem energetic and caring? Can I see myself and my child developing a good rapport with this agent? Does this manager have a solid reputation? If an agent or manager suggests that you take the time to read and understand the contract thoroughly before signing, this will be a clear sign of legitimacy. If possible, have a lawyer check out the contract, too.

There are some minor and some profound differences among agency and management contracts. For instance, "option clauses" can be confusing, since they give the agency or firm the periodic right to extend the length of a contract. For that reason, the option clause is frequently one-sided and definitely not in your favor. As grateful as you'll be to have your child signed, you may not want him or her accidentally committed to the same agent or manager for five or more years.

Firms usually offer a one-year contract with options for additional periods. This is because most agents and managers feel it takes at least a year to properly gauge and launch a child's career. Some will release you from the contract if you give them thirty days' written notice. Others may grant the manager a percentage of show business work that he or she actually doesn't help generate. Still other contracts may grant managers power of attorney, allowing them—among other things—to sign and collect checks.

Keep in mind also that an agent's or manager's commission may sometimes have to continue to be paid *after* the contract term has ended. If, for example, an agent lands a child on a TV series, he or she will collect a percentage of that child's residual payments for years to come—whether or not the child is still a client.

If you feel you've somehow been given a raw deal after signing with an agency or management firm, don't hesitate to call a lawyer to see what can be done.

The key point is that before you sign on the dotted line, know the precise legal obligations of all parties concerned.

MUTUAL ADMIRATION SOCIETY

Once your child is signed with an agent or manager, it won't be bad form or overly pushy to politely call every day. Older kids can call on their own. This way, you'll know in advance whether your child has an audition that day or soon (they often crop up with little notice). Follow up all auditions by letting your child's agent or manager know how everything went.

Although agents and managers will want you to stay in touch on a regular basis, they'll be on guard if you become overly demanding of their time and energy. Putting it bluntly, from the first day you meet your child's agent or manager, you too will be evaluated in a number of ways. Just as you'll be trying to imagine working with them, they will be picturing the pros and cons of a lengthy association with *you*. Is this a parent with whom I can work? Will this parent trust my judgment and let me do my job? These are questions that run through the minds of most agents and managers. And they will all tell you that no child is worth the nightmare of dealing with an unreasonable parent!

THE DIRECT APPROACH

A manager may not be in your plans right now, but you will very soon be making every effort to procure an agent to represent your child. It will be an important bridge to cross. However, the very process of finding the right agent and of that agent discovering your child will take time just when you are so anxious to move ahead. What will you do?

Most commercial, film, and theatrical productions employ casting directors to find the talent they need. Therefore, even without an agent, you may still contact the casting offices in your area on your own. The process of familiarizing a casting office with your child will be the same as if you apply to a talent agency for representation.

In large metropolitan areas, casting directors spend many evenings every month attending theater of every kind, including showcase productions, trying to spot fresh talent of all ages and types. This may sound as if aspiring youngsters in less-populated areas are at a disadvantage. The opposite probably is true, owing to the reduced competition in such areas. In light of that, your child's uniqueness may actually become more evident.

At the point that your child actually has video or film audition reels, you'll find that most casting offices have screening facilities. Those that deal in voice-overs will have high-quality audio facilities to hear cassettes of that kind.

In entertainment meccas such as New York, Nashville, and Los Angeles, the sheer volume of show business hopefuls has created a concern among casting directors and talent agents that once the general public finds out their telephone number, they'll be swamped with calls and uninvited visitors. Their message is plain and sometimes impolite: *Don't call! Don't send tapes or cassettes! Don't visit unless invited to do so! Stay away!*

Okay, you say, we'll play by the rules. But the regional

information section at the back of this book lists casting offices and modeling and talent agencies by city and phone number. Sounds like a catch-22, doesn't it? The idea is to let your fingers do the walking and let their office do the talking. If it's listed in your area phone directory, make a note of the casting office address and mail your material. If not, use the telephone numbers listed in this book and ask these questions in a brief, businesslike fashion:

1. What is your mailing address?
2. Do you take on children (or babies)?
3. Will you accept submissions through the mail from private individuals, or do you take agency submissions only?

The answers will provide you with your next, obvious step. Remember, this is *not* a call in which you exercise your selling skills. Its purpose is informational only. You don't even have to provide them with your name, unless it is requested. The U.S. Postal Service will do the follow-through for you.

Write the casting office to request registration and ask them if you and your child can come in at some point in the future. Enclose an 8 x 10" glossy or a picture postcard and résumé (details follow in the next chapter). List any union affiliations your child has, a phone number, and an address. As usual, don't forget to include the self-addressed, stamped envelope!

If your child does become registered, follow up monthly by sending in picture postcards with written reminders that he or she is currently available, and be sure to mention any upcoming appearances. If they're interested, most casting directors will remember to check the child out in action.

Going after casting offices on your own may be a long shot, but if just one approach leads to a job, that job may clinch a contract with an agent, and the time and trouble will obviously have paid off.

IN REVIEW: THE AGENT/MANAGER CHECKLIST

Here are some of the basic do's and don'ts of working with your child's future agent or manager.

1. *Don't be upset if your child doesn't get constant bookings.*
2. *Do stay in frequent contact.*

3. *Don't blame your agent or manager if a particular job fizzles out (he or she also wants your kid to succeed!).*
4. *Do try to trust the advice of your agent or manager (that's why you signed in the first place).*
5. *Don't be insulted if your child isn't fawned over by an agent or manager (as long as the jobs keep coming).*
6. *Do remember that you, too, are being judged.*
7. *Don't constantly remind your agent or manager of how incredibly gifted your child is; instead, assume that's why your kid is there!*
8. *In many areas, talent and modeling agencies also function as casting offices.*

Adam Hann-Byrd

Although the odds of an actor (of any age) being "discovered" out of the blue and catapulted to prominence on the big screen are comparable to the odds of winning the lottery, Adam Hann-Byrd can personally attest to the fact that such unlikely rags-to-riches experiences sometimes do occur. Always artistically inclined and a true natural as a performer, the now-teenaged Adam was spotted while costarring in a school play and subsequently cast—to great critical acclaim—as Jodie Foster's gifted son in the compelling film *Little Man Tate*.

Quickly impressing members of the industry, critics and audiences alike via his film debut as Fred Tate, Adam went on to a starring part in the feature film *Digger*, opposite Leslie Nielsen and Olympia Dukakis. Most recently, he brought his unique blend of intelligence and innocence to his role as the young Robin Williams in the highly popular film *Jumanji*. Adam has more recently costarred in such films as *Diabolique*, starring Sharon Stone, and the Ang Lee–directed *Ice Storm*, starring Kevin Kline, Sigourney Weaver, and Elijah Wood. In addition, the talented young actor also landed a recurring role on the hit TV series *NYPD Blue*.

Although his acting career and ongoing education keep him plenty busy, Adam also has earned a black belt in martial arts.

In a recent interview from his home in New York, Adam Hann-Byrd discussed his work and his plans.

Q: *How was your acting career first launched?*
A: It's interesting, because I wasn't really looking to be an actor before *Little Man Tate* came along. What happened was that the casting director of the movie saw me in a school play when I was eight. When I got home that night, my mom told me that this casting director had called and

wanted to know if I wanted to audition, and that's how it started. I didn't even know this casting director had seen me. I was sort of nonchalant about it at the time, actually, because I didn't quite understand what it all meant or what was going on, although I was always into movies. I'm a real movie buff. Anyway, I auditioned a couple of times after that and after the second time, they told me that Jodie [Foster, the film's director] wanted to meet me. She turned out to be great.

Q: *After* Little Man Tate *came out, much of the film's critical acclaim centered around your performance. How did you handle all of the praise and attention at such a young age?*

A: It was a little overwhelming, but I think of acting as a job, not as my life. I've always felt like a regular kid who just happens to be an actor. Of course, you have to enjoy what you're doing, but I don't think of it as my entire life, just part of it. You have to want to be an actor, though. It's not for the money; it's for doing work that you enjoy and that hopefully other people will enjoy.

Q: *What was the experience of working on* Jumanji *like for you?*

A: It was very different for me because there were a lot of special effects involved, but it was really great. Everyone was terrific and it was exciting to see a movie like that being put together. Robin Williams was wonderful, too.

Q: *Do you think young actors should be formally trained, or are they better off just acting naturally?*

A: I never took any classes. My feeling is that most kids are better off acting naturally, but it depends on the person and the role. I like to pick things up on my own by watching people and just observing life in general.

Q: *Why do you think you are so effectively making the transition from being a child actor to a young adult actor?*

A: I'm not sure, but I do think what you need to keep going in this business are a lot of different things happening in your life—you need a balance between acting and your real life. Especially since sometimes you can get spoiled and a little pampered, with everyone swarming around you and paying attention to you. On the other hand, all of that can fade away someday. What I do is practice karate, because it gives me a solid physical and mental foundation. Also, my parents are terrific, very supportive. That makes a lot of difference, too, when you're a young actor—whether you stay in the business as a young adult or move on to something else. If I told my parents I didn't want to act anymore, they'd say, "Okay, you don't have to. If you don't like it, don't do it." Whenever people ask me what advice I would give to aspiring young actors, I always say that the parents have to be supportive and the kid has to like it. Otherwise don't do it. I think kids have to look at acting as an experience, but not as their entire identity. They should stay normal kids no matter how successful they get.

CHAPTER

FIVE

YOUR ESSENTIAL TOOLS

There are certain essential tools of the trade that you will always need, regardless of the target career you and your child have selected. It's important that you devote thought and care in developing these tools and that you use them wisely along the way.

Some of those previously discussed include the trade papers and periodicals that will keep you informed about entertainment activities in your area, and the monologues and scenes that will help to develop your child's confidence and professionalism in interviews and auditions. Here are some more key essentials.

PICTURE PERFECT

Perhaps the most important tools of all are good photographs. Although amateur snapshots will get your child an agent, professional theatrical photographs will be a must after the child is signed. They'll be your calling card and your ticket to the inner circle of the industry. In some cases, it will be the photos alone that will land the child a job.

Whether your child is aiming to be a model or an actor, casting people are usually looking for a "type." Even with that in mind, *always let your child's personality come through.* Let his or her own style and looks determine the style of shots you have taken.

If for some reason your son looks silly holding a baseball bat, why take the chance on striking out by posing him at home plate? If your tomboyish little girl would rather be in an over-sized T-shirt and tennis shoes than in a clinging tutu and ballet slippers, don't force the issue. A posed photo will seem just that—posed.

In general, the type of theatrical photos you choose should be closely related to your child's age. Children under five, for instance, are usually best represented by composites (discussed below), whereas older kids seem to come off best in black and white 8 x 10"s. Combinations can be used as well. There are no set rules.

A theatrical portfolio is designed to show an actor's range and personality. In creating one, remember that children should appear as natural as possible—comfortable with whatever they're wearing, content with whatever they're doing. Many parents like to include an outdoor shot or two in their children's theatrical portfolio.

The photographer will take somewhere between 36 and 100 different frames. When you and your child's agent or manager have selected from these, the photographer will make a hundred 8 x 10" glossy reproductions with your child's name printed at the bottom (or "slugged"), above the names and phone numbers of agents and managers, and a union affiliation, if any.

Of the hundred glossies, you should give the agent about twenty-five and have the rest ready whenever you go out on calls. They can also be mailed to casting directors. Include a separate résumé (have résumés handy wherever you go—more on this later in the chapter). Don't write on the back of the glossy print, as the pressure of the pen or pencil can tarnish the photo surface.

Another important photographic tool to consider is the picture postcard. These resemble a traditional postcard but feature a shot of your child on front (often it's a smaller version of the glossy head shot). The child's name, union affiliation, and phone number for contact (the agent's number, most commonly) will be slugged on the front. Write whatever you want on the back, as long as your message is clear: *We're ready to work!*

If an agency recommends three photographers, call all three. See how they react to you, whether they seem rushed or bothered by the call. If you're not pleased, look elsewhere. No matter how good a photographer is, he or she must have a working rapport with your child. You'll want to ask to see samples of the photographer's work, too. Don't go by price. Go by gut feeling.

Sean Kenney started off as an actor (he appeared on the original *Star Trek* series, among other shows), but eventually built up a large business and solid reputation in Los Angeles as a photographer. Sean has worked extensively with children, and he usually tells parents to plan on spending about $1,000 to cover the initial outlay for photos and their duplication, for an answering service, and for résumés. "I tell them to bank about $250 for the pictures alone," says Sean, "including half again as much for the duplication or composites. Where else can you get into a business, let alone start a career for that amount? And these expenses are tax deductible!"

Commenting on the photos themselves, he says the best ones have a life of their own and a quality that instantly draws you in. "There has to be a spark of energy coming from the child. It can't just be a school type of picture or another nice shot the parents or grandparents will love. It must have an almost indefinable excitement."

To achieve this effect, good photographers do more than simply develop the photos. They try to develop communication with the child, often without the parent watching. And while some may apply a bit of blush here or fix a few strands of hair there, they go first for the natural look.

A few professional tips for your child:
- don't wear white on top or anything that's harsh on the face, such as busy prints or checks;
- wear solid colors if possible;
- refrain from using any heavy makeup; and
- try to schedule your session in the morning, when everyone is usually more refreshed, alert, and willing to work.

Another tip from Sean Kenney: Photo models who are interested in acting should avoid the typical model's pose in their photos. "I can always tell when a child comes in overly posed. He's become too trained as a model to be loose and relaxed for my kind of photograph. So I implore parents to keep their children from becoming too rigid and mannequin-like, if they're interested in being actors."

An important footnote: Whether modeling or acting, this is a business in which looks tell the whole story. So seek out a commercial photographer who specializes in models' or actors' composites and head shots, not one who specializes in weddings, bar mitzvahs, and graduations. Ask your child's agent or another person you trust for a recommendation. Again, try to have a few choices in mind so you're not stuck with the first photographer you find.

COMPOSITES

Your child's composite will be his or her passport to interviews, auditions, and readings. The idea behind a composite—a selection of poses, in various sizes, printed on an 8 x 10" glossy page—is to showcase an actor's versatility. So select poses that present your child as three or four definable types (e.g., the class brain, the athletic hero, the life of the party). Include one full-length, one close-up, and one profile shot. Let each separate shot represent a different facet of the child's personality (the use of props can help, whether it's a tennis racket or stuffed animal). The main goal as usual is to avoid phoniness. If the child looks awkward and uncomfortable, then keep experimenting until each pose projects naturalness.

When you go to the photographer's studio, bring along four or five sets of clothing. If the shoot is to take place outdoors, choose a location that is protected from the elements. You don't want your child's hair looking perfect in the car, and then suddenly gone with the wind when he or she steps outside.

After the shoot, you'll have the opportunity to look over the proofs, or "contacts." A magnifying glass will help considerably. And although your opinion counts for a lot, let your child's agent or manager make the final choices.

There may be a hundred or more shots on the contact sheet. Out of these, four or five will be made up as 8 x 10"s. If you have doubted the agent's or manager's selections, this will be the time to make your own final judgment concerning his or her choices.

The next step will be to take shots you have chosen to a photographic reproduction service that specializes in 8 x 10" glossy reproductions for actors and models. Here, your child's composite will be made, with a name, agency, and phone number slugged at the bottom. Order at least a hundred of these composites.

Next, take about thirty composites and staple a page to the back that lists your child's current age, clothing size (shoes, socks, and hats), weight and height, hair and eye color, agency, and union affiliation, if any, as well as a Social Security number. Of these composites, the agent or manager will want about twenty-five. You should keep the rest on hand both at home and wherever you go. You never know when a job prospect might present itself. A year later, after your child's vital statistics have changed enough to warrant it, be ready to prepare a new composite.

RESUMES

As your child's career gets under way, you will want to add recent job experiences to the aforementioned vital statistics. This will become his or her résumé. Once printed, the résumé can be stapled or pasted to the back of the 8 x 10" glossies, or printed directly on back.

A résumé should run no longer than a page. If all credits don't fit in that space, just list the key jobs to date and indicate that further credits are available upon request. Don't make up too many résumé copies at one time because the information will continually need to be updated.

Your child's name should be centered at the top of the page with a professional orientation (e.g., singer or actor) underneath. If he or she is an actor, list that first: Your child will fit into this category if he or she has been in a TV show, film, commercial, or stage play. If the child is more musically inclined, indicate whether he or she is primarily a singer or a dancer by listing one before the other. On the left side of the sheet, write your child's union affiliations (if any) and Social Security number.

Still at the top, but toward the center of the page, list more personal info, such as hair and eye color and the age range your child could realistically portray. On the top right, list the name, address, and phone number of your child's agent or manager (or both).

Next, list credits, grouped together according to category (television, stage, motion pictures) with the best credits on top.

Follow the credits with any other professional experiences: Anything from voice-over jobs to leading a hometown parade can be included.

At the bottom of the résumé, list all of your child's special skills and interests. Include virtually all of his or her talents: sports, languages, and the like. Finally, list any professional courses taken and coaches under whom your child has studied.

OTHER ESSENTIAL TOOLS

Once again, *be aware!* Especially of casting opportunities. All your hard work will be for naught if you're not home to receive those all-important calls for interviews or auditions once they do start coming in.

That's why *the telephone is really the most important tool of all*, and you should prepare to invest in an answering machine and check it frequently. An agent or manager may only call once! Moreover, once your child's career gets going, an answering service or even a beeper may be needed if you can handle it financially.

Along these lines, I remember once when the phone rang and it was my agent telling me that if I had a blue suit and could get to the airport in an hour, I could be en route to Kansas City to costar in a major Movie of the Week that had just come up. If I hadn't answered the phone or been accessible, I would have missed out on the part. You never know.

IN REVIEW

1. *Good photos will be your child's most valuable calling card.*
2. *Let all photos reflect your child's personality.*
3. *Carry your child's photos and résumés at all times.*
4. *Hire only those photographers who specialize in models' and actors' photos.*
5. *The purpose of composites is to show versatility.*
6. *Let your child's agent or manager make the final decision as to which shots are best.*
7. *Résumés should run no longer than one page.*
8. *Always be reachable by phone (which may require buying a beeper or an answering machine or hiring an answering service).*

CHAPTER

SIX

GETTING JOBS: THE AUDITION PROCESS

Agents and managers alert you to job opportunities and offer expert advice on how to improve your child's chances. They are your link to casting directors, who in turn make recommendations to the directors and producers. The idea, therefore, is to attract the attention of each of these people in any way you can. Well, *almost* any way.

"I had all kinds of bizarre things happen to me when I was casting director for John Huston on the film version of *Annie*," recalls Garrison True, who also conducted an international search for a young girl to play the title role in a remake of *Pippi Longstocking* (in which I costarred).

"I remember once in Cleveland, I was staying at a hotel and got a phone call from a woman who wanted me to see her daughter privately a couple of hours before the regular audition time. I told her I really couldn't do that, but she insisted that her daughter danced very well and that she was ready to prove it. What I soon found out was that they had taken the room directly above mine just so I could hear her tap dancing!"

In any case, casting directors send what are called "breakdowns" to agents with whom they have a working relationship. A breakdown is a cast list for a given production, with a description of each character. The agents in turn send back photos and résumés of clients who fit the bill. The casting directors select those they would like to see, and the agents call to let their client know when and where to show up. Often, it's the very next day. Thorough agents will find out as much as possible about the role and will try to read the script on behalf of their clients.

Here's a run-through of what you and your child can expect at most auditions. (Because they're more specialized, commercial and musical theater auditions will be detailed later.)

1. There will be a sign-up sheet at the site (be it a soundstage or office or whatever). The receptionist will have a schedule listing which children are set to audition that day and what their individual time slots are. Kids are usually seen every five minutes. You will be asked the name of the agent who arranged the interview, the time you were scheduled to arrive, and your child's Social Security number.

2. At this point, you will usually be handed a script. In the business they are referred to as "sides." If you are not given sides, check with the receptionist to make sure there hasn't been an oversight. As mentioned before, your child occasionally will face a cold audition with no material provided in advance. Hopefully, there will be sufficient time to get a feel for the character to be portrayed, if not all the lines. A good casting director can add to your child's grasp of the character with only a few sentences of explanation. Regardless of the circumstances, he or she won't expect a flawless reading.

3. Your child will then be escorted to the casting office. You'll be abandoned for what may seem like an eternity, so bring along a Walkman or something to read. Waiting is part of the whole process. *Try not to let your child see how anxious you are.* Sure, this will be important to both of you, but it will be only one of countless job opportunities for your child.

4. Once in the casting director's office, your child will be asked a few basic questions designed to draw him or her out. These questions will be much like those the agent or manager will have initially asked. How old are you? Do you like school? What makes you want to be an actor? How your kid answers will probably be more important than what he or she actually says. Your child may then be asked to read a scene with the casting director.

5. When the audition is finished, stop at the desk and leave your child's photo or composite with the appropriate casting people. In the case of an audition for a commercial, you will want to sign out, noting the time. This is because under the commercial contract, your child must be paid additional dollars if he or she spent more than an hour at the audition. Your child will be paid additionally for a third callback.

THE OPEN CALL

In many instances, casting directors will search region by region, seeing literally thousands of kids for a single film role. On these occasions, casting directors often resort to the "open call," wherein hundreds of would-be young actors may assemble in a single day.

CALLBACKS

When casting directors like what they see, your child will be asked to undergo one or more tougher auditions. These are known as "callbacks." In this situation, it's likely your child will see more strange faces, including those of the director and a variety of people representing the creative and business aspects of the project.

There's no one industry rule as to who makes the ultimate casting choices on a given project. Sometimes it's the director. Sometimes the producer. Sometimes the casting director. It's usually a matter of all three putting their heads together. If there's no consensus, *the producer tends to have the last word*, since he or she has probably made the biggest investment in time and money.

For film and television roles, children are sometimes videotaped or screen-tested during a callback.

One last tip: It's been my experience that it helps to wear the same or similar clothes and have the same hairstyle during callbacks as at the initial auditions, presumably since one's look had something to do with why he or she has been called back in the first place.

FINAL CALLS

By the time an auditioning actor reaches the producer, the weeding-out process is winding down fast. This is when your child will be asked in for a final call. Just as it sounds, this is the audition from which the final casting decision will be made. On hand will likely be the producer, director, casting director, and anyone else with a vested interest in the project.

In fact, the audience your child will face can often be fairly large.

As you might imagine, there is a powerful sense of competitiveness among finalists. You will need to help your child shrug off that feeling. Let other kids get distracted by what's going on and who they're up against. Have your kid keep his or her mind on the business at hand. *Encourage your child just to do his or her best and try to have fun.* That way, much of the tension will be eased. If it isn't, don't worry. Tension, of itself, is not necessarily an unhealthy frame of mind for an actor. Even the world's biggest stars often speak of becoming downright ill from nervousness before facing a crowd. More often than not, that state of mind gets channeled in a positive direction, resulting in a pumped-up, exciting performance.

COMMERCIAL AUDITIONS

Since commercials are targeted by most beginning young actors as an ideal starting place, the competition is formidable when it comes to landing commercial roles. As the commercial audition draws nearer, let your child know up front that he or she may be tested on film or videotape. For some kids, the first time in front of a camera is a confusing and frightening experience, not unlike how their first dates will be in a few years. Most kids, however, get a kick out of the whole thing. Chances are *you'll* be a wreck while your child is having a blast. The actor will want a candy bar, the parent a Valium.

In 1976, when Marsha Hervey's son Jason was four, her friends started suggesting that she somehow get him into show business. After a while, she finally agreed and, much to her surprise, she almost instantly got him a top agent. Since then, Jason has done over 200 commercials and dozens of print ads, played the young Rodney Dangerfield character in *Back to School*, been a regular on *The Wonder Years* and, most recently, launched his own production company. What's more, Marsha is a partner in the successful Hervey-Grimes Talent Agency, which has placed young clients in such network series as *Step by Step* and the respected *My So-Called Life*.

Marsha has been on more commercial shoots than she can even remember, and finds that most kids love the experience. "It's like a giant play group," she says. "But they must be prepared to do a lot of hard work. They need a great deal of stamina to be able to follow instructions down to the most minute detail."

Two audition calls might be necessary for your child to land a role in a commercial. Unfortunately, the first will provide little opportunity to display his or her talents. It's the session in which casting and advertising people check out the contenders to try to find the type they're out to hire.

Another likelihood, be it at the first or second call, is that your child will be asked to do a reading. This can involve anything from a full script to a single line. Props may be added to see if the kid can manage action *and* dialogue. (Some of the most seasoned actors have trouble doing both at the same time!) During this type of audition, it's less important for a child to execute a flawless delivery than to be believable, natural, and alert. These are the qualities that will help sell a product.

In most cases, your child will be given a script (one page or less, in large print) and told the role for which he or she is being considered. At some auditions, the child will be handed the commercial's storyboard. This is a frame-by-frame artist's conception of what the spot will look like when it eventually airs on TV.

Everything from the actor's dialogue to the precise positioning of the product is taken into consideration. Seeing it all laid out, children may find the reading process far less abstract and have a good sense of where they fit into the picture, literally.

Although there may not be a great deal of time for serious interpretation, *encourage your child to read over the dialogue several times before the audition.* Help your child to be comfortable with the lines and to deliver them smoothly, mindful that it should be *his* or *her* delivery, not yours.

Not every commercial featuring a child is light, bouncy, and upbeat. If you tell your child before the audition to be giggly and cutesy, there's big trouble ahead if it turns out to be a commercial that requires a somber-faced kid. Going back to the basics, your child will need to be energetic and enthusiastic, but also able to shift emotional gears if necessary. A perfect example of this is the classic Mikey spot for Life cereal. Here the mood was predictably sweet and warm, but the kid who stole the show was the one who didn't crack a single smile or speak a single word.

The Mikey spot, in fact, is an ideal illustration of the nonverbal brand of acting popular in many commercial spots. As you've seen over the years, many commercial actors are employed only to deliver a key reaction or handle a prop without speaking a word. In some instances, the actor's "sound" may be his or her primary asset. For example, there is an actress currently making a handsome living because she has a sultry, sexy laugh. You've heard her on radio selling everything from varietal wines to personal computers. There is no implication of sex in the commercial message, but the tone of her voice creates an excitement that goes beyond the message and helps make the spots memorable. Unique children's voices are sought after in the same way.

In commercials, it's frequently important for a child to seem to *like* the product (sometimes referred to as "the hero" in ad agency lingo, but often thought of as the villain by actors doing take after take over the course of one or more days). This can sometimes be difficult if the product being eaten, for example, happens to be ice cream, for the simple reason that *this* hero is usually finely mashed potatoes *masquerading* as ice cream! (Ice cream melts too quickly under the hot lights.)

Bottom line? Because so many spots can revolve around a simple gesture or perfectly timed double take, don't be put off by the idea of your child trying out for a role without dialogue. It may wind up that the part, even without any lines, is really the best in the whole commercial. And even if it does turn out to be a small role and nothing more, you have little reason to complain, given the big exposure and big money involved.

There's no great difference among preliminary auditions for films, TV shows and commercials, and the theatrical stage. However, stage auditions may occur in the office of a casting director or producer, or frequently on the stage itself. This can be an awesome experience, to say the least.

First, children to be seen that day will be gathered backstage. The stage manager will tell one child at a time to go to the center of the stage alone and face the audience. But there will be no audience, only the voice of the director. He or she will ask those few basic questions designed to assess the personality of the child, and then give that child the chance to read a few lines. The director will usually make up his or her mind either to see this child again or to dismiss the child with a quick thank-you then and there.

For stage *musical* roles, your child will generally be asked to show up either at the theater itself or in a rehearsal hall. He or she will be asked to appear on a given day at a particular time, and you will probably line up to fill out the usual informational and legal forms.

As in film auditions, the open call is also used for both plays and musicals, in which case it's sometimes referred to as the "cattle call" because of the undignified circumstances that often prevail. The producer and director open the doors of the theater to all actors who believe they qualify for an available role they've seen publicized in the trades or in a casting breakdown. Sometimes hundreds of people show up for a single role, although it's actually rare that an actor will be hired during an open call.

More commonly, actors will be hired to understudy the actor playing the role, which is an accomplishment in itself. After all, Dustin Hoffman understudied Martin Sheen in the 1964 Frank Gilroy play *The Subject Was Roses*. And that didn't exactly bring *his* career to a crashing halt! My understudy during the run of *Mister Roberts* was none other than Cliff Robertson, and such other stars as Shirley MacLaine and Carol Haney also were propelled to the top as a result of getting that big chance after being an understudy.

In the case of an open call for a musical, your child will be herded on stage with a hundred or so other kids to sing some familiar song. This can be tough on a young ego, not to mention your own, especially since your child won't even have the luxury of performing solo and may only be thanked and dismissed. Try not to regard it as a rejection. It may simply be that the child doesn't fit the physical type the producers have in mind, since so many children's roles require actors who resemble the performers playing their parents on stage.

If you're lucky, you'll escape the open call entirely, and your child will be asked to hand some sheet music to the accompanist and perform his or her own song. Here, at least, you will have the comfort of knowing every child was seen and heard individually—making it all the more gratifying when yours is invited back for a second round of auditions.

For musicals that require dancing, children who have been asked to return after their initial singing auditions will be grouped and taught a basic routine by the choreographer. After several group rehearsals, the elimination process will cut down the number of performers considerably. Each of the remaining kids will be told to come back on yet another day.

If the first meeting is in a casting agent's office instead of on stage, your child will be interviewed by the casting director first. If the chemistry is right, your child will be invited back to read, sing, dance—or all three.

Whatever form of audition is involved, *your child will more likely stand out from the crowd if he or she is at least somewhat familiar with the production* (assuming, of course, it's not brand-new). Without being too obvious about it, your child can even dress the part. By being comfortable with the material, he or she will express a level of determination, energy, and self-confidence that a director will notice. In this business, *that's* the key.

Before concluding this section, though, let me relate a personal stage audition story involving Dustin Hoffman. In the early '70s, I was costarring on stage with Marlo Thomas in the play *Thieves*, and a day before the last performance of the run, I got word that I had the chance to audition for Dustin the next day for a new drama by the illustrious playwright Murray Schisgal that Dustin was going to direct and in which he'd star.

The next day I showed up, having spent much of the previous night going over the lines of the role of a gruff general.

Well, I must tell you here that I am somewhat finicky about germs, and one of my least favorite things is to put something in my mouth that someone else has just had in theirs. The reason I mention this is because after reading through the part twice in front of Dustin and Murray, Dustin said I was good but needed to be a bit more "MacArthurish," toward which end he asked Murray to give me his pipe. Much to my horror, not only did Murray hand me the pipe fresh from his mouth, but it was dripping with saliva.

Needless to say, I tried everything I could to use the pipe without actually smoking it, but Dustin keep prompting me to put the darned thing in my mouth to see the effect. Here I was, getting physically sick at the sight and thought of what I was doing, and trying to impress two of the most important people for whom I had ever auditioned. So, through four pages of dialogue, I was several shades of green and probably as stiff and self-conscious as I've ever been. Believe it or not, they liked me, but I never went back to that theater again.

Anyway, to bring the story full circle, I later told that story to Johnny Carson on *The Tonight Show*, and who should call me the next day but an apologetic Dustin Hoffman, whom I met the next day for lunch. Dustin was so anxious to make it up to me, even though we were laughing about the whole thing, that he said he wanted me to play his agent in his next film, something called *Tootsie*. By the time the film was actually shot, though, I was tied up full time with *Eight Is Enough*, and a new director—Sydney Pollack—not only was attached to the project but ended up playing the role of the agent himself (and extremely well, as it happened).

As they say, that's show business.

A STAR IS BORN

Other possible sources of exposure for young performers over recent years have been talent programs such as TV's *Star Search*, the offspring of shows like *Arthur Godfrey* in earlier days.

Steve Stark was the casting director on *Star Search* before becoming producer of *Charles in Charge*, and remembers his days on the Ed McMahon–hosted show vividly.

"When I first started, I didn't want contestants to stand next to each other on stage and essentially be told one was a winner and others were losers. I found that offensive. In my estimation, no one was a loser. Frequently, winning or not winning didn't even make a difference, as with Tiffany, the first girl I cast on the show. She didn't win, but millions of record sales later, she had obviously proven herself. But I would never claim to have 'discovered' Tiffany. I found Sam Harris in a little club, but I never feel like I discovered him. His music teacher discovered him back in Oklahoma. I simply put these people on the show and whatever happened, happened."

You never know how near your child's big break is. So you really can't go wrong trying to *increase your chances by exploring each and every possibility available to you.* Perhaps an invitation for your child to appear on a television show is a long shot right now. But work toward it anyway. Over and over. Until that long shot eventually turns into a sure thing.

Steve has an anecdote similar to Garrison True's. He remembers being in a New Orleans hotel while casting *Star Search,* and having some four hundred people vying for the next day's auditions. Around eleven o'clock he heard a knock on his door.

"I opened it—in my robe and totally exhausted—and there's a guy saying, 'Room Service!' Well, I told him I hadn't ordered anything, at which point he said it was compliments of the hotel, then promptly wheeled in the cart, pushed it aside, locked the door, and went into a monologue from *Macbeth*!

"He'd actually gone to a costume shop, rented the busboy uniform, bought the food at his own expense, stolen the cart from the hotel kitchen, and brought it up to me. In a way it was very funny. But it was also frightening. We had people who ate dog food and barked for auditions. On another open call, a man did a fire dance and his hair caught on fire in the middle of the performance. It's a strange business."

The point is to keep your sense of perspective. If today's audition doesn't go well, start planning for tomorrow's. Nora Eckstein often has told her clients that interviews and auditions are like buses. There's always going to be another one coming along.

"There are countless opportunities and there's always something else worth exploring," Nora says. "You just can't take it personally. Too many people and too many factors are involved in these decisions. If it doesn't work out, it's on to the next thing. That's how you must deal with it. If parents and children get bitter or overly sensitive every time someone else gets a role, they're really not cut out for this kind of work. The roles will come, but you may have to pay your dues along the way. Also consider that each audition, whether your child is selected or not, is another opportunity for valuable experience."

IN REVIEW

1. *A good agent probably will help acquaint your child with a role before an interview or audition.*
2. *Bring something to occupy your mind while your child is being interviewed or auditioned.*
3. *Your child's actions and attitudes when answering interview questions will be more of a factor than what he or she actually says.*
4. *Leave a photo or composite of your child with all the appropriate people.*
5. *Don't let your child get caught up in nonproductive competitiveness during auditions.*
6. *Prepare your child for the possibility of being filmed or videotaped on short notice.*
7. *Encourage your child to review the script several times before an audition.*
8. *Remind your child to be energetic and enthusiastic, unless the role requires a more serious approach.*
9. *Many top actors began as theatrical understudies.*
10. *Explore all possibilities.*

Jason Hervey

◻f the current crop of young actors, few have enjoyed as much success, visibility, and variety in their careers as Jason Hervey. Although most familiar to television viewers as the sometimes less-than-lovable Wayne (Fred Savage's older brother) on ABC's Emmy-winning *The Wonder Years*, he has also starred or appeared on such series as *Diff'rent Strokes, Punky Brewster, Taxi,* and *Trapper John, M.D.,* and has a remarkable 250 commercials to his credit. On the big screen, Jason has had featured roles in several box-office winners, including *Back to the Future, Pee-wee's Big Adventure, Police Academy II,* and *Back to School.*

It was a persistent family friend who convinced Jason's mother, Marsha, to audition him for a Japanese commercial in 1976 (despite the language barrier, he got the job). What followed was not only his own growth as one of the busiest child actors of the '80s, but his mother's rise as a successful personal manager as well. Over the years, the two maintained a busy schedule both separately and together, but found the time to devote to several key charities such as Mothers Against Drunk Driving, the Make-a-Wish Foundation, Variety Clubs International, and the Jerry Lewis Muscular Dystrophy Telethon (for which Jason was selected National Youth Host in 1988). Over time, Jason has also managed to excel as an athlete, be it on the slopes, the tennis court, the soccer field, or even behind the wheel of a racing car.

For other young performers hoping to launch similar careers, here's what this accomplished young actor had to say about his own career and the state of the industry when interviewed after the run of *The Wonder Years*.

Q: *What are your first memories of the business?*
A: My first real memory of acting is having to drive out to Ojai (a farming and resort community near Ventura, California) to do a commercial for a company called Chip Star in Japan.

All I really remember is spending a very long day in the potato fields in Hemet, California. I was four at the time and had no idea what I was doing. Now, having grown up in front of the camera, I don't know anything *but* that life.

Q: *Do you find that many of your contemporaries have been pushed into acting, or is this what they want to be doing?*

A: It's a mixture, I suppose. There's no question that some of them are pushed for all the wrong reasons. Mainly because their parents want to be in the business, and they're living out that fantasy through their children.

Fortunately, that's not at all what it was or is in my case. From the very beginning, it was made clear to me that if I wanted to quit tomorrow, my mom wouldn't care. She's just always been behind me in whatever I wanted to do. The entire situation with her, in fact, has been great all along. At first, she was another mom on the set, looking out for my best interests and making everything go smoothly. Then, after being there and watching and learning for eleven and a half hours every day over fourteen years, she became a professional herself. After all, being right on the scene like that is the best training anyone could hope for. So, the bottom line is that I've been lucky.

As for kids who *are* being pressured by their parents, they'll probably have to put up with it until they just can't take it any more—then blow up and say, "No, I don't want to do this!" It's like Emilio Estevez's father in *The Breakfast Club*, who wanted his son to become the star wrestler that *he* never was, and so pushed the kid from day one.

Q: *You and your mom are the perfect example of a successful parent/child show business combination. What can people reading this do to improve their chances of enjoying a similar level of success?*

A: First, I would strongly urge everyone to avoid any place that says it can *promise* you success, or claims it can make you a star and get you on the covers of national magazines. That place doesn't exist. No one can really make that happen. The right way, of course, is for parents to go out and find agents for their children, and then work closely with those agents to find out what the child is doing right and what he or she is doing wrong. The parents have to be involved and know exactly what's going on. This doesn't mean interfering or trying to run everyone's life. But they can't just drop off kids at auditions.

My advice to kids is real simple: just have fun. Don't let yourself lose touch with who you are and how old you are. If I were a director or casting agent talking to an eight-year-old boy and he was sitting there telling me about the Stanislavsky method of acting or how he's been in fifty different acting programs around the world, he'd probably be the *last* person I would hire. I do think young actors should go to one or two acting coaches to become polished, but after that they need to stand on their own two feet and be as natural as possible. That's what will get them jobs in the long run.

Q: *You began your career in commercials. Despite the competition, do you think that's the best place for most kids to start?*

A: Yes, definitely. If not commercials, then print jobs. From there, they will hopefully build to TV, then Movies of the Week, then films and TV series. That's how it happened with me. Of course, lots of young actors would want to think in terms of theater, too, though it's just never seemed right for me.

Q: *How should young performers deal with success when it comes their way?*

A: You have to keep reminding yourself that it could all go away tomorrow, which is absolutely true. Enjoy it while you have it. Don't squander your money, either. Save it for a rainy day, because there may well be one at some point.

I always try to keep things in perspective, realizing that success came relatively easily and could disappear the same way. Naturally, parents have a huge impact on how their kids handle success, or rejection for that matter. If they have the attitude, "Hey, you didn't get the part, but don't worry about it. There's always the next time," kids will be cool. That's what my mom always said. If I didn't get a role, it was because they wanted a kid with brown hair or brown eyes. She'd always tell me I was the best.

Then, if you *do* make it, you can't—or your parents

can't let you—start acting differently at home or with friends. It's that way with my older brother, who's going to be a lawyer. He tells me how proud of me he is, but if I ever mouthed off to him, I'd get thrown around the room in a second! Believe me, if your friends really are your friends, they'll keep you in your place. If you start having a "star" attitude, they'll tell you to knock it off fast.

It's never happened to me, though, since I've worked hard to maintain a sense of perspective. But it's your friends' and family's job to keep you in line and let you know the world doesn't revolve around you.

Q: *Has your education suffered in any way as a result of your hectic work schedule?*
A: No. Having teachers work with you one on one can be a real plus, even though I do miss being in public school. I had some of the best times I've ever had in my life when I was going to school. I just haven't been able to do that over the last three years or so. But no matter how working kids are getting their education, I'm a big believer in having something else to fall back on, whether or not it's industry related.

For instance, recently I've been the host, cowriter, associate producer, and creative consultant on Bob Bennett Productions' *Wide World of Kids*, a nationally syndicated half-hour TV show for ABC that profiles the lifestyles and cultures of different kids around the world. My point is that if someone can explore as many areas as possible, they might discover they enjoy something else even more than acting. You just never know.

Q: *Someone like Ron Howard would seem an ideal case in point.*
A: He's one of my idols, along with Tim Burton, who directed *Batman*, and I. W. Harper, the director of *Wide World of Kids*.

Q: *Do you think the business and the types of roles available have improved lately for young actors?*
A: Absolutely. People are putting their faith so much more now in young actors and actresses. It's a great thing to see. I think writers are finally creating three-dimensional roles

for kids, instead of having them deliver one-liners just to get a laugh from the audience. Look at Neil Patrick Harris in *Doogie Howser.* I love that show. And *The Wonder Years* is his favorite show. The industry seems ready to deal with the real issues young people face, and that means even more doors opening up for good young actors in the '90s. After all, it's a kid's world. We're the next leaders. And Hollywood is reflecting that.

Q: *Any favorite shows from over the years?*

A: I was on *Diff'rent Strokes* for two years and there was one episode in which I had to dress up as Madonna. It meant I had to walk around the set all day between takes looking like Madonna—wig, makeup, and all. Trust me, it was very funny. But, in case you're wondering: No, Warren Beatty *didn't* ask me out!

CHAPTER
SEVEN

WHAT TO EXPECT AND
HOW TO BEHAVE ON THE SET

Filming is filming, whether it's for a theatrical motion picture, a television program, or a commercial. Your child's first experience in a studio or on location for any one of these purposes is likely to be a bit mind-boggling.

When you arrive at the studio or location (some location shoots can involve traveling with the cast and crew and perhaps spending the night), you'll soon be asked to sign a contract and fill out a W-4 Income Tax Withholding Form. If you choose, you can claim zero dependents, since your child will probably be a full-time student. Most of the time, you will be asked to bring a selection of clothes for your child, unless you're told beforehand that outfits will be provided.

Next will come an unavoidable period of waiting. Take advantage of this free time to help your child memorize lines and to convey your love, support, and pride.

A voice-level check may follow, after which the first scene will usually be blocked out by the director, cast, and crew. *It's essential that you listen carefully to what the director has to say.* Many takes later, you'll at last be ready to move on, this time perhaps for a close-up of one or more actors, a stunt, or a special effect of some kind. Your child may or may not be given a break during this phase, depending on what work remains to be done. The break can be fifteen minutes or as long as two hours. Then it's time for the whole process to begin again for a new scene.

Although the director is in charge, there are many other people with crucial responsibilities on the set. The first assistant director, for example, helps the director line up actors and extras, and makes sure all the props, special effects, and other elements are in place on time and ready to go. A second assistant director (of which there are sometimes more than one) assists the assistant director and often has a trainee of his or her own. Either the second assistant director or the trainee is responsible for ensuring that all actors sign their W-4 forms and complete their time cards. A production manager hires and pays the crew and arranges for food and transportation needs, among other things.

The basic crew includes the camera operator (plus an assistant), a makeup artist, hairstylist, sound operator, and several gaffers (who handle lights) and grips (who lift and move equipment).

When your child's first filming experience draws near, *expect the unexpected.* In television especially, a script is never finished until shooting is finished. In this business, writing means rewriting. So don't be surprised if the day before your child is to appear before the camera for the first time, a script appears on your doorstep with rewritten pages. These will be printed on a different color paper, with the specific changes marked with an asterisk in the margin to help you spot deletions from or additions to the dialogue.

Of course, most filming today does not involve the incomparable *L* word—*live!* During my entire eight-year run of *I Remember Mama,* those of us in the cast weren't so much worried about remembering Mama as we were about remembering our lines. After all, in those days there were no retakes—and that's why stories of "corpses" miraculously sneezing or walking off stage, of doors that wouldn't open, and of vanishing dialogue lost in the twilight zone even before there *was* a *Twilight Zone* are still legendary.

Once on *Mama,* the actor playing my father left the theater halfway through our live broadcast, believing his part was done for that episode, but forgetting a key scene he was supposed to be in later on. With no other recourse, the show's director, Ralph Nelson, did the actor's lines from off-camera, with us hastily explaining that our dad was working on the lawn outside.

In a similar vein, I once walked onstage during a play some two pages too early, which was bad enough but was all the worse because I burst in on the play's big love scene. And during one performance of *Mister Roberts*, I was supposed to exit a scene through the audience but step slightly aside so that two prop people could cover me with a bucket full of soap suds. Instead, the two were so overanxious that they threw the soapy water too soon, totally missing me and completely drenching someone in the audience. As I said: expect the unexpected.

Anyway, in filming, as in any commercial endeavor, time is money. When you look around a set, just notice the number of people involved and consider the technology required to create the proper illusion of reality and you'll understand how important saving time is.

In theatrical films, budgets are typically much larger and shooting schedules are much longer, although the pace is frequently more relaxed. After all, nobody's going to tell a Steven Spielberg to hurry up if he's not happy with the way a scene is going. What it comes down to is this: The bigger the director is, the bigger the budget and the longer the schedule.

Whereas a Spielberg may shoot only two script pages a day, a television director is expected to complete from six to ten. Understandably, every minute on a television soundstage is a premium minute, and *your child will be counted on not to delay the filming*.

When your child is cast in a regular series, the demands on your time and his or hers will be almost literally around the clock. Production can often take twelve hours a day, six days a week, depending on whether the show is filmed, taped, done live, or on location. Certain states have child labor laws that limit the number of hours minors can work, but the pace will be hectic nonetheless.

This will be the time for your child to establish him- or herself as a complete pro. Help your child maintain a high energy level. Provide nourishing, high-energy snacks. Once children demonstrate consistent attentiveness and a general maturity over such long hours, their reputation for reliability will get around the industry (and don't panic if they're nervous: Many longtime pros feel the same way to this day). Once a child is viewed favorably, you can bet there will be other jobs down the road.

The director Les Martinson certainly knew what it's like to work with young television performers. He helmed many episodes of *Eight Is Enough*, *The Brady Bunch*, and *Small Wonder*, and also directed the Cliff Robertson film *PT 109* as well as the popular *Rescue From Gilligan's Island*. In an interview several years back, he said he found that the main problem with child actors is their limited attention span, which is why he always tried to make everything as enjoyable as possible and build up their confidence in the process.

Although Les was reluctant to credit himself, he said his years directing television shows with young actors were remarkably free of strife. Instead of accumulating ulcers, he was storing up what became wonderful memories. Recalling the *Brady Bunch* set, he remarked, "One child was more exemplary than the next, and so were the mothers. Never a problem. I've never seen anything like it. On *Eight Is Enough*, the same unusual situation existed. Never any temper tantrums or difficulties. This usually comes from the top. It's the executive producer in charge of a show who sets the tone and creates the atmosphere on the set. When you walk on a happy set, you know it right away. It's not common, but it's wonderful when it happens."

Being on a film set day in and day out can sometimes best be compared to sitting on a roller coaster that isn't moving. You know a wild adventure is just around the corner, but you also know you may have to wait before you get there. Even so, the last thing a director needs is a whiny kid disrupting the set by complaining that he has nothing to do.

A flip side: Instead of growing bored, children sometimes become overstimulated and hyperactive on the set. If that happens to your child, it will probably stem from a feeling of being lost among the cast and crew swirling around the set, in which case the child will need your soothing reassurance. *If there are other kids on the set, by all means encourage yours to join them and be a part of a group.* If your child still can't seem to acclimate, try to show him or her around (without interfering with filming). Explain what's going on, if you can. Perhaps there will be an assistant director, on-set tutor, welfare worker, or other industry-wise adult who can help give your child a sense of how he or she fits in.

Never forget that one's behavior on the set will be judged as much as one's talent. There are simply too many young performers out there scrambling to get ahead for anyone in the business to put up with an unstable kid. Of all the four-letter words used in entertainment circles, *brat* is certainly one that nobody ever wants to hear.

Don't let any of this scare you off for a second, though. These situations are the exceptions, not the rule. Most kids won't be bored, overwhelmed, *or* disruptive during filming. They'll get a huge thrill out of the new sights, sounds, and people and anxiously look forward to each day's work.

All this applies to parents as well, who must also get used to complying with what they're told to do and staying out of the way. Along these lines, parents on the set who have complaints are urged *not* to bother the director merely to vent a gripe. If you have a problem that needs to be dealt with immediately, go to the assistant director. If it isn't urgent, let your agent take care of it through the production office. Of course, if your child's health is being jeopardized, go immediately to the welfare worker who is on the set for that very purpose. If you feel a stunt person should be doubling for your child in a given scene, for instance, the person to talk to, again, is the welfare worker. You and the welfare worker are there to protect this minor who can't protect him- or herself.

As do all experienced agents or managers, Diane Hardin stresses that *just as there are professional young actors, there are also professional stage parents.* Parents who are professional go about their business so the cast and crew can do the same. You can stand and watch your child, she says, if you can do so without hindering the crew's work in any way. But you don't need to have your face three inches from your child's at all times. As a matter of fact, Diane thinks it's better for the children if they *don't* see their parents all that much while they're working. As parents, you don't think *you're* being watched, but you are. And more than one child has been fired and replaced over the years because a parent was impossible to deal with.

"Don't get a 'star' attitude," says Diane. "You're very lucky to have a child working in this business. You should be grateful."

Soaps, like game, talk, and news shows and most sitcoms, are shot on videotape. The experience for the actor is very different from that of working with film. If you've ever followed a day-time drama, you will have noticed that most of the regulars have a day or two off per week. This is understandable, considering the long hours and intense pacing involved. Having been on two soaps myself—*Young Dr. Malone* and *The Nurses*—I can speak from personal experience when I say that they are nothing less than exhausting.

Your child's schedule on a soap will depend on two factors: the size of the role and the terms of the contract (a contract may not figure into it at all, in which case your child will just be told when he or she is needed).

For budgetary and scheduling reasons, soaps aren't shot piecemeal like films, but almost straight through. For an actor, it becomes the equivalent of doing a stage play or live TV show every day. That's why there is near-constant pressure on everyone to do the job right.

Your child will have to be ready to deal with the pressure. Hopefully, the on-set atmosphere will be loose, friendly, and supportive, even though so much has to be done in so little time. There *will* be directors or producers, however, who forget that their cast is human and that human beings make mistakes.

Every director, regardless of his or her disposition, will at least expect your son or daughter to give it his or her all. If your child has a scene the next day, the night before can't be spent watching TV. On the set, *he must know his lines, know his cues, and thoroughly know the character he's playing.*

A brief rundown of a day in the life of a soap:

• Rehearsal begins early, usually about 8 a.m., followed by another rehearsal with blocking. Here, the director lays out the camera and character movements step by step ("Celia, you'll look at the window when Rick tells you he's leaving you for another man. Then you'll turn and walk to the cabinet, grab the gun, cry furiously, and announce that you're pregnant but don't know who the father is. Johnny, that's when you run in and tell them both that your mommy's memory is coming back and she knows who tried to run her over with the lawn mower.").

- Lunch follows either on the stage or in the commissary.
- Next up is a dress rehearsal, followed by the real thing. By the end of the day (around five or six o'clock), your child may well be exhausted. But when the episode airs two or three weeks later and you realize millions of loyal viewers are enjoying your child's work, it will have been more than worth it.

COMMERCIALS

A commercial may take all day to film and require numerous run-throughs, all of which may appear identical to the untrained eye. Nevertheless, it's vital that your child act professionally and be patient. Once again, think of the millions of people who will see the final results, and you'll understand how important the smallest detail is, given the limitations of a thirty-second time frame.

Beyond the personnel common to all filming, expect also to find an ad agency producer on the set of a commercial. This is someone who oversees the business end of the shoot in his or her capacity as the advertising agency's representative. Frequently, your child will have met the agency producer during the audition. If serious (and only serious) problems arise during shooting, he or she is a person who can help. On the set you'll also see other representatives from the ad agency and from the company that makes the product.

Most commercials are shot in segments, so your child probably won't have to memorize each word and movement for the entire spot. After a practice run-through or two, the action will be recorded on film or on tape. An assistant will be on hand timing everything to the split-second.

As your busy day begins to wind down, your child (along with other cast members) may be asked to record what are known as "wild lines" or a "wild track." That means another run through the dialogue of the commercial, but in this case it is only recorded on audiotape, not on videotape. Later, these lines will be laid into the regular sound track wherever voice levels are found to be too low or muffled.

Another sound-related trick is for actors to prerecord their dialogue at the top of the day, and then mouth the words for the camera during shooting. As it is for any form of filming, "lip sync" (short for *lip synchronization*) may be used when a song is being sung during the spot, for instance.

The very last element recorded at the end of the shooting day is called a "presence track." For this, the audio recorder asks everyone on the set to observe about a minute of total silence. This is recorded and later used during editing. Even silence has its own "sound" as far as both a film editor and a Paul Simon are concerned.

Some commercials are never meant to be aired on television at all. Called "demos" (short for *demonstrations*), these are made by ad agencies to test the reactions of either a sample audience or of the clients themselves, who frequently want to see several different ad campaigns from a given agency before giving the final go-ahead. Because these commercials don't actually air, your child will receive a smaller fee. Nevertheless, it's still nice work if you can get it.

If you'd like a copy of your child's commercial once it's completed, most ad agencies will provide one for a minimal charge. Your best bet will be to make this request to the agency producer before you leave the set, and then follow up on the phone a week or so later. Don't be annoyed if the answer is no at first. Some ad campaigns are cloaked in secrecy until all the pieces are in place. As soon as the spot hits the air, you should have no trouble getting a copy of it.

Landing a spot in a commercial will give your child a chance to learn how to work in front of a camera and to gain exposure that would otherwise take years. It's no accident that so many experts recommend that children look to commercials as a good way to start a show business career.

STAGE CHILDREN

Any child who is a principal, an understudy, or a "swing" person in a stage show is expected to go to the theater for every performance. A swing person fills in when needed and can be called upon to try a variety of minor roles (sometimes within the same performance). Since these are live productions, it goes without saying that *promptness is a must* (when I was in *O Mistress Mine*, the rule was clearly laid out: if you were more than two minutes late, you could instead say, "O Unemployment Mine").

You'll be told to arrive at the theater at least a half hour before curtain. Once there, you will get verbal updates every fifteen minutes to remind you it's almost showtime. And when it *is* showtime, your child will have to be physically and emotionally prepared and ready to go.

Most kids find a long-running show gives them a definite sense of continuity in their lives—a familiar character to play, a home away from home, and a regular group of people with whom to work and socialize.

In fact, children are often more comfortable in stage shows because their performances can be delivered sequentially. Unlike films and many TV shows, in which scenes may be shot out of sequence, a play is presented in "real time." For many young performers, this leads to a much more secure feeling.

IN REVIEW

1. *Be prepared for last-minute script changes.*
2. *Filming will be as demanding as it is rewarding for your child.*
3. *Remember that time is money on the set.*
4. *Behave professionally—remember, there are professional stage parents as well as professional children.*
5. *Never interfere with filming, but help your child get his or her bearings on the set.*
6. *Try to learn how everyone functions on the set.*
7. *Shooting a soap is much like doing a live play, so your child must be able to handle the pressure.*
8. *Commercials require expert timing, many takes, and considerable patience.*
9. *Promptness is an absolute must in the theater.*
10. *Use "waiting time" to offer emotional support and to help your child perfect his or her lines.*

Jackie Cooper

By the time he was a teenager in the mid-'30s, Jackie Cooper wasn't simply a child star, he was a national institution.

Jackie's first taste of acting began when he was only three, but just four years later—in 1929—he emerged as a star once and for all as a member of the classic *Our Gang* comedies (rerun on television as *The Little Rascals*). One short year after that, he enjoyed his first starring role in the Academy Award–winning film *Skippy*.

Another Oscar winner followed in 1931 when MGM teamed young Jackie with noted actor Wallace Beery in the emotionally wrenching film *The Champ*. They were also to costar again in the superb 1934 adaptation of *Treasure Island*.

Jackie proved as skilled at playing a streetwise tough kid as he was in the role of a sweet young innocent and over subsequent years became both a critically *and* publicly heralded young actor. He worked in just about every major studio and with most of the major adult stars, including Jimmy Stewart, Henry Fonda, and Lana Turner. At twenty, he enlisted in the U.S. Navy to serve in World War II, leading to a lifetime devotion to that branch of the military and to numerous honors from the government.

Although many of his contemporaries failed to sustain the quality of their careers as they matured, Jackie made a smooth transition into the adult world of acting. In addition to the countless stage, film, and TV roles that came over time, he went on to establish himself as a top director. In recent years, he has helmed such TV movies and series as the award-winning *M*A*S*H*, *Magnum, P.I.*, *Cagney and Lacey*, *Rainbow* (about Judy Garland's early years), *Izzy and Moe* (starring Jackie Gleason and Art Carney), and *The Night They Saved Christmas* (starring Carney, Jaclyn Smith, and a young R.J. Williams).

In 1981, Jackie turned his talents to writing, coauthoring

(with Dick Kleiner) a powerfully honest autobiography, *Please Don't Shoot My Dog*. Film audiences are most familiar with Jackie's recurring role as *Daily Planet* editor Perry White in all four *Superman* films.

Here, then, is an in-depth conversation with this unique master of all trades.

Q: *How has the business changed for young actors from when you got started?*

A: Both from personal experience and based on what I was told and what I've read, one big difference is that in the early days, a producer-director like Hal Roach went out *personally* and looked for young talent. Sure, someone would occasionally tell him about a cute child they'd seen, but he usually found kids on his own. Today, it seems that it's almost entirely up to the child, parent, and agent to generate jobs.

A couple of things never change, though. For instance, kids between five and twelve still tend to get most of the work. Secondly, it's still essential—more so than ever before, in fact—that these children have a natural style that audiences can relate to. That's why I strongly believe kids should experience normal social and school-related activities in their lives before their parents try to put them into the business.

There used to be professional acting schools that children attended from the first grade on. A lot of them were going to these schools when I started in the industry. But those kids had no idea what the average child's life was like at all, so as performers they had no real life to draw on. Maybe that's why at twelve years old I was uncomfortable around kids my own age. Since I'd spent most of my life with older people, I wanted to be with adults. At fifteen, I was interested only in girls at least three or four years older, which was tough, because eighteen-year-old girls aren't particularly interested in going out with fifteen-year-old boys! Before I moved to New York in 1947, John Garfield and Keenan Wynn were two of my closest friends, and they were both six or seven years older than I was.

So I think kids today shouldn't even consider going to a professional acting school until they're twelve years old or so. They need to have time to be kids first. If the business could regulate the use of kids as vigorously as it regulates the use of animals, we'd all be better off. Things have improved, but not all that much. Even the "Coogan Law" has loopholes a mile wide, so clearly there's still work to be done. How about an ASPCC—American Society for the Prevention of Cruelty to *Children*?

Q: *Was the studio system you grew up with better or worse for kids than what we have today?*

A: In one way it was better because it offered a form of protection for kids, in that the studio watched what the *parents* did. They didn't want any bad publicity stemming from the misbehavior of the parents. In another way, however, it wasn't so good because the studios had such far-reaching control over all their contract players, kids included. They also controlled the studio doctors, who gave pills to the kids to make sure their performances remained full of energy. Judy Garland became a terrible pill freak, and it wasn't of her own doing. I remember her talking about rehearsing with people like Busby Berkeley until 4 or 5 a.m. to be ready to shoot the big production number at 8:30. And her mother allowed it! So did the studio boss, Louis B. Mayer. So overall I guess today is safer, considering all the pros and cons. There isn't an ASPCC, but people have access to a great deal more information, this book being an example.

Q: *How did your career first get off the ground?*

A: Like most kids with a broken family, money was tight. My mother was off playing the piano with a singer on the vaudeville circuit and was hardly ever home—home being right here in Hollywood. My grandmother raised me. By the time I was three, I'm told, she was taking me along to stand in line outside the studios for extra work. That's what you did in those days. There was no Extras Guild. People would literally just stand outside the studio hoping they'd get called in. They'd hear that a Western was being made, so they'd dress up as a cowboy or an Indian. Once in a while, my grandmother and I would be asked in. Everyone would assume she was my mother, since she was only in her thirties. After working here and there for two dollars a day and a boxed lunch, one thing led to another and the roles began getting bigger.

The truth is, I really don't remember that period very well, including waiting outside the studios. Evidently, there were some directors who noticed that I would do whatever they asked me to. I can't even tell you how I got into *Our Gang* or if we even had an agent at that point. Then in 1929, I was in a sound musical at Fox Movietone. It was supposed to be the first sound picture, but Warner Bros. beat it with *The Jazz Singer.* Now, *that* I remember very well because I had to sing a song in the film.

Q: *Did the experience scare you?*

A: I knew the song and the melody, so I was fine. Most kids don't have those kinds of fears. It would have been frightening if any experience went badly, and then I had to go back and do it again around the same people. But I have no memories of being afraid that I wouldn't do well. Looking at some of my old pictures today, I wish I had!

Q: *It was* Our Gang *that made you a star, but what do you think sustained your success over the following years?*

A: I've always felt that I was only as good as the director. I've seen pictures of mine in which I think I was just terrible. But in the same year, working for a director like Victor Fleming (*Treasure Island*), I would be a different kid. The thing I learned later on was that directors had actually been impressed with *me*, because I would offer to do scenes over again until I felt I had given my best performance.

Q: *What was it like to be a national idol, and how can successful young actors today learn to keep their egos in check?*

A: I've certainly had to direct my share of egomaniacal kids who were unheard of a year ago and are now telling *me* how to direct a scene. It's something parents can keep an eye on, but ultimately it's up to the kids to monitor themselves, or else they're in for some tough times.

In terms of my own experience, I always think of what Sid Grauman did the day we put my hand- and footprints in the wet cement at the old Grauman's Chinese Theater (now Mann's). He took a stick and he wrote, "America's Boy." I still get a tremendous kick out of that. But I don't think it was until 1940, when I went back to the Chinese and took another look, that I realized what it had all meant.

I guess my name was biggest through the age of thirteen, during the Wallace Beery era. But it was a time in my life when I wasn't fully aware of what that level of success meant. Sure, the kids I played with would tease me and say, "Hey, you think you're such a big shot!" But I was able to get them beyond that just by being one of them and not behaving differently. That's something I would strongly suggest to successful kids now.

It was when I was seventeen and eighteen that I became really conscious of what my career meant. Of course, by then the name wasn't quite what it had been, and I knew I'd have to work extra hard to keep it alive. In any case, if I *did* have any inflated thoughts about myself (which I don't remember having), they wouldn't have lasted long in the Navy! Whatever happened there, they were more likely to blame *me*, because I was supposed to set the example for the others. That helped put everything in perspective for me.

It is amazing, though, how much impact this medium has. I can stop for gas somewhere in the middle of Mexico and be recognized to this day. Not from TV or *Superman*, but from the old movies. I've never *needed* to be recognized, but it's a joy if you can make six or seven people smile who otherwise weren't going to smile. As my mother always said, "If you don't want to be nice, don't go out and be seen." And that advice still applies in the business today, for working kids *or* adults.

Q: *How were you able to make that often difficult transition from child star to successful adult in the business?*

A: Ironically, I've always said that to a large extent I was saved by the war. I grew up in the Navy. Even so, some of the less pleasant facets of the business do stay with you for many years. I went through therapy for three years. I went through a period of loneliness. I was distrustful of people, and with pretty good reason. My mother wasn't dead five minutes when relatives were fighting over my money. Fortunately, she and my uncle (noted director Norman Taurog) had made all kinds of plans for me and I was protected against those relatives. The money had been put away and was properly invested.

I was protected from the kind of thing that happened to Jackie Coogan. In fact, Jackie and I made a couple of movies together after the war, and he advised me how I could best spend and invest my money. Over the years, wise money management and conservative financial planning ensured that I would never go to the poorhouse. This in turn enabled me to do the kind of work I wanted to do, like taking a chance on live television. It didn't pay that much, but it was a wonderful creative opportunity.

Q: *What message would you send to kids looking for a show business career?*

A: Ideally, that they not do it solely for the money, but for the satisfaction of trying to do the best they can at the job. Again, I think it's essential that they have a few years of traditional schooling behind them. They should know what normal relationships and activities are for a child. If it's not solely for the money, and if they can find out objectively if this is the career they want, then they're off to the best start possible.

Q: *As a director, have you found the mothers of young actors easy or difficult to work with?*

A: Frankly, I don't work with kids that often, but when I do, I usually confine the talk with their mothers to the next day's work. If the child has a bad habit that affects our work together, I'll discuss that. But I ask the mother not to punish the child for a bad habit, because the fear of punishment will be on the kid's mind instead of the scene.

I'm probably not objective enough on this whole subject, but I can't help that. I directed a picture in 1981 called *Leave 'Em Laughing*, starring Mickey Rooney and a child who played an autistic little boy. Mickey played a clown who could make all the kids laugh except this one kid. It was a sweet story and quite dramatic in spots. I also knew the kind of performance I could get out of this young actor if I wanted to scare him or lie to him or scold him, or whatever. But I couldn't do it. It was done to me, but I just couldn't do it to him.

So when I see some of the more demanding mothers during auditions or during filming, I can't help but remember my own grandmother saying over and over, "Be nice, be nice, be nice." That's why to this day I can never remember people's names. It goes back to when the director or producer or casting director were headed my way, and my grandmother would pinch me in the back and say, "That's Mr. or Mrs. So-and-So. Say hello, be nice."

Ever since, the minute someone is introduced to me, I suffer some kind of subconscious memory block.

Q: *Are there any memories you especially cherish over others from your early career?*

A: MGM used to make short films for publicity purposes and then run them in the theaters with full-length features. One of these shorts was called *Jackie Cooper's Birthday*. It was my tenth, I think. Clark Gable was in it, Jean Harlow was in it. But even though they had assembled over a hundred of the biggest MGM stars on this huge soundstage—for *my* birthday—I barely remember being there. What I *do* remember is not being the slightest bit impressed. It was another day's work to me.

Many of my nicer memories of that time have to do with some of the men who played my fathers and subsequently became real-life father figures to me. People like Ralph Bellamy and Richard Dix. I had a stepfather for about ten minutes at one point, but we didn't exactly get along. So these actors had a profound impact on me. And a lot of them stayed in touch for years after our working relationship ended. I guess mine was the classic case of a kid wanting a man to look up to and love. As distrustful as I was of adults—are they lying to get me to smile or to cry?—it was wonderful to have guys like that in my life.

Those are the memories that make me say, as I wrote in my book, that with all the ups and downs, I'm not bitter. I benefited from those experiences and I learned a lot during those years.

CHAPTER

EIGHT

BALLET—THE ULTIMATE CHALLENGE

No theatrical art form boasts the tradition and mystique of ballet. No other makes such demands on both teacher and student. Ballet is the ultimate challenge, blending grace and stamina with well-rounded athletic ability.

Maybe you wonder whose child will voluntarily submit to the kind of mental and physical discipline that ballet requires. Well, probably the same child who suffers every kind of mental and physical discipline to play first-string football, volleyball, tennis, or any other sport. It's simply a matter of channeling all that energy and determination in a new direction.

Teacher Natalia Clare heads a highly regarded dance studio in Los Angeles where Patrick Swayze and his mother, Patsy, taught jazz classes. Natalia has grown very concerned lately about the unfortunate decline of interest in ballet.

A student of the renowned Bronislava Nijinska and one-time principal ballerina with the Ballet Russe de Monte Carlo, she recalls the '70s, when television popularized ballet for mass audiences. During that period, for example, Edward Villella and Jacques D'Amboise of the New York City Ballet performed in specials that clearly showed the extraordinary athletic ability demanded of the great male dancers, with D'Amboise actually taking kids off the streets of New York and training them for performances in Madison Square Garden.

Several years later, with Rudolf Nureyev's defection from

Russia, Mikhail Baryshnikov's appearance in the motion picture *The Turning Point*, and Gregory Hines's in *White Nights*, ballet's widespread popularity and accessibility reached even greater heights. In particular, people like Arthur Mitchell and Alvin Ailey, as well as the members of the Dance Theater of Harlem (a superb classical ballet company) showed formerly reluctant boys and young men that ballet could indeed be a "macho" form of art.

Why, then, has all that enthusiasm for ballet diminished? Natalia worries about today's kids, because "nothing seems to stimulate them. Becoming a professional dancer takes extremely hard work and dedication. I can't really put my finger on what happened. Maybe it's considered too passive compared with some other types of entertainment. To me, though, ballet is a complete art form that embraces music, art, and drama. As a ballerina and teacher, I know it has opened up an entire world and so many different cultures to me, with dance as the common language wherever I go."

Whatever is to blame, the great American ballet companies are finding it increasingly difficult to develop the would-be stars of tomorrow. There simply aren't enough students, which clearly suggests *there's a major opportunity for those children who show a willingness and ability to learn ballet*—and for those parents who have the resolve to stick out up to ten years of training!

Most good teachers agree *that the earliest and best age to start any kind of dance training is at eight years.* Younger children's bones haven't had the time to develop properly. However, there are preballet classes specifically designed for six- and seven-year-olds where the basics are taught with none of the more stressful positions required.

Although ballet teachers tend to expect a longer commitment of time and a greater degree of passion from their students, they look for basically the same things that all dance teachers look for in their pupils. The physical ideal is the "perfect dancer's body": a small head, long neck, long limbs, and lean physique.

This so-called perfect body, however, is far less critical in contemporary forms of dance. Natalia's own former student, Melora Hardin—Diane's daughter—landed the lead in the TV version of *Dirty Dancing*, though Natalia points out that she "has a most lovely body, but not quite the ideal legs for a tutu."

Mentally, dance students should have a tenaciousness in the face of occasional frustration, a singleness of purpose, a compulsion to continue the training for many years to come, and an overall love for dance almost to the exclusion of everything else.

Unfortunately, it's frequently the *parents* who don't have the patience needed, regardless of how physically and mentally qualified their children are. They want success to come right away for their kids. Fathers in particular frequently want a backup in case dance training doesn't pan out. In addition to taking strenuous ballet classes, they expect their children to excel in school and sports as well.

"You can't have it both ways," says Natalia. "Ballet requires total commitment from parent and child. It's something both must want very much."

Those who *do* want it very much usually find their ballet training well worth the effort, whether they stay in ballet or move on to other forms of dance or the musical theater. Some of Natalia's own students over the years reflect this: Laura Desiree became a principal ballerina with the Pittsburgh Ballet. Heather Watts became a star with the New York City Ballet. Others went on to dance with the Joffrey Ballet and other major international companies. Among Natalia's students who have used their training as an element of their acting and musical theater careers are Tracy Wells of *Mr. Belvedere* and Lisa Lackwood, a former soloist with the American Ballet Theater who has been featured in the stage version of *The Phantom of the Opera*.

MARKETING YOUR CHILD'S BALLET TALENT

As you might imagine, auditions will represent the next step after your child has been through the requisite years of training. How many audition opportunities your teenager will have will depend greatly on your location. The good news is that there are some twenty to twenty-five auditions held every year in large population centers such as Los Angeles, Chicago, Boston, and New York, since most major American ballet companies are always seeking the stars of tomorrow.

When your child is accepted by one of these companies as a student, he or she will probably attend its summer sessions for a month to six weeks. Some students are lucky enough to win a scholarship, while others must pay tuition for the session and cover their own food and lodging. Classes are typically large. Still, remember that *the major companies do eventually place top students in their professional ranks.*

An example is the New York City Ballet, which will take on exceptional students in its work-training program. With progress, those students are then invited back for a second year. If they still show promise, they're asked to stay on a full season and are ultimately asked to join the company. In other words, being a student with a ballet company can and frequently does open the door to a full-fledged career.

To find when and where such auditions are going to be held, and possibly to find good beginning ballet schools in your area, the best source of information is *Dance Magazine*. The April edition is especially useful in that it carries scores of announcements concerning auditions, schools, contests, and camps for the upcoming summer. A directory lists schools, teachers, and regional companies in every state, complete with addresses and phone numbers.

Beyond leading to a career as a performer, ballet (and other) dance training often leads to a career in teaching. Natalia points out that a professional dance career is not a prerequisite for becoming a good teacher. "A good teacher is a good teacher, and students and parents instantly recognize that. In fact, some of the greatest dancers make terrible teachers because great dancers are inherently performers, not necessarily teachers."

Natalia considers herself fortunate to have had the brilliant Nijinska as her teacher. In her youth, Los Angeles was a back-water where ballet was concerned. The ballet center in America was almost solely on the East Coast and the one important company was the Ballet Russe de Monte Carlo. "There were no auditions as we have today," Natalia recalls. "They came to the studios to seek out dancers for their companies. The great ballerinas Marjorie and Maria Tallchief and Cyd Charisse were in the same class with me. I knew Cyd then as Tula Ellice Finklea, and she was the first one chosen by the Ballet Russe. Few people know that this led her to London where she met and fell in love with Nico Charisse, bringing a quick end to her ballet career but a wonderful beginning to her very successful film career. The second student chosen happened to be me."

Natalia's is an obvious success story. But what happens to the teenager who has worked hard for eight or ten years, attended a company's summer session, and then fails to be accepted professionally? Naturally, it can be devastating, much as it is for the athlete who trains all his or her life for the Olympics, only to perform poorly at the trials. But a lot of kids *do* fight back, refuse to take no for an answer, and eventually are accepted in a company. These are the ones who inevitably find success not only in ballet, but in all of life.

A young girl once asked the legendary Martha Graham whether or not she should be a dancer. Graham simply but profoundly answered, "If you have to ask, don't dance." Maybe that says it all.

IN REVIEW

1. *Most top American ballet companies need students, which means there are major opportunities out there to explore.*
2. *Most teachers agree that eight is the best age to start ballet (or any) dance training.*
3. *Be prepared for your child to study ballet for up to ten years before he or she is ready to pursue a professional career.*
4. *Major ballet companies in large cities frequently hold auditions for prospective new students.*
5. *Dance training often leads to a career as a dance teacher.*

CHAPTER

NINE

PHOTO MODELING

☐bviously, modeling is the most looks-oriented field of all. Your child's teeth, in particular, will have a part in determining how much work he or she gets (but note that false teeth can sometimes be used for a shoot). In fact, at the age when one's teeth are undergoing the greatest change—between six and eight—you may find that modeling calls drop out as fast as the teeth themselves! It's true that a dentist or orthodontist can come to the rescue, but any decision of this sort must be well thought out. Don't act out of panic. Once the teeth return, so do the jobs. Especially for children wearing clothing sizes 8, 10, 12, and 14.

The clothing modeled for fashion assignments is provided, but with most other modeling jobs, it will probably be up to you to bring the appropriate outfits. If it turns out the type of clothing you are asked to bring isn't what your child would normally wear, you might consider borrowing from a friend. If luck is on your side, your brother-in-law owns a children's clothing shop, your cousin is a photographer, and your neighbor's mother-in-law is a talent agent. For some curious reason though, it rarely works out that way.

In teen-fashion modeling, it's next to impossible to get away from the fact that a tall, lean figure, though not always essential, is a definite plus. The concept of the ideal young model has varied over the years, but your child will almost certainly need to be at least 5'6" in the teen-fashion modeling field, or 5'7" (for females) and 6' (for males) in the high-fashion modeling field where the average age is 19.

At any age, traditional good looks are a prime asset. But there are also those intangibles that create the mystique successful models of all ages seem to share. Consider the photo models you see pictured most frequently, male or female. They all have a natural rapport with the camera. Effortlessly, they exude a sense of intelligence, grace of movement, confidence, and, if the job calls for it, a sexuality that immediately catches your eye.

When your child lands a modeling agent and starts getting assignments, be ready to provide transportation at a moment's notice and to bring grooming aids, shoes, socks, clothing (if needed), and a composite to every shoot.

Also, remember to compliment your child on achieving this important first step. Whatever these early assignments are— even if they're low paying and local in nature—they represent a wonderful sign of things to come.

CELEBRITY CLOSE-UP

Rodney Allen Rippy

Although he devoted recent years to his education and not his career, Rodney Allen Rippy (now in his twenties) still enjoys a special place in the hearts of countless Americans who fondly remember his classic series of Jack-in-the-Box commercials in the '70s. As a child performer, Rodney took the art of unpretentious naturalism to a new height not only in those and other commercials, but in feature films (including *Blazing Saddles*) and on such diverse television programs as *Laugh-In*, *The Tonight Show Starring Johnny Carson*, *The Merv Griffin Show*, and *The Dinah Shore Show*. Indeed, Rodney proved that the rise to stardom *can* sometimes be just a commercial away.

Born and raised in Southern California, Rodney was all of three when he went on a fateful audition for the Jack-in-the-Box commercial that would launch his career and change his life. Over the subsequent years, and thanks in great part to the enduring love and support of his mother, Flossie (who regrettably passed away in 1986), he enjoyed a level of popularity few actors of *any* age could ever hope to enjoy in their careers. Despite his accomplishments, however, Rodney decided in his teens not to let his professional success interfere with his personal growth, and therefore packed up and headed off to North Carolina to live and study before returning to Los Angeles.

Q: *What are your earliest recollections of the business?*

A: Well, there certainly was no tradition of show business in the family, but since my two brothers, my sister, and I were all young at the time, my mother thought it might be enjoyable for us. I distinctly remember one day when I was about three years old, I was sitting about two feet from the television set and cracking up from *The Little Rascals* when my mom walked in the room to see why I was laughing and said, "Rodney, do you think *you* could be on TV?" I nodded my head, but she wanted to be certain, so she asked, "Are you sure you wouldn't be scared?" I just shook my head, and she said, "Alright, let me see what I can do about that."

From that day, she started going through the Yellow Pages and just about everything else that could help, and calling people throughout the industry, not just for me, but for the other kids in the family, too. Up until that point, she hadn't been a professional of any kind, but she suddenly gave this her all, with Pop's encouragement. Of course, I was really young at the time, so to this day, I don't have an exact picture of what she did or whom she called back then—only that it seemed to work out. Eventually, I met up with the woman who became my agent, Dorothy Day Otis. I suppose she liked the fact that we—and this included my brother Kenneth and my sister Beverley—weren't fearful of anything and just had our own, natural personalities. And, soon after that, the very first audition I went out on was for Jack-in-the-Box.

Q: *Do you remember that audition to any extent?*

A: Actually, I remember that and just about everything else from that point on as if it were yesterday. It was a very exciting time for all of us. After all, my sister landed a Banquet Fried Chicken commercial after *her* very first audition, and it was the exact same story with my brother, who did voice-over work for the "I'd Like to Teach the World to Sing" commercial for Coke. It was incredible. As for my audition, which like I said was actually my first, there were tons of kids there, as you might imagine. Right before I went in, my mom said, "Now, Rodney, remember, this is for food. I brought you up right, so whatever you do, don't talk with your mouth full! Be real nice and just do your best. If you have any problems, don't worry. There will be other auditions." She gave me a big kiss and in I went. In fact, that would always be her attitude. There was never any pressure put on me, not once. Actually, the very day of my audition, my sister was filming her own commercial, so my mom was racing across town to check up on both of us. Obviously, *she* must have felt a lot of pressure, but she never let it affect her treatment of us, then or ever.

Anyway, when I went in for my audition, one of the men on the set asked his associate to go ahead and flip on the camera, which wasn't one of the cameras they planned to shoot the commercial with. It was just a video camera on a tripod. There was a lady on the set making Jumbo Jacks, and so they slid a fresh burger in front of each kid who came in.

After I was sitting and the camera was on, the man asked what my name was, and I told him. Then he asked what the burger was, and I said, "That's the Jumbo Jack from Jack-in-the-Box." He told me to pick it up and take a bite, which I did. And he said, "Well, Rodney, how do you like it?" But just then it hit me that my mom had told me not to talk with my mouth full! So, with my mouth totally full, I finally put down the burger, leaned to one side and said, "I can't talk, my mouth's full!" Well, they all cracked up, but I figured I had really blown it. They thanked me and I went out to meet my mom, who naturally asked me excitedly how it went. When I told her the whole story, she said, "Oh, well. You tried, honey. Let's go on home."

Q: *How and when did you find out you got the job?*

A: It was a few weeks later. Before we heard, though, my mom had sat all three of us down—my oldest brother, Ray, was never in the business, by the way—and asked how we liked it. I told her I loved it, just based on the audition. My sister, on the other hand, was indifferent and said she'd probably rather just be a "regular" girl. My brother wasn't at all impressed by the so-called glamour of Hollywood, and still isn't. So Mom again told us she wasn't going to push us or make us do anything we didn't want to do, and that's why Kenneth and Beverley never went back into the business again. Meanwhile, a few days later, Dorothy called us and said the Jack-in-the-Box people had liked me and were actually considering turning the audition interview into the final *commercial*, which is exactly what they did. I guess they felt it had gone so perfectly that, even given the relatively poor quality of the footage, it would be pointless to try it again. It was really thrilling for me.

Q: *How many Jack-in-the-Box spots did you end up doing?*

A: I think I wound up doing eight or ten, all basically in the same off-the-cuff style. I remember one in which I literally did nothing but laugh throughout the entire commercial. They sat me down, put the Jumbo Jack in front of me, and had a guy I couldn't see come up behind me and start tickling me. Naturally, I was hysterically laughing, at which point, the director casually said, "Roll 'em."

In another one, I was describing the contents of the Jumbo Jack, and for some reason, instead of saying "tomato," I kept saying "chomato." That's what they seemed to love, and those national commercials for Jack-in-the-Box alone spanned something like twelve years. Then, they brought me back in 1986 to do one more. I was happy about that, but was especially appreciative toward the company for bringing back the same original crew that had shot all the other commercials years before.

Q: *Over the years, there were many other commercials and jobs, but it was that hugely successful stint with Jack-in-the-Box that almost literally made you an overnight star. How did that affect you, as well as your relationships with your friends and family?*

A: I never felt like a celebrity of any sort. I have even had people tell me I'm *too* down to earth for this business. But it was wonderful. I was like a kid in a candy store, with the United States as my playground. We traveled everywhere and were treated extremely well wherever we went. There were never any problems or rivalries with my brothers or sisters, which also made it fabulous. From day one, they were nothing but supportive. Everybody seemed to be pulling for me. I had a great childhood.

Sure, there were kids who would try to provoke me because of what was going on in my life, but they stopped just as soon as they realized I was still one of them and didn't have an overinflated ego. I was going to public school and playing in the front yard just like everybody else, which unfortunately made my mom a nervous wreck. I guess I can't blame her in retrospect; when things really got hot, you could flip the channels and find me on two or three different commercials at the same time, so she was always terrified that I was a kidnap victim waiting to happen. Still I was able to lead a normal life, and it all worked out beautifully.

Even though the roles did slow down after I was thirteen or so, and even though this can be a cruel business— where you drive two hours for an audition, only to be in and out in less than five minutes—I've always said and still believe that I'm very fortunate to have had what I had as a kid. I'm so grateful for the fun and experiences I enjoyed during those years. If I never, ever had another job in the industry, I'd still feel blessed. To this day, people recognize me, my voice, or my name, and that's still wonderful. One of these days, I know I'll have the right opportunity to show people what I can do and to have even better experiences than before.

Q: *On a more general level, how do you feel the opportunities for blacks have changed over time in the industry?*

A: I would say the industry as a whole has become somewhat more receptive to African-Americans in front of and behind the camera, but only to an extent. I feel there remains very little room for advancement for African-Americans in the business, that doors are still being closed for no apparent reason. When I auditioned for that first Jack-in-the-Box commercial, there were kids of virtually all ethnic backgrounds trying out, because they weren't looking for a white kid or a black kid, just the best kid for the part. I wish it could be like that more often.

Q: *As someone who truly grew up in the business, what message would you most like to impart to parents today who are considering a show business career for their children?*

A: I would tell them that if they feel their child is talented in some way, that's wonderful, but they must be prepared to do a lot of work and spend a lot of time. Most of all, they have to support their child emotionally, and not make that child believe his or her self-worth is on the line with every interview. Finally, if the child is successful, the parents must remember that this is their son or daughter, not some product or commodity. Speaking from my own point of view, I can only say that I didn't miss out on a thing. I saw this and other countries, I met some of the most interesting people in the world, ate in some of the finest restaurants, and even—literally—was given the red-carpet treatment. Not that I ever felt I really deserved all of that, but it would be impossible for me to forget the fun and excitement of those years.

Q: *Now that you're back in Southern California, on your own and resuming your work, what do you see ahead in your career?*

A: It's great being on my own and going out on as many auditions as I can. Best of all, though, I can honestly say that with all that has happened in the past, I still believe in my heart that the best is yet to come.

CHAPTER

TEN

BABY STARS

Many parents decide to launch show business careers for their children while they're still babies. Certainly, the work is out there and the payoff can be substantial, both professionally and financially.

Most likely, your baby isn't quite ready to recite lines, model a new outfit, hold up a bottle of juice, pirouette across the stage, or sing the best of Broadway. If he or she is, call the *Guinness Book of World Records!* But if not, it doesn't mean your baby isn't "talented." Time again to ask yourself, Why not *my* child? After all, what do all those working babies have that yours doesn't? Not a thing.

Babies are more in demand in the job market than ever before, as such recent popular films as *Parenthood*, *Look Who's Talking*, *Baby Boom*, and *Three Men and a Baby* clearly show. Television commercials have become an especially lucrative field for babies as well. In fact, infants and toddlers have turned into TV's most charming "salespeople," pitching everything from food to diapers to steel-belted radial tires.

If you do choose to go pro with your baby, your opening move, as usual, will be to check out any and all magazines containing baby-related ads and everything from billboards to cereal boxes on which infants are prominently featured. This will quickly tell you what look is "in" and give you a fix as to where your baby will fit into the market.

Fine acting is obviously not an issue at this age (though some babies do appear to be "performing" deliberately). Your child's job security will therefore depend upon two very basic qualities: looks and disposition.

Understandably, most advertisers want a happy, healthy-looking baby associated with their product, usually one with a round face and equally round behind. Most babies have both, so the business is open to infants of all sizes and colors. Also, there's no sex discrimination in the employment of babies, unless the role specifically requires one sex or the other.

The baby who is expressive, smiley, and apparently comfortable in front of strangers will always be in demand. Crying is par for the course in a baby's life, and no director or casting director expects nonstop sweetness and light from a baby. Nevertheless, the contented baby is obviously going to be the working baby.

Although babies are often signed in Hollywood, it's New York, the nation's advertising center, where they are most frequently sought out. In general, agents and managers who handle babies look for potential clients by searching through ads in local newspapers and magazines. Some have been known to "discover" babies in everyday settings such as supermarkets and pediatrician's offices.

Needless to say, thoroughly check out any agent or manager who simply walks up to you on the street flashing a card and praising your baby. He or she is probably legit, but look into it anyway. Anyone who's genuinely interested will wait.

YOUR FIRST STEPS:
MODELING AND COMMERCIALS

If you're positive about moving ahead, your first goal will be to get a reliable agent as detailed in Chapter Four. If possible, find an agency that specializes in babies, as many do. You'll probably have the best chance with a modeling agency, since many agents and managers don't handle babies at all. The work your baby does in this field will serve as ideal training for what's ahead in TV and film.

With luck on your side, your baby's entire modeling session will run only an hour or so, without a nap or bottle missed. As you well know, however, the only predictable thing about a baby is complete *unpredictability*. The baby may be playful at a certain time of day at home, but fourteen pounds of terror during the same time of day at a photographer's studio.

Because patience can run out faster than formula, sometimes a cranky baby—cruel as it sounds—has to be replaced on the job. In all likelihood, this won't happen to your baby. But if it does, just set your sights on the next assignment.

There's work to be found for your baby in television commercials, but it's a very competitive field for which you'll have to be all the more motivated and determined. Hundreds of babies may be considered for each commercial role. Of these hundreds, just four are usually selected. Three of these are chosen solely as backups in case the first choice "goes Hollywood" and decides to throw a tantrum on the set.

Since a commercial takes far longer to shoot than a print ad and involves a sizable crew, time out for naps and feedings is a costly proposition. For this reason, some directors like to shoot footage with each of the four finalists while they're in pleasant moods instead of waiting for the "star" baby to eat, sleep, or de-grump.

ON THE SET

Just because a director yells "Action!" doesn't mean that babies are suddenly going to stop what they're doing and launch into character. Babies do precisely what they want. At their own pace. In their own time. Whether or not it happens to coincide with a director's particular needs.

That's why trained pros known as "baby wranglers" are often brought in on shoots of all kinds to help minimize the chance of a baby being disruptive on the set. Their job is to find new ways to amuse babies and keep their attention. Food, props, gestures, funny faces—all of these are tools of the baby-wrangling trade. And since *mothers generally aren't allowed to be in sight of a baby during filming* (babies need all the concentration they can muster), one of the key services baby wranglers provide is to create an atmosphere of love and security even though Mommy is off in the shadows.

Most pros agree that it's counterproductive to overrehearse a baby, since many quickly get bored and refuse to do what's needed. With that in mind, directors will simply start shooting right away and on a good day can capture a "performance" that is better than anything in the script. For example, if the scene calls for a baby boy to drop an ice cream cone on the floor, and he instead drops it on the lead actor's lap, chances are everyone will be pleased. After all, that's exactly the kind of unexpected thing kids do at home, and a surefire audience-pleaser on film.

Happily, most babies actually adapt well to the camera and aren't prone to show fear or tension. Indifference, maybe, but not fear or tension. So unless the baby's nap and feeding schedule work against you, odds are your baby will show star potential from the very first day on the job. The entire shoot will be a fascinating experience for you and, with a stageful of fawning adults, an exciting one for your baby, too.

MIRROR IMAGES

If you happen to be the parent of twin babies, your chances for landing work for them are, appropriately enough, doubled. Twins are used throughout the industry, but they are especially welcome on movie sets, since they guarantee an identical backup baby on call at any given time. Ideally, one baby will be cheery and ready to go if the other is sleepy and ready for bed.

Screen Actors Guild regulations are understandably strict regarding the use of babies:

- Children between the age of fifteen days and six months may be permitted to remain at the workplace for only two hours, and only twenty minutes of this time may be devoted to actual filming.
- Children between the age of six months and two years may be permitted at the workplace for a maximum of four hours. But this period must not include more than two hours of actual work and must be balanced with two hours of rest and recreation.

With these rules in mind, you can see why it helps a producer and director to be able to excuse one infant and bring in his look-alike without losing precious time and money.

Hollywood is currently undergoing a kind of twin-mania,

with some of the films mentioned at the beginning of the chapter as prime examples. Consider that twins were used on each production and you begin to see the possibilities. Talk about making genetics work in your favor!

Only *you* can know how well your baby will adapt to the world of lights, cameras, and constant action. But keep in mind that if you act now to help your young child act now, he might have enough money for college while he's still learning how to *spell* college. When that happens, the whole family benefits. Now, and for many, many years to come.

TODDLERS

For toddlers through children of age four or five, a key factor is height and clothing size. To get an idea of the kinds of kids being employed, once again scan brochures, magazines, and papers. Try to identify the common threads that run through all of them. Then do the same with television commercials. Watch them carefully to detect similarities in both appearance and temperament.

What you'll find is a surprisingly broad selection of types among the children working today. An important concern for the advertiser is to match the child to the product. But since there are so many different kinds of products out there fighting for the attention of consumers, it stands to reason there are numerous casting opportunities to explore.

Your child's rapidly developing personality will have a big impact on his or her professional chances. Looks alone won't get your child a job if he or she is tough to control. Even when a young child is hired, that child is counted on to take direction with at least some degree of maturity.

In film work of any kind, kids of any age sometimes aren't the most welcome addition to the cast. This is because they are expensive to work with, owing to the legal and guild restraints that figure into their hours of work. A production schedule must therefore be planned around their availability. And it's not always the most economically sound schedule, either, often necessitating many extra hours or even days. So when a child comes on a set, the obvious hope is that he or she will be professional enough to do the job and do it well in the time allotted. When that happens, the child will establish a reputation that will get around to casting directors and producers in no time at all.

IN REVIEW
----

1. *Babies are more in demand than ever.*
2. *The contented baby will be the working baby.*
3. *Babies are most frequently sought in New York.*
4. *Not all agents and managers handle babies.*
5. *Modeling is generally the best field for babies to start in.*
6. *Hundreds of babies may be looked at for a single TV commercial role.*
7. *Most babies adapt very well to the camera.*
8. *Twin babies are particularly in demand.*
9. *Looks alone won't keep your toddler or young child working if he or she is trouble on the set.*

CHAPTER
ELEVEN

THE BUSINESS OF SHOW BUSINESS

People go into show business for many reasons, and money is certainly one of them. While this shouldn't be the primary motivation for getting your child into the industry, you *will* eventually have to know how to deal with managing and keeping money, which is often more difficult than making it.

TURNING TO THE PROS

There are many members of the Screen Actors Guild who don't make enough income to live on, whereas others, including kids, can earn in the $100,000-a-year range or far more. When your child's earnings reach that point or get close to it, you'll definitely be in need of financial management. If you're an experienced businessperson, this may not be a problem for you. Because of the specialized nature of the entertainment industry, however, it's likely you'll require some professional financial help.

At the very least, you'll need professional advice in preparing and filing income tax returns. In addition to the overall complexity of current tax laws that affect everyone, there are numerous very specific rules that apply only to those in show business. Some examples include claiming deductions for lessons, as well as tax write-offs for everything from wardrobe, travel expenses (to auditions and jobs), management and agency fees, production and publicity expenses, to using your home as an office. And the list goes on.

Determining how many deductions to claim requires expert knowledge about the business of show business. A perfect illustration is the case of wardrobe expenses, because whether such costs are deductible or not is based on exactly how the clothes are—or can be—used. For example, if your son's day-to-day clothes are all that he's asked to wear for a given part, chances are the cost of those clothes can't be claimed as a deductible business expense. However, if you have to buy a costume for a role that he wouldn't otherwise wear, you have a legitimate write-off.

You can see there's often a thin line between the allowable and nonallowable expenses in this instance, and the legalities are just as complex in all other areas as well.

MANAGING ON YOUR OWN

If you choose to manage your child's career yourself, remember you'll literally be going into business with him or her. This may sound simple, but few parents really think it through, and they ultimately pay the price down the line. In short, you'd best be ready, willing, and—most of all—*able* to understand contracts, manage money, and file tax returns, among many other responsibilities.

Managing your child's career will become *your* career. And this is a tough, sometimes merciless industry. For that very reason, if you're not entirely sure you can handle both the endless details and the constant pressure of management, don't let pride keep you from seeking out someone who can. *A wrong move now could jeopardize your child's career before it even gets off the ground.*

BUSINESS MANAGERS:
WHEN AND WHY TO GET ONE

Generally, *you should start considering a professional business manager when your child's income reaches about $50,000 a year.* Anything less than that and you'll probably have a tough time justifying the cost, although it may pay if you're unable to get a fix on the basics of money and business management.

Business managers are widely used in the entertainment world. A great many people employ them—not just performers, but athletes, newscasters, producers, writers, directors, record executives, and studio heads as well, to name a few. Business managers are usually certified public accountants, attorneys, or people with considerable insight into the workings of the entertainment industry. Most commonly, however, they are accountants, since the services they perform include keeping financial records, paying bills, banking, and filing tax returns. At the point where your child's earnings make tax-related matters complicated, you are strongly advised to retain a qualified tax adviser with experience in the entertainment industry. There are also audit functions that occasionally need to be conducted for certain clients. For instance, if your child's earnings are contractually tied to the gross income of a film, your business manager will audit the studio's records to ensure that the figures all add up correctly.

Typically, all clients' earnings and bills are sent directly to their business manager's office. The bills are reviewed carefully for accuracy and paid. Earnings are deposited to the client's account, which is maintained by the business manager. Tax records are also kept at his or her office. These generally include a personal set of books and files for paid bills, and other documentation (e.g., contracts and agreements) that support the income and expenses involved.

In addition, business managers establish and maintain banking relationships for their clients, arranging for loans when necessary and negotiating the terms of repayment. Because business managers normally represent a large number of clients, they tend to have substantial bargaining power with particular banks. This can work very much to the advantage of a client, who may not yet enjoy a solid history with a financial institution.

Business managers usually supervise and coordinate other professional services, such as legal and tax advice, that will have an impact on the business affairs of a client.

Business managers also play a vital role in negotiating some contracts. However, they can't represent a client in obtaining or negotiating work assignments in certain states since this falls under the exclusive legal domain of talent agents. Nevertheless, actors frequently have to consult their business manager when contracts have tax or accounting implications (proper documentation is a must), because most talent agents and personal managers lack expertise in these areas.

Other services business managers may provide include arranging personal purchases; negotiating, coordinating, and implementing escrows; representing clients in investment matters; preparing business plans for new ventures; organizing and running the business side of clients' ventures; and putting clients in touch with top pros in virtually all facets of the entertainment business.

BUSINESS MANAGERS: HOW TO GET ONE

Given how important they will be in your child's career, finding the *right* business manager is essential. The industry abounds with stories about business managers who were actually business *mis*managers, sometimes accidentally or intentionally leaving their clients flat broke.

Among the headline-grabbing examples of late was the case of Kareem Abdul-Jabbar, who was reported to have lost $10 million as a result of his business manager's misconduct. In the late 1960s, Doris Day—after the death of her husband—was more than shocked to learn she was literally broke after a career that had garnered her millions. All she had left for her years of work was a sizable tax bill. Fortunately, she found her way back to financial health, but many others have not and will never be quite as lucky.

The difficulty in choosing *any* professional is always the same. You're never really comfortable until you have a sense of their character as well as their abilities. One tried-and-true means of accomplishing this is through referrals. For that reason, when the time comes, ask someone you know in the business who has been through the process how they found their child's business manager and who it is. Ask as many people as you can whose judgment you trust. If one manager's name crops up again and again, he or she is obviously well worth contacting first.

Attorneys who specialize in the entertainment industry and deal with a number of business managers can be among the best sources for referrals. You may also get in touch with professional associations such as the American Bar Association or Society of Certified Public Accountants.

After you have the name and phone number of several possible business managers, call and request a personal interview. Right up front, make sure to tell the receptionist or secretary, as well as the business manager, who referred you. This will help you get past the business manager's initial reluctance to make an appointment with an inexperienced prospective client.

If possible, have the person who referred you to the business manager call ahead either to arrange the interview or at least to put in a good word for you. Remember, successful managers are busy and are often hesitant to take on new clients whose earnings are—even temporarily—limited. But don't let that deter you from doing everything you can to schedule a meeting, if you're convinced this person is worth the effort.

Be sure you're adequately prepared for the interview, just as you would be for any business meeting. Dress in business attire and don't take your child with you. Bring copies of relevant documents with you, such as income tax returns for the past few years, along with your child's résumé, credits, and photos.

During the interview, try to find relationships you have in common, such as those with talent agents, personal managers, and attorneys. This will further help you to open the lines of communication.

These are some questions you will want to ask your child's prospective business manager:

- How long have you been in business?
- What types of clients do you represent, and do you specialize?
- How many management clients do you have?
- What kinds of services do you offer (paying bills, income tax planning, reviewing contracts, etc.)?
- What are your professional affiliations?
- How do you charge for your services and what specific services are included in a standard fee?

When the business manager shows an interest in accepting your child as a client, ask for a brief tour of his or her offices to meet some of the people working there. This will help you feel more at home in these new surroundings and give you more of a feel for how things are done.

When the interview is over, don't be afraid to ask for some references. Leave without making a final commitment. By all means, call those references, even if you already were referred to this business manager by someone you know.

Lastly, thank the potential manager for his or her time and don't overstay your welcome.

BUSINESS MANAGERS: HOW THEY CHARGE

As do related professionals, business managers earn either a steep hourly wage (generally between $150 and $200) or a percentage of a client's annual gross income (usually 5 percent).

Under the 5 percent method, if a client's income is $50,000, the business manager's annual fee would be $2,500, paid only from the income when it's received. In other words, there's no obligation to pay for services until the money comes in. Since business managers obviously do better with clients who are earning more, they must average the costs of running their offices across the spectrum of all their clients, giving those clients who earn less better results. The smaller clients still get the benefit of the office's full range of services, but pay only in proportion to their earnings.

Business managers sometimes accept smaller clients in the hope that they'll become big earners and will stay with the firm. That's why many are willing to make that initial investment in aspiring young performers and why your finding a good *and* reasonably priced business manager early on isn't out of the question.

In the case of high-earning clients, business managers may occasionally agree to lower their percentage fee, or more likely, set a maximum annual fee. This is particularly true when the client is moving from another management office and already has a thriving career. Therefore, don't forget that when the time comes, you may want to talk to your child's business manager about an hourly rate or maximum annual fee.

THE "BOTTOM LINE"

Many people hear of the enormous salaries often paid to actors, and are under the impression that each dollar made is another dollar in the bank. The truth is, however, that expenses and taxes must be paid out of these earnings, and it will help you to know how the figures break down.

This example profiles the income and expenses of a successful actor making $1 million a year. It should serve to illustrate how things *really* work in the entertainment industry:

INCOME (*before any deductions*)	**$1,000,000**

LESS:	
PERSONAL MANAGER'S FEES (15%)	– 150,000
AGENT'S FEES (10%)	– 100,000
BUSINESS MANAGER'S FEES (5%)	– 50,000

NET EARNINGS BEFORE BUSINESS EXPENSES	**$700,000**

ESTIMATED BUSINESS EXPENSES	
PUBLICIST OR PR FIRM *(usually hired after success is attained)*	– 25,000
LESSONS	– 10,000
ASSORTED EXPENSES *(travel, office, secretarial, legal, etc.)*	– 60,000
BUSINESS ENTERTAINMENT	– 5,000

NET EARNINGS BEFORE TAXES	**$600,000**

ESTIMATED FEDERAL AND STATE INCOME TAXES	– $210,000

NET INCOME AFTER TAXES	**$390,000**

As you can see from a quick review of these figures, even a successful actor doesn't take a million-dollar income to the bank. Instead, he or she winds up with just under 40 percent of that income, roughly the same percentage an actor making $100,000 a year takes home (or $40,000).

PROTECTING YOUR CHILD'S INCOME

In 1939, California enacted the Child Actors Bill, giving the courts power to set aside up to half a child's entertainment-industry earnings in a trust fund or some other type of protected savings until he or she is no longer a minor. You may have heard of this legal milestone by the name the press gave it at the time of its creation: the "Coogan Law." The name came about as the result of a lawsuit filed by the late Jackie Coogan (best known to some audiences as Uncle Fester on *The Addams Family* in the '60s) against his mother and step-father in 1939 for alleged mismanagement of his earnings while he was a child star.

Today, under the California Civil Code (secs. 36, 36.1, 36.2), all employment contracts for minors must be approved by the court. Therefore, when a child does have a job opportunity, it's usually desirable for the employer to have the contract legally approved and thus avoid the chance of being sued later.

Once a contract is approved, the court can rule that up to 70 percent of a child's earnings be put in a trust fund or other form of savings until he or she reaches twenty-one, but only if that child is on a series (this rule, in my opinion, should be industry-wide and still doesn't protect kids from having almost a third of their income turned over to potentially unscrupulous parents).

The Domestic Relations Law of New York State offers similar protection for children working there. Strangely enough, however, it isn't considered a criminal offense for contracts of this type to go unapproved by the court. And in reality, many aren't.

In California, it's also possible under some conditions to have a young performer declared an "emancipated minor" by an appropriate court. This means he or she is no longer a minor and can enter into contracts and manage personal affairs without parental or court approval. However, discuss such a critical step—and all other important money-related decisions—with your attorney and business manager when the time comes.

IN REVIEW

---

1. *You'll need professional advice in preparing and filing income tax returns.*
2. *Only manage your child's career if you are very well-versed in the business of show business.*
3. *Consider hiring a business manager when your child's annual income reaches the $50,000 mark.*
4. *Finding the right business manager is essential.*
5. *Bring all relevant records, as well as your child's résumé and credits, to an interview with a prospective business manager.*
6. *Remember that roughly only 40 percent of every dollar earned winds up in the bank.*
7. *The so-called "Coogan Law" in California is the best legal protection for show business children thus far.*

The Jackie Coogan Story

The history behind this landmark case is a story worth telling because it provides a lesson to parents well worth learning.

This riveting Hollywood drama unfolded on April 11, 1938, when twenty-three-year-old Jackie Coogan shocked the movie world and delighted the gossip columnists by filing a lawsuit in Los Angeles Superior Court. Not against his agent, his manager, or some tyrannical studio mogul, but against Mr. and Mrs. Arthur L. Bernstein, his own mother and stepfather. The claim: They had denied him $4 million of his past earnings as a movie star. In the suit, Coogan's attorneys asked the court to order an accounting of the Bernsteins' financial holdings in an effort to determine where all his earnings were (a fortune today, but worth many times more back then) and whether or not he was in fact entitled to it.

For this famous young actor, it was an ironic and unfortunate by-product of a career that had been meteoric ever since he was chosen to make his screen debut at age five opposite Charlie Chaplin in *The Kid*. Instead of becoming just another one-shot wonder, he went on to star in a succession of critically and publicly acclaimed films, including *Peck's Bad Boy*, *Robinson Crusoe*, and *Oliver Twist*. As a result, he quickly became the nation's first genuine child star—before anyone had even heard the name Shirley Temple.

By the time he was nine, Coogan had traveled the world and even met the pope. Around this time, he was handed a $500,000 check by Metro designed to lure him away from First National Pictures, along with an unprecedented offer guaranteeing him $22,500 a week *plus* a percentage of every film he made. All of this naturally made Coogan a millionaire overnight, prompting his financially minded father to form Jackie Coogan Productions (set up in part for the purchase of valuable Los Angeles real estate).

With Coogan's twenty-first birthday approaching in 1935,

the press began speculating that the young star was about to inherit a $1 million trust fund created for him by his father to be disbursed to him in quarterly payments. Everything seemed carefully planned and decidedly aboveboard.

Just then, however, fate intervened in a manner more suited to a Coogan movie than to real life. Only months before his son's twenty-first birthday, Coogan's father was killed in a car crash. But that was only the first shock. The second shock was that he hadn't mentioned a word in his will about a trust fund for his son. Jackie Coogan Productions went solely to Coogan's mother, Lillian, while he personally didn't receive a dime.

Complicating this dramatic scenario further was the marriage shortly thereafter of Lillian to Arthur Bernstein, the family's business manager. At the same time, young Coogan was himself married to Betty Grable. As a newlywed facing the usual monetary problems of trying to buy a home and raise a family, he suddenly realized just how cash poor he was. The Bernsteins, on the other hand, were living like royalty.

Thus the lawsuit was filed and one of Hollywood's most important chapters was written.

It turned out that during Coogan's most active and lucrative period as a film star, his actual weekly allowance had been only a paltry $6.25. Even as he grew older, nothing but the basics had been provided, except when his parents—in a rare burst of generosity—had given him $1,000 in Christmas and birthday gifts. It was later revealed that he had been given another $1,000 upon his twenty-first birthday, but no more. The big question remained: Where was the four million?

As the story came to light, it was learned that Bernstein was a horseplayer and over the years had incurred a series of hefty gambling debts. Jackie Coogan Productions had been footing the bill. Moreover, Bernstein apparently had been taking some rather expensive gifts for himself that had actually been intended for Coogan.

Supporting Coogan's allegations was the erratic behavior of Lillian, who theatrically and repeatedly claimed to be the helpless victim of her son's domineering personality. The young actor's case revolved around his consistent assertion that his late father had planned to turn Jackie Coogan Productions over to him, a claim validated by the testimony of esteemed actor Wallace Beery, a friend of Coogan's father. Beery told the court he had definitely heard that just such a trust fund was intended for young Coogan, even if the legal documentation had never been completed.

Also in support of Coogan's case, documents were found by his attorneys having to do with the all-important claim about an intended trust. One, dated fifteen years earlier, showed that his mother had petitioned the court to appoint her the guardian of her son's estate. The other, dated a short time later, showed that the first petition had been denied because Coogan's father had stated his plans to create a trust fund for his son.

Throughout this real-life soap opera, however, there was one fact working in the Bernsteins' favor. According to widely followed English common law, the parents of a working minor could legally collect and handle any and all monies a minor earned.

In the end, there was to be no last-minute breakthrough or shattering confession in the case. In fact, the world would never know what Coogan's father really intended for his son's financial future. Despite all the public attention, the case never even went before a jury. Instead, Coogan and his mother agreed to settle out of court eleven months after the entire matter had come to light. By then, Coogan's estate had shrunk to $291,715, no doubt due largely to the Bernsteins' misman-agement. The settlement was announced on March 19, 1939, calling for Lillian to pay $126,307.50 to her son, an odd fig-ure no one could ever explain.

As mentioned, the payoff for Coogan's contemporaries and for countless other young actors over the decades proved far more satisfactory. And while many feel the "Coogan Law" still isn't effective enough, everyone agrees that some protection is better than none.

Jane Withers

Jane Withers's remarkable career can quite easily be separated into two distinct phases: the first being the '30s and '40s when she was a child film star and the second being her equally popular reign in film and on television as an adult. Whatever the medium has been, America's love affair with this special lady certainly has never subsided.

Born in Atlanta in 1926, Jane had already become a highly proficient dancer, singer, and impersonator three short years later. Raised in a loving and religious home, she also turned out to be a casting agent's dream come true: a young performer with all the makings of stardom but none of the ego that sometimes comes with talent.

After attracting the kind of attention in her home state that only the premiere of *Gone With the Wind* would surpass, Jane headed for Hollywood in 1932 with her mother, Ruth. Her father, Walter, stayed behind to support the family. Jane herself will describe some of what happened next, but her big break was to come just two years later when she was cast opposite Shirley Temple in *Bright Eyes*. Suddenly, the country was just as smitten with the lovably scrappy and mischievous Jane Withers as it was with her costar, though that perception of Jane had more to do with "reel" life than real life.

While the years and films that followed (*Ginger, The Farmer Takes a Wife, Checkers,* and *Pack Up Your Troubles* among them) secured her a place as one of the industry's most beloved child stars, in 1947 Jane decided to take a holiday from films to get married. She and her first husband were to have three children together, and a subsequent marriage would result in two more kids. Proving she was more than able to sustain her appeal as an adult actress, she returned to the screen in 1955 for one of her most successful motion picture outings: the James Dean classic *Giant*.

Making a smooth transition to television soon after, Jane

went on to appear in everything from sitcoms to dramas to game shows, while also making a mark as one of the most charitably minded celebrities in Hollywood and, of all things, a premier collector of miniatures and dolls.

Despite Jane's range of credits, younger generations most readily associate her with a 1963–75 stint as Josephine, the Lady Plumber, in TV commercials for the cleanser Comet. In fact, by the time she left the role, she had earned the distinction of having starred in the longest-running series of commercials in the history of television.

Today, able to look back on her years as a child star and on an adulthood that thus far has seen her enjoy success in such varied fields as performing, real estate, production, and doll collecting, Jane Withers is as sprightly and energetic as the little girl who captured so many hearts all those years ago. Best of all, though, she remains as active as ever in show business (frequently on tour or guesting on TV shows) and charity. And based on her track record, Jane is sure to have more than a few added surprises in store for us down the line.

Q: *What were your beginnings in show business?*

A: I can honestly tell you that every day in my life, I thank God my mother thought it would be interesting to have a child in show business. There was no history of it in our family whatsoever, but Mama just loved the movies; she adored Colleen Moore, and I later had a Dutch Boy haircut just like hers. Mama was absolutely incredible—totally unlike any kind of so-called "stage mother." She was a fine, elegant Southern lady with great morals and integrity and truly believed with all her heart and soul that she was bringing a child into the world who would have talent to share with others.

Long before I was born, she wanted a little girl. My father would ask her, "Suppose it's a little boy?" And she'd say, "No, Walter, it's going to be a little girl." She also told him, "I want you to please understand this, but we're only going to have time for this one child. I believe this child will be special." Anyway, the key to everything that was to happen later was visualization—her uncanny ability to visualize who I would be and what was going to happen. She literally used to study the marquee at the Fox Theater in

Atlanta and say to herself, "Withers is a rather long last name, so she will need to have a short first name for it to look right." First it was going to be *Jayne*, but she knew *instinctively* that was not it! Finally she arrived at *Jane* and knew right away that *was* it!

Q: *What are your first memories of performing in public?*

A: I literally started working at the age of two and a half years old, and I remember it as if it were still yesterday. You've heard of "amateur night in Dixie"? Well, every Saturday night in the different neighboring theaters, they would have amateur night. I started out singing and dancing and doing impersonations. And started winning, to the point where eventually I was known throughout the South as— are you ready for this?—Dixie's Dainty Dewdrop! Isn't that a doozy of a title?! Anyway, Mama later told me that every week, other parents would ask her if I was going to enter that Saturday's contest, because if I was, they wouldn't bother entering their own kids that night.

It was fun to win, but sometimes it bothered me, too. I clearly remember one time when they were about to open the envelope and announce the winner, and all I could think about was this wonderful elderly dancer who I thought was so special. You know something? I cried like a baby when I won because I felt *he* deserved it. That really upset me. I said, "Mama, it doesn't seem fair if I always win." And she said, "Well, sweetheart, the people love you. And even though we know that all of the other people competing are winners, you must learn that some people will just go through life more liked than others, and it's a blessing that you're one of them." I'm mentioning all this because it's an example of how she would always take time, no matter where or when, to share things like that with me. I feel that was so important in my life. The point is that even if I hadn't won, she would have been there to love and support me.

Q: *Was there ever a time when you didn't want to perform?*

A: Yes, actually. In the very beginning, I didn't want to go on stage at all. I've always loved flowers, and before the first contest I was going to compete in, friends had sent me a bunch for good luck. Well, when it came Saturday night, I didn't want to go out in front of all those people. My mother said, "But Jane, we talked about it and you said you wanted to do this." And I said, "Yes, ma'am, I love performing, but there are all these people out there I don't know, and I'm afraid they won't like me." So she said, "Honey, you mustn't be afraid they won't like you. You just do the best you can. If they don't like you, naturally you'll feel bad. But you have to realize that there will always be times in life when people like what you do and times when they don't. The important thing is to remember that if you really want to do something, you have to believe in yourself and try again and again and again." Keep in mind I was only two and a half, and this was the very first Saturday night amateur contest I was going to compete in. Anyway, I still didn't want to go on, so I said, "Let's take the flowers and go home." And she said, "Oh, no. They sent you flowers for a reason, and now it wouldn't be fair for you to keep them. They're for the people going onstage tonight. But I also want you to know that it's alright if you don't want to perform now. You know I still love you, so let's just go on home." We did go home, and she didn't mention amateur night after that. She didn't try to prod me or force me into it.

I still continued practicing my singing and dancing and taking my lessons, but Mama never tried to push. She even asked me whether I wanted to stop practicing and taking my lessons altogether. "You've got to love what you do," she said. "And part of that should be a desire to share your talent with other people. If you don't think you will ever feel that way about it, just let me know and we can stop now." Well, I thought about it, and about three weeks after that first contest night, I went to her and said, "Mama, now I want to perform on Saturday night. I talked to the Lord and made my decision." She always told me to talk to the Lord when in doubt and I'd get an answer, and I always have. And that was the beginning of my wonderful friendship and understanding with my mom and dad, who always allowed me to make my own decisions.

From the very beginning, my mother told me, "I think you're going to be very successful, dear, because you're talented and special and have something to share. But any-time you don't really enjoy what you're doing, then you shouldn't have to do it. Always remember that." It's what every child in this business must understand. Most of all, it's what every parent must understand. My parents never did anything but encourage me from the start. My mother would say that God gave me something special. Actually, I knew I was different. I could just look in the mirror and know that! Nobody in the world looked like I did. All the other little girls had their blond curls and I was always very plain and tailored. I was never upset by it, though. I knew my looks and style were different, but I also liked it that way. Instead of trying to change me, my parents would tell me *never* to try to be like anyone else but only to be who I am. This was a family that truly worked together as a unit, and it wasn't until many years later that I realized not every family was like ours.

I thought all parents were wonderful like mine, and just as thoughtful and conscientious. As time went on and I had opportunity to share memories with different children who had grown up in the business with me, I couldn't believe some of the stories I heard. My parents were always there for me 100 percent, but I found out that a lot of people weren't anywhere near as fortunate.

Q: *When did you first come to Hollywood?*
A: Mama and I came out here on March 10, 1932. My Daddy, who was a manager for Goodrich Tire and Rubber in Atlanta, insisted on staying back to support the family. I guess my parents felt I'd gone as far as I could in Atlanta, including guesting on a radio show a couple of years earlier, when I was three. But as far as Hollywood was concerned, I didn't have a thing lined up and we didn't know a soul. We didn't even know what hotel to go to, but my mother said, "The only place I know is Hollywood and Vine. So I guess that's where we should be." Anyway, we found a place to stay. But we couldn't afford that place more than one night. Daddy was sending us $100 a month to live on.

Everything seemed so far apart in Hollywood, and it was very confusing for us. But everyone told us we had to get into something called Central Casting, so that's where we headed the day after we arrived. When we got there, we found all kinds of children. Many of them were so rude I couldn't believe it. They were yelling and screaming and getting into fights. Oh, what I learned, even that first week in Hollywood! I said, "Mother, I don't think these children have had any proper training." They were all fighting to get the first place in line, probably because their parents had told them, "You'd better not fail us!" I tried to talk to these kids, to tell them they were wrong to push and shove, that their talent would determine whether they made it or not. But they were convinced the only way to make it was to plow ahead of everyone else and fight their way to the top. "No," I said. "Maybe you *do* have to fight for yourself in some ways. But if you have the ability, if you have something to share, you'll have your chance." I couldn't understand their way of thinking. *I* didn't mind being last in line. If fact, it was a pattern that would last for many years, especially if we were in alphabetical order. Even as a star, I was always introduced last, unless Loretta Young, Darryl Zanuck, or Efrem Zimbalist Jr. were there, too!

Q: *Later, after you not only landed jobs but eventually became a national treasure, how did you avoid getting carried away with success?*

A: Oh, good gracious, I was tickled to pieces, and I still am! It makes my heart so happy. I think this business is fantastic. Thousands of people around the world have told me I was very much a part of their lives growing up, and there's no way that wouldn't make someone feel proud. But the joy wasn't in thinking I was "great." It was, and still is, in maybe helping to brighten up other people's lives. The most important sense of pride I had was in accomplishing what Mama and Daddy believed I could do. That's what mattered most. I'm very grateful for that. It means the world to me that I didn't disappoint them after all the love and time and energy they put into raising me and making me so happy.

There's one thing I would like to stress for those parents who are thinking of starting a child in show business: Success is not necessarily something that can be judged by how much money you make. Sure, I did make a good deal as a child—though we continued to live off my father's income even then. But that's not where the satisfaction came from. As an example of what I'm talking about, from the very first week we arrived in Hollywood, my mother and I went to the Hollywood Presbyterian Church on Gower Street. What used to bother me was that after I became well-known, hundreds of kids started coming to my Sunday school. They were there for my autograph. So I went in and talked to my minister about it and told him it bothered me that this was the reason these children were coming to church. At the same time, I told him I didn't see myself staying in show business and that I wanted to become a medical missionary. "Well, Jane," he said in all sincerity, "we've always thought of you as our missionary of love and laughter. That's very special. You are reaching hundreds of thousands of children now and making them happy. That's why they come to this Sunday school to see you." I said it still troubled me that they should be asking for an autograph in church. "But I notice you never sign them in church," he said. And that was true. I always waited until after Sunday school, and then I'd go outside and meet with the kids. "You see," the minister said, "you already are a missionary, but just of a different kind. Please think carefully before you abandon your career. You're giving the medicine of laughter and that's one of the greatest gifts of all."

All of a sudden I started looking at it in a different way and feeling especially proud of what I was doing. And you know something? I've never looked back since.

CHAPTER
TWELVE

YOUR CHILD'S EDUCATION:
HOW TO BALANCE IT
WITH A SHOW BUSINESS CAREER

Young performers are thrust into the adult world ahead of schedule. The only way to give them the kind of balance they need in life will be to have them keep doing the things they'd normally be doing *without* a show business career. This should include giving them an education equal to that of any child outside the industry. However successful they become, they must know that there's more to read than a script and more to learn than the next day's lines.

Fortunately, over the years the entertainment community has developed ways to accommodate the educational needs of its child performers. That's why many of the interviews your child will be asked to give will be scheduled for *after* schooltime hours. On those occasions when a young actor is forced to miss a class or an entire day of school, that child will be able to compensate as if he or she had been sick. The child will simply find out what assignments are pending and do the work as soon as scheduling permits. There is usually ample free time on a film set, which will give a child an opportunity to get much of that schoolwork done. It has been my experience, in fact, that kids can often learn more about life on the set and out in the world than in a traditional educational environment. Once your child's career is off and running, you may ultimately have to remove him or her from a normal school situation altogether.

Many parents of successful professional children like to give their kids a combination of regular schooling and personal tutoring. You will need an education of sorts yourself when it comes to picking that tutor. Take the time to do some research. A tutor will have to be someone who not only keeps your son or daughter up on the schoolwork, but also reminds him or her that there was life before television and movies and that understanding geography takes more than just knowing where to find Hollywood on the map!

Another option is the on-set tutor. Because they are required by law on California sets, most young performers have benefited from this unusual form of education. For a busy young actor with little time to spend at public school, it makes a great deal of sense. Especially given the fact that on-set tutors are highly skilled teachers familiar with the distractions and crises on a set.

One of the most active and accomplished of these teachers is Sid Sharron, whose years as an on-set tutor (specializing in mathematics) have given him a clear insight into the inner workings of this vital profession. The first and most important factor, he says, is to leave no doubt among students that this *is* school, however untraditional it may be.

"Whether I'm working with a child in a trailer on the studio lot or in the most exotic location imaginable," says Sid, "I make certain that schooltime is just that. Not a time to play, not a time to relax, not a time to memorize lines, and not a time to tell me about that day's work—but a time to *learn.* Once that ground rule has been established, the results can be remarkable and the one-on-one attention can be extremely helpful."

Although Sid by and large has found his students to be very receptive to learning, regardless of the harried circumstances, he has occasionally come across the odd rebel who believes him- or herself to be above the need for schooling. That's why he also makes it clear from the outset that there are no "stars" in his classroom. "Mind you, I understand what some of these children are going through and I'm happy to work with them in whatever way I can to get them to *want* to learn. But I could never allow any student to set aside his schoolwork because his job is keeping him too busy. I may not be able to provide the social atmosphere of a traditional school environment, but I want to guarantee that each student receives a well-rounded education, no matter who they are or how successful they've become."

Another alternative is a special arts school, such as the *Fame* school in New York, although you may not find one in your hometown (as mentioned, I had the chance to attend such a school). If you do, however, by all means check it out *if* your child simply can't put in a normal day at a public school. Special arts schools are, by definition, devoted to the arts. Unlike other schools, they *are* prepared to deal with a child's unorthodox schedule on a daily basis.

In many states, working children have to keep up a C average to be granted work permits, so it's not as if an education isn't taken seriously in the business. However, it's not always easy for young performers on the set to fulfill the minimum three hours of schooling required by law.

If a child is working under the jurisdiction of the Screen Actors Guild, he or she has certain protection under their regulations concerning the education of minors.

- If a minor is guaranteed more than three days of employment, the producer agrees to employ a teacher whenever the minor is engaged on any day during which the primary or secondary school normally attended is in session.
- If a minor is not guaranteed more than three days of employment but winds up working for more than three, the producer must also employ a teacher—after the initial three days of work—on standard school days.
- On any day a minor is employed but isn't entitled to have a teacher (as spelled out above), the producer must still provide a teacher if it's a standard school day *and* a teacher has already been hired for another minor on the set.
- All teachers must have proper credentials from at least one U.S. state.
- Teachers are paid by producers.
- No more than ten minors may be taught by one teacher, unless there are no more than two grade levels represented. If that's the case, no more than twenty minors may be instructed by one teacher.
- If the young actor's main language is not English, it's up to the producer to find a teacher who speaks that child's native language.

- Instruction may take place on a soundstage, on location, or in either the student's or teacher's home.
- A producer must provide a school environment (schoolhouse, special trailer, etc.) that includes proper equipment and supplies. Only the teacher and students are allowed in this area.
- Teachers must determine the required number of instruction hours per day. The minimum, however, is three hours a day, with no learning session lasting less than twenty minutes.
- Teachers must prepare written reports for each minor taught, covering attendance, grades, attitude, and the like. These reports are then given to each student's own regular school officials.

IN REVIEW
----

1. *No matter how successful he or she becomes, your child should enjoy the normal experiences of childhood.*
2. *Most interviews or auditions are scheduled for* after *school hours.*
3. *Your child should use breaks from filming to get homework done.*
4. *Take your child out of school* only *if there's no other choice.*
5. *If possible, give your child a combination of regular school and personal tutoring.*
6. *Thoroughly check out all potential tutors.*
7. *Other possibilities include on-set tutors and special arts schools.*
8. *Working children have the chance to learn about life long before their contemporaries.*

Soleil Moon Frye

Though best known for her long-standing title role in the popular '80s sitcom *Punky Brewster*, young actress Soleil Moon Frye managed to attain an enviable reputation for versatility within the entertainment community.

Unlike many young performers, however, Soleil actually had a difficult time overcoming almost painful shyness when she was a child. Nevertheless, once she was able to rid herself of these inhibitions, what emerged was a girl more than ready to share her talents both in front of live audiences and in front of the camera.

An actress who obviously has that mystical "certain something" to which casting agents often refer, Soleil went on to appear over the years in television series and films as diverse as *Who Will Love My Children?*, *Ernie Kovacs: Between the Laughter, Invitation to Hell, Missing Children, The Wonder Years, Diff'rent Strokes, CHiPs, Magruder and Loud,* and, of course, *Punky Brewster.* In between live-action appearances, she provided voice-overs for a cartoon spin-off of *Punky* as well.

Along the way, Soleil also turned up on everything from *Mickey's 60th Anniversary Special* and *Night of 1000 Stars* to the Emmy Awards and *The Tonight Show Starring Johnny Carson.*

With a personality as animated as that of Punky herself, Soleil provided us with these interesting recollections and still-helpful suggestions after the run of *Punky Brewster.*

Q: *How did your first launch your career as an actress?*
A: Well, my brothers were actors. One of them starred in a show called *Voyagers,* and the other was in *E.T.* So I grew up in that atmosphere; in fact, my father's an actor, too. But I was a very, very shy little girl, although you'd never know it today! I was always the type who would hide behind my mom on the set. Finally, though, when I was about five

years old, I started talking more and breaking out of that shell little by little, until I told my mom I was ready to try the business. Because I had been so shy, she asked me if I was sure this is what I wanted, but I told her I was positive it was. And, soon after, I went in to try out for a part and they told my mom I was great. It was my first time, and I got the role.

Q: *Do you have any idea what helped you break out of that pattern of shyness?*

A: I guess it just came naturally. I also think that watching my brothers and sisters over the years influenced me. Being on the set so many times, I eventually started to feel at ease and even at home. Sure, my first day on the job was nerve-racking. You just have to try your best to feel as natural as possible, and that's usually the quality they want you to convey most, anyway. You have to enjoy what you're doing and to see how much fun it can be to slip into a different character and really learn about acting.

There was never any jealousy from my brothers, only encouragement. It was something I did on my own. My mom never pushed me. Deciding to act was entirely my choice. And once I landed that first job right away, which I guess is pretty rare, it gave me the confidence to go on to do other film and TV work. Then, one day, I went up for a TV show called *Punky Brewster*, and got the part!

Q: *As exciting as it was to star in a series, it must have been a great deal of work, too.*

A: It was definitely hard work, and didn't leave me time to do much of anything else, personally *or* professionally. That lasted for about four and a half years. A lot of people just don't realize what difficult work it can be, and so they aren't prepared for it. They also have to understand that while things may not come easily or immediately, they mustn't take it personally. They may have the wrong color eyes or hair or may not be the right height for a role. But they shouldn't give up. In my case, acting was something I really wanted to do. Even if it had taken years more for me to make it, I would have stayed with it. I love acting; it's something I'm very comfortable with.

I love being in front of the camera, but I love even more the idea of possibly influencing kids out there. In fact, since *Punky*, I've been doing a lot of work to help children who are suffering from preventable diseases. Even when I was doing *Punky*, I would have lunch every day with a child from the Make-a-Wish Foundation. It's nice to give something back, no matter how busy you are.

Q: *Do you feel your education suffered in any way as a result of your success?*

A: No, not at all. Actually, one of my brothers at one point decided to put his acting aside to go to college. He realized, and I feel the same way, that acting isn't all there is. For any young actor, education should always remain a top priority. You have to think ahead and plan for the possibility that you may someday want to do something else or that you may not be working as much as you are now.

Q: *When you did make it to the top, how did it affect your friendships with kids your age?*

A: It didn't really, at least not with my longtime friends. Sure, there are going to be a couple of kids you know or meet who will start acting jealous or have a bad feeling about you, but you learn how to avoid those kids. You just have to be sure you don't develop the kind of "star attitude" that's going to cause that sort of reaction. Unless you're performing, the idea is to be yourself.

Q: *Do you feel there are more or fewer opportunities for hopeful young actors today than when you started in the industry?*

A: I think there are more good possibilities out there for different types of children. You just have to try and stay real with yourself, and remember that it will take a lot of effort to get what you want. If you really want to do it, you'll probably get your chance someday.

At age 7, I starred in my first Broadway play, *Tapestry in Grey*. I played the son of the great Melvyn Douglas.

Here I am as Isaac in the Broadway play, *The Eternal Road*, directed by Max Reinhardt.

I played Nels on the television show, *I Remember Mama*, which aired on CBS from 1949 to 1958.

In the hit Broadway play, *O Mistress Mine*, I played Alfred Lunt and Lynn Fontanne's son. It was one of the largest parts ever written for a juvenile actor. I beat out Marlon Brando for the role.

I costarred in Thornton Wilder's *The Skin of Our Teeth* with Florence Eldridge and Tallulah Bankhead.

My son Vincent was 14 when he costarred in his third TV series, *Three for the Road*, with Alex Rocco and Leif Garrett.

Here I am with Betty Buckley and the exceptionally talented young cast of *Eight Is Enough*. Clockwise left to right: Laurie Walters, Susan Richardson, Grant Goodeve, Dianne Kay, Connie Needham, Lani O'Grady, Adam Rich, and Willie Aames.

The immortal team of Mickey Rooney and Judy Garland. In reel life, they were saying, "Let's put on a show," but in real life they reached the pinnacles of youthful stardom both together and apart.

Carl Switzer as Alfalfa in *The Little Rascals*.

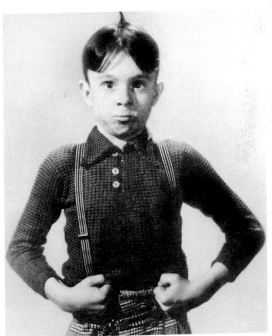

Charlie Chaplin and Jackie Coogan, who played the title role in *The Kid*. The part would catapult Jackie to fame, but not fortune. In later years, Jackie triumphed once again as Uncle Fester on *The Addams Family*.

Today's audiences perhaps know her best for her long-running "Josephine the Plumber" commercials, but Jane Withers was one of the industry's most popular young performers at the outset of her illustrious career.

A Dog's Best Friend. Jon Provost has both childhood and adult memories of working with the world's most famous canine celebrity, Lassie. Jon played Timmy in the original TV series from 1957–1964. He then had a recurring role in the show's 1989 revival.

Having grown up right before our eyes and enjoyed huge success as a young actor in, among others, *The Music Man*, *The Andy Griffith Show*, *American Graffiti*, and *Happy Days*, Ron Howard launched a powerhouse directing career which includes such hits as *Splash*, *Parenthood*, *Apollo 13*, and *Ransom*.

(Below) Don Grady with his *My Three Sons* costars, Barry and Stanley Livingston.

Like Ron Howard, Don Grady has parlayed his success as a young actor into a second successful career in show business. In Don's case, his second profession was actually his first love: music. After the run of *My Three Sons*, he launched a new career which has made him one of today's most sought-after film and television composers.

(Top) With a successful career that has taken him from his teens to adulthood, and which includes such TV series and films as *Family Ties*, *Back to the Future*, and *Spin City*, Michael J. Fox is one of the most accomplished former child actors of his generation.

One of today's most popular young actors, Jonathan Taylor Thomas is familiar to television and movie audiences alike, with credits including *Home Improvement*, *Man of the House*, and the live-action *The Adventures of Pinocchio*.

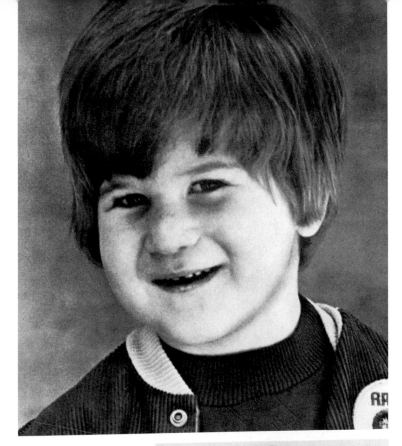

Jason Hervey has been a familiar face to audiences over many years and many projects, and includes among his film and TV credits such titles as *Back to School* and *The Wonder Years*. Today, Jason is also a fast-rising producer with his own entertainment company.

Before enjoying consistent success as an adult actor with roles in such hit films as *Superman*, Jackie Cooper was one of the leading child and young adult actors of his time.

Anyone old enough to remember will never forget Rodney Allen Rippy in his classic series of Jack-in-the-Box commercials.

Adam Hann-Byrd truly was an overnight sensation, going from a role in a school play to the title role (opposite star/director Jodie Foster) in *Little Man Tate*. Adam has also appeared on *NYPD Blue* and played the young Robin Williams character in *Jumanji*.

Reaffirming star Bill Cosby's popularity and launching the careers of several young actors, *The Cosby Show* was one of the biggest and most influential hits of the '80s.

(Below) Many of Kurt Russell's current fans may not recall that he first enjoyed tremendous success as a child actor. A Disney favorite, he's pictured here making an "executive decision" in the studio's feature film release, *The Barefoot Executive*.

Soleil Moon Frye captured the hearts (and Nielsen ratings) of millions with her
starring role in TV's *Punky Brewster*.

Looking absolutely nothing
like her Nellie Oleson alter
ego on TV's *Little House on
the Prairie*, actress Alison
Arngrim has become one of
the most prominent national
activists for AIDS research
and patient's rights.

CHAPTER

THIRTEEN

□nce your child has representation and is getting work, it will be time to become a member of one or more talent unions. There isn't a specific union for models, but many join the Screen Actors Guild (SAG) or the American Federation of Television and Radio Artists (AFTRA) to do commercials and other types of work (actually SAG and AFTRA are on the brink of a likely merger to better serve their combined membership).

Union activities within the entertainment world are governed by what is called the Four A's: the Associated Actors and Artists of America. This comprises nine distinct branches, including SAG, AFTRA, the Actors' Equity Association (AEA), the American Guild of Variety Artists (AGVA), the American Guild of Musical Artists (AGMA), the Screen Extras Guild (SEG), the Hebrew Actors' Union (HAU), and the Italian Actors' Union (IAU). In Canada, actors are represented by ACTRA, which comprises the equivalent of SAG and AFTRA.

For your purposes, the key ones to consider are SAG and AFTRA. Either can be joined with a minimum of difficulty, simply by showing the union your child's work contract and paying an initiation fee and first semiannual dues. Incidentally, a performer without union affiliation can work for up to 30 days under any union jurisdiction thanks to a law called the Taft-Hartley Act.

Joining a union may not be difficult contractually, but it can be financially, especially when payments are going out but money isn't coming in. To relieve that problem, several unions allow their members to suspend paying dues if those members haven't worked under union jurisdiction for a year. It's a risky proposition, however, since a child in that situation isn't eligible to audition at union calls. Beyond that, if a job suddenly comes up, reinstatement may not come in time for the child to be able to accept the job.

Nevertheless, the advantages of union membership far outweigh the disadvantages. *Union affiliations on a résumé have a highly positive effect on casting people.* In fact, have your child carry his or her union card(s) to all auditions, interviews, and jobs.

Union benefits ultimately include health insurance, pension plans, free classes and seminars, informative newsletters, and discounts on everything from performing arts schools to basic everyday supplies. In other words, you can expect to get your money's worth, and more.

Also worth noting here: don't depend on your child's agent to check on whether the company hiring your son or daughter is a union signatory—find out for yourself. I should know—I was once fined $10,000 for working on a nonunion production because my (former!) agent didn't check first.

SCREEN ACTORS GUILD (SAG)

SAG had its origin in 1933, when a small group of Hollywood actors joined forces to form a self-governing guild that would provide all performers with one voice. Today, this most familiar of show business unions represents some seventy thousand professional actors and performing artists nationwide.

SAG has exclusive jurisdiction over principal performers appearing in feature films and in all other types of productions shot on film. In addition, SAG shares videotape jurisdiction with AFTRA with respect to television programming, TV commercials, and industrial/educational programs. SAG also represents extras in feature films, SAG television programming, SAG nonbroadcast films, and commercials in certain areas.

SAG's primary functions include
- negotiating industry-wide contracts with motion picture and television producers to establish minimum wage scales;

- enforcing all legal contracts;
- determining working conditions;
- handling the payment of residuals;
- franchising and regulating talent agents; and
- offering its members medical insurance and pension plans.

An actor may become eligible for SAG membership either:

1. upon presentation of a letter, no more than two weeks before filming, from a signatory (guild-recognized) producer or authorized representative, or from a signatory company stating that the applicant is wanted for a particular role;
2. upon presentation of proof of employment by a SAG signatory film, TV, or commercial company (this must state the applicant's name, the production on which he or she worked, the dates worked, and the salary received; this proof can be a signed contract, a payroll check, or a letter from the company on its own letterhead); or
3. if the applicant has been a paying member of an affiliated Four A guild for a year or longer, and has had at least one job as a principal performer with that guild.

SAG's main number is (213) 954-1600. Branch offices are listed in the Appendix, state by state, under regional information. Any office will gladly provide you with whatever information or material you might need.

AFTRA

This union has sole jurisdiction over performers in live television, radio programs, radio commercials, and musical recordings. In addition, AFTRA shares videotape jurisdiction with SAG with respect to TV programming, TV commercials, and industrial/educational programs. With autonomous local branches located throughout the country, AFTRA represents performer categories such as actors, announcers, dancers, disc jockeys, newspersons, singers, specialty acts, sportscasters, and stunt people. AFTRA contracts also cover extra performers in some situations.

AFTRA was created and is run solely by performers, and also offers life insurance, medical benefits, and a pension plan.

Membership requirements are similar to those of SAG. AFTRA offices are also listed in the Appendix under regional information. The best advice is to call or write for all the necessary information.

The union your child joins will depend on the type of work he or she secures. As confusing as it may seem now, you will almost certainly have an agent or manager to consult with by the time joining a union becomes necessary. Once your child is a member, be sure to take full advantage of all that union has to offer. SAG and AFTRA, for example (along with other unions), have bulletin boards and casting information lines to let you know about some of the roles available. Bear in mind that even if your child does have an agent, it will still be up to you to explore every conceivable job opportunity. Making use of a union's considerable resources therefore will be clearly advisable.

IN REVIEW
----

1. *The unions that will likely be of greatest importance in your child's career are the Screen Actors Guild (SAG) and the American Federation of Television and Radio Artists (AFTRA).*
2. *The Taft-Hartley Act allows actors to work without union affiliation for up to 30 days.*
3. *The pluses of union membership far outweigh the minuses.*
4. *Your child should carry his or her union card(s) to all auditions, interviews, and jobs.*
5. *Be sure to consult with your child's agent or manager about when and how to join a union.*

CHAPTER
FOURTEEN

PLAYING BY THE RULES

If your child is working without the protection of the SAG rules outlined in the previous chapter, make a point to investigate the labor laws and educational requirements in your area. If your child's agent, manager, or school principal can't provide the answers, seek them out for yourself.

In the Appendix, you'll find a section that lists the appropriate agency in each state that deals with the rules, laws, and regulations governing the employment of minors as performers. The laws vary from state to state. Some have few, if any, regulations. For instance, certain states exempt minors who are performers from child labor restrictions altogether. In other states, minors under a certain age are prohibited from working in the entertainment industry at all, although waivers are common. In many cases, a decision rests with a school principal or superintendent, and a student's grades frequently come into play.

Canadian child labor laws are regulated by ACTRA, which leaves the child actor's educational decisions up to his school principal. In Canada, a minor is defined as a child under 16.

Given California's place in movie history, it's not coincidental that it has always been a step ahead in regard to the laws affecting show business children. Over six decades ago, the California state legislature passed what was and is called the Blue Book, the legal bible of the entertainment industry.

One key rule stipulates that a minor can't work without a permit, and can't get a permit without a job offer. To obtain an Entertainment Work Permit in California, one must

- get an application card signed and filled in by the employer or casting director connected with your child's imminent job;
- take the application to the school so an official can verify that the child has at least a C average and provide a copy of a report card;
- take the application to a physician for signature and affirmation of the child's physical well-being; and
- personally take the application to the Division of Labor Standards Enforcement or the nearest labor commissioner's office.

If all is in order, a permit will be issued then and there, which is valid for six months for children six months old and up (the permit for younger babies is usually just for one month). Renewing the permit involves going through the entire process again, although you won't have to deliver the application in person.

California labor laws particularly come into play in regulating the number of hours children of various ages can work. These laws mandate that

- babies between the age of fifteen days and six months may be on the set a maximum of two hours, with the workday not to exceed 20 minutes;
- children between six months and two years may remain at the workplace a total of four hours, with half the time devoted to rest and recreation;
- kids between two and six may be at the workplace for a maximum of six hours, with half set aside for play and/or schooling;
- six-to-nine-year-old kids may be on the set eight hours, with at least three of those hours allotted to schooling (when it's a regular school day) and one to rest and recreation;
- minors between nine and sixteen may be at the workplace up to nine hours, with at least three hours of schooling and one hour of R and R;
- teens between sixteen and eighteen can be at the workplace for ten hours, with three hours of schooling and one hour of R and R;

- twelve hours must elapse between the minor's time of dismissal and call time the next day; and
- all time spent traveling from a studio to a location or vice versa counts as part of a child's working day.

California makes it mandatory that not only a parent or guardian be in the company of a minor on the set, but also a studio teacher or welfare worker. The law requires producers to set aside a special room or trailer away from the set where kids can attend to their schooling and enjoy some well-deserved playtime. This teacher or welfare worker must turn in a report at the end of each day spelling out each child's activities and general demeanor. If the report creates a negative picture, his or her work permit can be nullified. In addition, the teacher or welfare worker supervises all non-school-age children on the shoot.

Babies are also well cared for in California, legally speaking. The employer must hire one qualified nurse for every three babies under six weeks old, and one nurse for every ten babies over six weeks old. In addition, a studio teacher or welfare worker must be on the scene.

IN REVIEW

1. *Child labor regulations differ greatly from state to state.*
2. *California has the most comprehensive laws with regard to show business children.*
3. *Be sure to research what the specific laws are in your home state by contacting the State Department of Labor, Employment Standards Division, or SAG, AFTRA, or ACTRA office nearest you.*

Alison Arngrim

As an actress, Alison Arngrim is best known for her long-standing role as the self-absorbed and nasty—oh, let's just say it: *bitchy*—Nellie Oleson on the hugely successful TV series *Little House on the Prairie* (which she left in 1981). As it happens, the beautiful real-life Alison Arngrim bears no resemblance in appearance or demeanor to her former television counterpart. Indeed, for more than a decade, she has been among the most selfless people both within or outside of the entertainment industry, devoting her time, talent, and energies to an issue as far removed from the idyllic town of Walnut Grove as imaginable: AIDS.

Alison first began volunteering at AIDS Project Los Angeles (APLA) in 1986 following the death of her *Little House* "husband," actor Steve Tracy. Though relatively ignorant about AIDS, like virtually everyone else at the time, she decided, *unlike* most everyone else, to do more than read a few articles on the subject. Instead, she quickly became one of the most productive and active forces in the quest to fight AIDS and educate people about the disease. Over the years, this devotion has seen Alison be named chairperson for the AIDS Project Los Angeles volunteer speakers bureau; provide AIDS education to nurses, service clubs, churches, and schools; participate in numerous AIDS conferences throughout and outside of the country; speak before the Presidential Commission on AIDS; and become the first woman to receive the Friend in Deed Award from AIDS Project Los Angeles, among many other honors.

Alison, who continues to serve on the board of governors of AIDS Project Los Angeles, has over recent years hosted the APLA TV show, *AIDS Visions*, and has written articles for several national magazines. Still acting as well as performing stand-up comedy in diverse venues nationwide, she had this to say about her life and work thus far.

Q: *How did get started in the business?*

A: My family is in the business. My parents actually met in the theater in Canada and were running a theater at one point, with my father producing as well as acting. They were a big hit. After my brother was born, our parents continued working in Canadian radio and television; then they moved to New York, where my father was on Broadway and my mother started doing a lot of voice-over work. She was the voice of Gumby, Casper, and Davey in *Davey and Goliath*. This was in the late '50s through the mid-'60s, during which time I was born [in New York]. My brother started working when he was five and soon landed a role on *Search for Tomorrow*. Then we all moved to California, and my brother wound up in several TV shows, including a series role on *Land of the Giants*. My mom continued working in commercials and doing voice-overs, but my dad went into personal management, ultimately managing people such as Liberace and Debbie Reynolds. So we were the show biz family. I was going on auditions when I was a baby, but the first ones I remember were when I was five and six years old. In fact, I got my first commercial when I was six—for Hunt's Catsup. I was one of the kids trying to put a tomato into a bottle, but my tomato broke and splattered all over me.

Q: *When you were going to those early auditions, were you excited, uncertain, terrified, or combinations of all three?*

A: Despite being a show business family, my parents didn't really want us kids to be actors, but my brother kept begging them to take him on an audition. When they agreed, they figured he'd hate it and get over it. Instead, he went and got the part, and he loved it. By the time I was six years old, my brother was on *Land of the Giants*. Between that and the fact that my mother was doing voice-over work in cartoons, I sort of felt that everybody was on TV, so I wanted to do the same thing. I had a performing bent anyway, so I had no problem going out on auditions. Some I really liked, some were boring, some were difficult because they wanted you to do elaborate things, like play a musical instrument, which I don't do. The ones where they just wanted me to come in and read were always fun. I remember there was a strange reason why I didn't end up getting a lot of parts. Very often, the standards by which you're judged as a child actor are totally different from the standards by which you're judged as an adult actor. The standard of beauty, for one. For example, a gorgeous child actor doesn't always make a pretty adult, and vice versa. To a kid, they'll say, "Oh, you're really cute," and have you work a lot—maybe you have freckles and buck teeth, and you'll be considered adorable until you're five. If you're twenty-five with freckles and buck teeth, you're not exactly going to be considered a gorgeous leading man. I had sort of the opposite problem as a kid. I had big blue eyes set pretty far apart, and long blond hair. I was thin with high cheek bones and a pointy chin, and I looked like some kind of miniature fashion model. Had I been 19, I would have worked a lot more. But I was six, and I didn't look like the girl next door. So, they would actually say things like, "You're too pretty." It's an odd form of rejection. They wanted plain little girls and I didn't fit that image.

Q: *But your well-defined looks actually wound up helping you land the part of Nellie on* Little House *to some extent, didn't they?*

A: Absolutely. I was eleven when Michael Landon was first thinking of making a series out of the *Little House* books. When the show became a reality, I went and read for the parts of Laura and Mary, but I knew there was no way on Earth I was going to get either of those parts. Laura was a tomboyish, freckle-faced, rough-and-tumble kid—it wasn't me. I knew I wasn't the farm-girl type. But they did call me back to read for Nellie. I hadn't read the books, so I had no idea who this character was, but I read the script and it said this girl was supposed to look like a little prim and proper china doll, so I was all set. One of my parents always went with me to an audition. When I went to read for Nellie, my dad was with me, and when I started going over the script, the first thing I said is, "Dad, this girl's a little bitch." I started reading the dialogue to him and he started cracking up and said, "Don't change a thing. Just do that." So I went in and did the scene for Michael and the casting director, and they started laughing hysterically and asked me to read it again. I said, "What do you want me to change?" and they said, "Just read it the same again." I was hired that day. By the time I got home, my agent was calling to say I'd already gotten the part. And that's how I became Nellie Oleson.

Q: *Did you have any sense of how popular the series would become?*

A: No, not at all. Michael had a solid track record with *Bonanza,* and had gotten this fabulous deal to develop a family series. But no one was sure Little Joe Cartwright could carry a show on his own, and whether this concept would work. *The Waltons* had just been on a year or so, and the family series syndrome hadn't kicked in. Actually, the *Charlie's Angels* syndrome had started to happen, so *Little House* was a very uncertain prospect. NBC, in fact, wanted Michael to do a detective show or cop show, but he said no. He wanted to do *Little House,* and they thought he was crazy, just like they thought he was crazy many years later when he had a great idea for a show about an angel [*Highway to Heaven*]. We never thought the show would be a hit or even make it to the air.

Q: *What was your initial reaction to being cast?*

A: On the one hand, having grown up in the business, the idea of being on a TV series was almost an expectation in a way. It wasn't something foreign to me. So I had certainly given thought in my short life to that point as to what I would do if I was cast in a series. On the other hand, there was the reaction: "Oh, my God, I'm actually on a show." So, I was somewhat in shock the first day on the set. The other thing was that I had gotten the marvelous part of this bitchy girl, although I tended to be a little shy. So it was this great revenge on every bully who had ever tormented me in real life.

What helped a lot was that Melissa Gilbert and I immediately became friends, like sisters. We decided to become each other's allies. Once that happened, I never had any trouble.

We had an advantage on that show. There were a lot of other kids. When my brother was in *Land of the Giants*, he was the only child. He hung out with kids from other TV shows sometimes, but he wasn't working with other children. *Little House* had ten regular cast members who were kids. I was around more people my age on that show than I had been before I got the show! When I was in school on the set, there were a lot of people in the room. My brother went in and was by himself. So an experience for a kid working on a film or a television show can be radically different based on whether they're the only child actor in the cast. Because we had a large group of kids, we were able to create our own little society when we needed to. We didn't face a lot of the pressures that are sometimes put on children in the business to take on adult responsibilities.

First of all, we had Michael Landon, who was essentially a child himself, and was bound and determined that we were going to have a good time. But anytime any of the other adults were trying to constrain us, we would get around it. We managed to have all of the same kind of fun kids would have in summer camp. We made our own fun. We were getting away with murder. We were very lucky. Melissa Gilbert really laid down the law on our not getting into rivalries. She's a very smart person. She was practically running the place by age nine. The only instance when there seemed to be a rivalry turned out to have been a rumor started by some actress's mother. I don't know how long it took the adults to figure out the source of the rumor, but the kids all knew within days.

Q: *How were you able to separate yourself from the Nellie character at the end of each day?*

A: Nellie, to some extent, came from within. I tell people now that Nellie Oleson lives for ten minutes every morning before I've had my coffee. She is a legitimate part of my personality. I had no trouble whipping that up. It was a great release. Strangely, though, Nellie had the opposite effect on me than most people would have thought. The role didn't make me more bitchy, it made me less bitchy. In fact, the calmest I've ever been was right after doing an episode when I was really vicious. I would come home at the end of the day and be exhausted from working all day, and I was drained of all hostility after screaming at people and throwing things all day. I was professionally "de-bitched" for eight hours a day. It was fabulous. Can you imagine having a job where you're paid to scream and throw things? I was in a great mood when I got home. If I had had to play Laura or Mary or be someone nice, I probably would have gone stark raving mad. But there I was—thirteen, fourteen, fifteen years old—with all of the pressures of a series and people constantly telling me what to do, but with the perfect emotional outlet. I knew I had it made. Child actors are, once again, held to a different standard—they're supposed to be cute and adorable and sweet all the time. And there I was being congratulated for being vicious and rotten. I knew I had lucked out.

Of course, off the set, I still had the problem of some people thinking I was Nellie. But I had known most of my friends since third grade. They just thought it was hilarious that I was Nellie Oleson. They were totally indifferent, because I hadn't interrupted my normal social and educational life for the show. I had maintained continuity in my life. I was kept in the same school I had been going to before the series, which is something I would strongly recommend to parents of child actors.

Q: *You had the advantage of growing up with parents who understood the industry, but what other qualities do you think made them so effective as the parents of child actors?*

A: First of all, both of my parents are brutal realists. They would just tell things the way they were, and they encouraged us to be the same way. If we'd ask whether a series would be a big hit, they'd say, "Well, probably not. It might sell, but it might not. You might make a bunch of money, but then again, maybe not." Everything, good and bad, was clearly laid out for us in advance. They would tell us the truth. My dad would always ask me to get feedback from a casting director, whether or not I got the part. In fact, I think it's perfectly reasonable for parents to ask for feed-back; that way they can find out whether their child did something weird at the audition or whether they just weren't tall enough. My parents would always tell me what they had been told—you're too pretty, you're not pretty enough, you were too tall, whatever. They also gave me my money and gave me the responsibility for handling it and spending it. They trusted me. They knew I had done the work; I had earned it.

Q: *While many celebrities lend their names or some of their time to a cause, few, if any, have become as devoted as you in regard to your AIDS work. How do you keep that commitment going strong year after year?*

A: Because we can all make a difference if we want to. I gave a talk about AIDS a few years back in Walnut Grove, Minnesota—the actual home of *Little House*—and it was the first time the subject had been addressed in a public forum there. Months later, I got a letter telling me that a group had been formed in Walnut Grove to make quilts for babies with AIDS to be sent around the country. That wasn't happening before I went, so a person can make a difference.

Q: *What advice would you give to parents reading this book?*

A: Try to remember that a child going into show business may have a hundred agents, managers, producers, and others working with them over the years, but they're only going to have one set of parents. The temptation for a parent of a child performer may be to jump in as their manager or pub-licist or whatever, but don't forget that you're still that child's parent. One of two things is going to happen to young performers—either they'll be a huge star like Roddy McDowall or Elizabeth Taylor, or they'll be active for a few years and then be done. Either way, you'll still be that child's parents. Your relationship with a kid as a parent is far more important than whatever is going on profession-ally, no matter how much money is coming in. I've seen two extremes: totally ignoring a kid's behavior and deciding all rules go out the window because the child is successful; or putting kids in a hothouse like an orchid and never letting him or her have any fun. Kids are still kids, still human beings, still the people they were before their career happened. When it's all over, either they're an adult who's famous or an adult who's not. In any case, they still have the same basic needs all people have. There has to be a grounding in reality. It may be fabulous and your kid might be making a bucket of money and becoming famous. If that happens and it's what your kid wants, great. It can be a great ride and a lot of fun. But your kid is still your kid. If you can keep that in your mind, you really won't have any problems.

CHAPTER
FIFTEEN

FROM DR. SPOCK TO DR. FREUD:
WATCHING OUT FOR YOUR CHILD'S
MENTAL WELL-BEING

Through all the steps you take to launch your child's show business career, always be aware of his or her mental well-being. After all, this is still a little kid, one who will suddenly be saddled with big responsibilities. You know what you're doing and you know your own child, but by way of a reminder, here are some of the key emotional factors to be on the lookout for along the way.

ARE YOU DOING THIS FOR YOUR CHILD
OR FOR YOURSELF?

No single question is more important than this. Your child's emotional future is at stake, and it's vital that you and your child be on the same wavelength and after the same goals. Any child old enough to understand must share your eagerness to experience this wonderful but complex new adventure.

If you instinctively feel your child is reluctant about an acting career, then it's time to examine your own motives. If you have to admit you're secretly doing it for yourself, then you also must know it's best to back off, at least for now. Turning over a child's paychecks to a therapist is hardly what this is all about.

Try plain, old-fashioned honesty. *Regularly take the time to ask your child if a career in show business is what he or she wants.* You can't foresee all the emotional ups and downs that lie ahead, but if every feeling and every possibility is discussed, you'll be able to head off the more serious psychological setbacks that occasionally crop up.

ENCOURAGE, DON'T PUSH

Whatever you do, don't change from a loving parent to an obsessed tyrant overnight!

One of the cardinal parent-child rules is that the more an adult pushes, the less the child will want to oblige. When my parents were divorced, my mother became all the more obsessed with launching a career for me and my sister Joyce, but fortunately we were excited by show business ourselves and she always knew where to draw the line.

Quite simply, if you have to drag your child to auditions and lessons every week, you'll only be planting the seeds of resentment. The ideal arrangement will be a mutual one. Together, you will have mapped out a game plan up front. As part of that planning, you will have prepared your son or daughter to give up a certain chunk of time to pursue this new career. This way there will be no surprises where your child is concerned. The pros and cons will have been spelled out in advance and the terms agreed upon.

"I've seen people push their kids and leave everybody very unhappy," says Bob Williams. "It's much like what I've seen in Little League baseball. All of this should be a growth process for the child, not an endurance test. One thing I've always said—and my son works a lot—is that if he ever finds he's not enjoying it, he shouldn't do it. He should never feel pushed. There are times when kids get tired and need a break. They need a normal life. I think parents should be on guard for that. If the child doesn't like it now, you can bet it's going to cause big problems later on."

You may have it in your mind that only the pushy stage parent is the one who sees positive results. Certainly, it does take a lot of drive and determination to get ahead. But don't expect your child always to share your level of ambition. The world can see the fire in your eyes, but he or she should only see the love in them.

Whatever their age, even the toughest of kids will need constant support as they embark on this new adventure. Even as an adult, imagine going from the security of home one minute into the alien world of show business the next. That's why it's important to remind children at the earliest stages of a career that you'll always be there, proud and loving, regardless of what happens. It amounts to keeping life's priorities straight. They must continue to see that *family* comes first—not next week's casting call or acting lesson.

Dr. Michael Peck is a noted psychologist in Los Angeles with extensive experience in dealing with show business children. He is also the father of an actress. He feels the most important task of childhood and adolescence is the process of growing up. Some of the most disturbed teenagers he's seen are those who've grown too fast for their age. But a successful child actor can still maintain priorities, still have school friends, play softball, have friends over, and live as normal a life as possible.

"My feeling," Dr. Peck says, "is that the closer a working child can simulate the normal life of his peers, the better off that child will be. Responsibility for creating that sense of normalcy lies with the parents. They must set the example and show the way."

Armed with assurance that nothing has changed in the home environment, your child will be ready to go out there and show 'em all. That's when he or she will begin having a real blast. Meeting fascinating new people, visiting exciting new places, learning how to relate to others, and thriving on being the center of so much attention. As I have said, I really think you'll find that your child has learned more about life and the real world by his or her teen years than most kids have by their mid-twenties. That alone will have made it all worthwhile.

SPELL OUT REALITIES

Make it clear to your child what lies ahead *before* you get started. If you promise your son a lot of money and a bright red sports car before he's even old enough to drive, you're contributing to his living in a fantasy world. *Tell it like it is:* On the one hand, it's a lot of hard work, some occasional sacrifices, and a fair amount of competition. On the other, it's the chance for a thrilling career, an invaluable growing experience, and, just possibly, financial security for life.

If the realities seem too overwhelming for your child, leave it alone. You can always try again down the line, when he or she *is* ready. And even if your child *seems* to be going along, be sure this isn't his or her first "acting job" and that the enthusiasm displayed is not just to please you. You're the one who knows your own child best, so unless your kid is an even better performer than you think, you'll see through the false bravado soon enough.

While it's a mistake to promise children fame and fortune, it's equally wrong to convey that they will probably never have a chance. Find a middle ground between irrational optimism and doomsday pessimism. Simply ask them to do their best, enjoy themselves, and *look for success to come in gradual stages, not in leaps and bounds.* You'll be teaching children to believe in themselves and to be patient, qualities that will stay with them the rest of their lives.

SHORT-TERM GOALS

As a means of giving your child the kind of discipline required for a show business career, consider setting up short-term goals now. For example, have your child read a particular book, learn a favorite song, or master a new dance step within, say, a two-week period (*without* making it sound like homework). Choose activities he or she will enjoy and in which you can participate as well.

Even if these short-term goals have little or no bearing on a child's new career as a performer (building a model plane, completing a jigsaw puzzle, and the like), you'll be demonstrating the satisfaction and pride that come with finishing what one has started. It's this sort of pride that will help your child become a true professional and grow as a person.

POSITIVE FAMILY EXPERIENCES

As your child's world grows more and more exciting, remember to reinforce that sense of normalcy and security. *Provide balance in your child's life with regular family outings and activities.*

Once a career begins to take off and he or she is enjoying those accomplishments, your child's perspective may become a bit unfocused. As such, he or she will need a few jolts of reality, reminders that there's more to life than acting, singing, dancing, or modeling. Whether it's a meal out, a weekend matinee, or a trip to the park, give your child the chance to enjoy the company of the family. I can certainly attest to the fact that positive parental support made all the difference in the world to me when I was getting started.

OH, BROTHER! (OR SISTER)

Once your child is bound for stardom, what will you do if jealousy crops up in his or her siblings? Even under ordinary circumstances, it's difficult to keep young siblings civil toward each other. Naturally, the problem is aggravated all the more when one of the children is somehow being set apart from the rest.

The reality is that some jealousy and resentment will be inevitable. However, it can be tolerable so long as you don't treat your young celebrity as being somehow superior to his or her brothers and sisters. In other words, be as proud as you want, but don't show this child any special favoritism. And don't be afraid to punish your little thespian just because he or she is on a first-name basis with Sylvester Stallone or Bill Cosby!

WATCH THAT EGO

Once your child's a professional, guard against two undesirable possibilities. The first is that your child will take unsuccessful auditions or casting calls as personal rejections. The second is the opposite—that with every new day and every new job, your child will be that much more convinced he or she is the greatest thing since the invention of the wheel.

Again, it will be up to you to help restore balance. If one loses out on a job after giving it the best possible shot, do what you can to ensure that your child still feels good about him- or herself. Build up that confidence for the next time. It will be no good if your child thinks you're disappointed. Talk it over, express your pride, and go about your business.

Bob Williams says the key is for parents to consistently tell their children that *losing out on a part usually has nothing whatsoever to do with a lack of talent.* When it gets down to the finalists, they're probably all very close in terms of ability and experience. Unfortunately, one child may be just the right age or size or have the right look. "It can be very dangerous emotionally," Bob stresses. "Especially if a parent is constantly prodding the child, pressuring the kid to succeed and expressing disappointment every time a job doesn't work out."

At Disneyland several years ago, Bob's son R.J. joined a group of friends for a birthday party. Half the kids were actors. "As we got to the front entrance, the mother of the birthday child turned to the other children and said, 'OK, all the kids who are *somebody* over here, and all the *nobodys* over there.' You can see where that kind of thing can stay in a child's mind for a very long time."

Not surprisingly, Dr. Peck agrees. "How parents and agents handle rejection, or *perceived* rejection, will really determine a great deal in terms of how the child reacts. If the parents put constant pressure on kids, and a job doesn't happen to work out, the child believes he's 'failed' his parents. Maybe at a young age, around five to eight years, he doesn't care that much about what a casting agent, producer, or director says. These are people who have a minimal personal impact on him. But it's an entirely different scenario once the parents figure into the picture."

Andrea Pruett certainly saw her son, Harold, face the usual rejections, even given his unique versatility as a performer. "Sure, you get dejected," Andrea admits. "But then, you have to stop and understand that no matter how talented your child is, he may just not be right for a certain part. Maybe he's too tall or too short. Very likely, it will simply be because he doesn't look enough like the other actors playing the members of his family. *Whatever* the reason, you have to see it through all the way. We did in Harold's case, and it couldn't have worked out better."

If the other extreme comes into play and you feel your child is becoming something of an egomaniac, get his or her act together fast! It will be understandable if your child is proud of having landed jobs and earned money, but not to the point of suddenly thinking the world revolves around him or her. *If a child behaves obnoxiously, he or she must be told.* Your child may be bringing home more money than you are, but won't be beyond having a little repair work done on his or her personality.

Dr. Peck says parents in such a situation should talk to the child's agent or manager, cut down on roles, send the child out on fewer calls, and place him or her right back into a normal school environment. "One of the interesting things I've observed along the way is that kids from about eight to fourteen, when they have a same-age peer in school who's an actor, don't treat him with kid gloves. They treat him like any other child, sometimes even with a fair degree of resentment. Once the child actor realizes his star status isn't helping, it's a good way to control his ego and make him understand that there's a whole other life going on that has nothing to do with his profession."

Dr. Peck adds, "The kids that do best are those whose friends are not impressed by their celebrity status, but are impressed only by open and sharing people. If the child actor can fill that role and be that kind of person, he won't get an overblown ego. And this must be reinforced at home, with his parents telling him, in essence, 'We're thrilled you have a successful career and financial security, but the idea isn't to make you into a screen idol.' Kids who see show business solely as a vehicle to a rewarding career will be fine. The ones who see it as an opportunity to be famous, have their pictures taken, and feel more important than everyone else will be in trouble."

"My youngest son worked all the time and was quite a celebrity," Judy Savage recalls, "so we just treated it as a hobby that he was lucky enough to get paid for. That's the right attitude to adopt. I knew [*Family Affair*'s] Johnnie Whitaker all the time he was growing up and he was a great kid. Ronnie Howard turned out just fabulous. He has a terrific family. Kirk Cameron's family is one of the nicest you would ever want to meet. And no one turned out better than Shirley Temple! It really all depends on the family."

IN REVIEW
----

1. *However successful children become, remember they are still children.*

2. *Make certain a show business career is what they want, not what you want.*
3. *Support and encourage, but don't push, children.*
4. *Tell it like it is so that children know what lies ahead.*
5. *Set up short-term goals to promote their sense of accomplishment and self-worth.*
6. *Maintain balance in their lives through quality family time.*
7. *Never treat professional children as superior to their brothers and sisters or peers.*
8. *Guard against children becoming either too egotistical or too insecure as a result of their careers.*

CELEBRITY CLOSE-UP

Jon Provost

From 1957 to 1964, America's most beloved canine star made Jon Provost one of the country's most beloved child actors. The dog, of course, was Lassie, and it was on the classic series of the same name that young Provost, from seven to fourteen, starred as Timmy.

Even before *Lassie*, Jon had launched his career at the age of two in *So Big* with Jane Wyman and Sterling Hayden. His numerous film and TV credits before and after *Lassie* included *The Country Girl*, starring Bing Crosby and Grace Kelly, *This Property Is Condemned*, starring Natalie Wood and Robert Redford, *The Jack Benny Show*, and *Mr. Ed*.

Though Jon later opted for a career in real estate, his show business career came full circle several years ago when he was cast in the recurring role of Uncle Steve in MCA TV's all-new *Lassie* series.

Here are some of Jon's recollections of being a child star.

Q: *How did you get your start in the business?*
A: My kindergarten teacher had read an ad in the paper that said Warner Bros. was looking for a blond, two-to-three-year-old boy who wouldn't mind taking direction—and evidently I didn't. One of the stars of the movie was Teresa Wright, whom my mom idolized. So actually it was an opportunity for my mom to possibly get to see one of her favorite stars. Nobody in my family had ever been in the business, and my dad thought the whole thing was a silly waste of time. Sure enough, though, after auditioning with close to four hundred other little boys, I ended up getting the job. It was just a fluke. Then one thing led to another, culminating with *Lassie* in 1957.

Q: *Was your mother acting as your agent at the start of your career?*

JON PROVOST   185

A: Not the way the story was related to me. After we'd been at one particular audition for a couple of hours, a lady walked over to my mom and said, "You know, I think your son might just get this job. Does he have an agent?" My mother didn't even know exactly what an agent was, much less have one for me. So this woman said, "He'll need to have an agent to represent him. *I'm* an agent. Sign on the dotted line." That agent was Lola Moore, one of the biggest in the industry as it turned out, and I was with her for fifteen years!

Q: *In your early career, did you ever feel you were being pushed or were you doing what you wanted to do?*
A: Actually, from as far back as I can remember, the experience always seemed a normal one to me. It was no different from going to school. Sure, there were times when the hours were long or it was boring, but the truth is I always did enjoy it.

Q: *Why do you think you have such positive memories of those days?*
A: I think I owe it to my family. Ninety-nine percent of how a child reacts to a career in show business has to do with his or her home life. Unfortunately, one or both parents frequently will quit working once a child is successful and can support the family. I don't think that's right. It puts a strain on the child and distorts what a normal family upbringing is supposed to be. Luckily, it wasn't that way at all for me.

As obvious as it sounds, the main thing is to enjoy what you're doing. If you can't have fun, you shouldn't be doing it. That's the bottom line in all professions. And in great part it's up to the parents to instill that sense of fun, to let a child know that work and enjoyment *can* go together.

One time on *Lassie* we had a kid who was hired to be my double. There was a scene in which a boat Lassie and I were on was supposed to tip over. Even though this kid was a good swimmer, when it came time for the stunt, there was no way in the world he was going to do it. He started freaking out. Instead of understanding what her son was going through, though, his mother just kept saying, "You're going to do it!" Over and over. I ended up doing the scene myself. Not because I had to, but because I wanted to. The whole incident was a textbook example of how a parent *shouldn't* handle a show business child.

Q: *Were you nervous or relaxed during interviews and auditions?*
A: I just went in, did what I had to do, tried to do my best, and left it at that. I was lucky in that I really didn't have to deal with too much rejection. Things were almost always just handed to me. Of course, when I was older I was turned down more frequently. But for the seven years of *Lassie*, I was spared all that. You just have to deal with the rejection, or what seems like rejection, up front. And the same goes for the interviews and auditions themselves. Simply do what you can and hope for the best. If it doesn't work out this time, there's always the next time.

Q: *Were you able to maintain a relatively normal social life with kids outside the business?*
A: Pretty much so, except for the fact that I was busier than my friends. There were guys in the neighborhood whom I hung around with whenever I had the time. On the other hand, everywhere I went, people knew me from the series, so I really didn't have the usual anonymity most others have.

Q: *How does a young performer avoid letting that kind of success go to his or her head?*
A: I can only speak from my own experience. When I was home, I was never treated any differently from my brother and sister. My parents didn't go for the so-called Hollywood scene. I got fifty cents a week allowance, and I had to take out the trash and keep my room clean just like my brother and sister. Sure, my mom enjoyed what I was doing. I was her "star." But the key was she never let all that affect the way she dealt with me.

Q: Lassie *was more than just another series. It was almost like a national treasure. How did that make you feel?*
A: I used to watch the show when Tommy Rettig starred in

it before me, and naturally I had no idea I'd wind up in his place one day. A few years ago, my kids watched the old shows on Nickelodeon, and I must say they still hold up. I'm fortunate to have been on a show that doesn't make me cower when I watch it today. The series is a classic. It really is.

Q: *How was it working with Lassie?*

A: There were three dogs on the set at all times. A main dog, a stand-in, and a double. Over the seven years, I worked with three main Lassies. The one I worked with the longest was the last. He—they were all males—and I had a great relationship. He was just an incredible dog. I would go home with (trainer) Rudd Weatherwax on weekends and play with the dogs. We always had animals at home, too, and I have three dogs today. No collies, though.

Q: *Any favorite anecdote from your years on* Lassie?

A: Toward the end of the series, we did a five-parter called "Lassie's Great Adventure." We were shooting up in Northern California in Sonora. One scene had me coming down a river on a raft I had built—not the boat scene I mentioned earlier, incidentally—and it called for me and Lassie to fall off the raft and swim to safety. Obviously, that wasn't something we could really rehearse. And since the scene required close-ups, we couldn't use a double even if I wanted one. Anyway, when we got thrown into the water, I went under and hit my chest on a rock. It knocked all the air out of me, and when I came up, I yelled for help as loud as I could. Wouldn't you know everyone assumed I was acting! Instead of giving me a hand, they were complimenting me on such a convincing performance. It wasn't until later that they really knew *why* it was so convincing.

Q: *What advice would you give kids starting in the business today?*

A: First, they have to want to do it for themselves, not for someone else. As I said before, they need to have fun and to remember that getting turned down isn't the end of the world. Each time that happens, it's possible to learn something from the experience and increase their chances the next time around.

People used to ask me if it was difficult working with a dog, but the truth is that human performers would make many more mistakes than Lassie. That's the nature of this and every other business: No one's perfect. And it's a terrible mistake to get down on yourself every time you experience a disappointment. The secret is not to focus on those disappointments, but always to look ahead to what's next and keep moving forward.

CHAPTER

SIXTEEN

A QUESTIONNAIRE JUST FOR CHILD ACTORS

(NO PARENTS ALLOWED!)
----

1. *Do you really want to be in show business?*
2. *If you do, why?*
3. *What area of show business would you enjoy most as a performer?*
4. *Do you like performing in front of other people?*
5. *Have you ever performed in public, or even just in front of your family?*
6. *Was it scary? If so,* how *scary?*
7. *Are you nervous in front of strangers?*
8. *Would you rather perform in front of a camera or onstage?*
9. *Do you like to read?*
10. *Are you willing to take acting, singing, or dancing lessons?*
11. *Are you willing to work hard to become successful?*
12. *Would you be able to take instructions from a director?*
13. *Do you think your parents will be angry with you if you don't succeed right away?*
14. *Even if you make a lot of money, would you still want to go to college?*
15. *Do you think you would change if you made a lot of money?*
16. *Who are your favorite young actors on TV and in the movies?*
17. *Who are your favorite older actors on TV and in the movies?*
18. *If you could play any character, who would it be? Why?*
19. *Do you think you'll be good as a performer?*
20. *Is there anything about yourself you would change?*

CHAPTER
SEVENTEEN

AND IN CONCLUSION . . .

Every child is special.
Every child is talented.
Every child has what it takes.

The secret to success in show business is having a child who projects those qualities from the moment you meet him or her. Diane Hardin represented the late River Phoenix for a while when he was about ten, and says she knew from the moment she first saw him improvise that he was going to be a big star. "He just had it, whatever *it* is," says Diane. "The ideal combination of personality, looks, and talent, and an obvious joy for the art of acting."

Unfortunately, many parents think their only chance of promoting that "ideal combination" in *their* children is to clone another Macaulay Culkin, Jonathan Taylor Thomas, or Olsen twin. The problem with that is twofold. First, by the time you've changed your child into the sort of performer you think he or she should be, the industry may very well be on to an entirely new type. Second, and most significantly, in attempting to convert your child into someone *else's* child, you will instantly be taking away the very individuality casting directors appreciate the most.

Quite simply, your child is an individual. Any industry professional who has been around the block more than once has seen and heard it all. You might say these experts have developed bionic vision when it comes to seeing through children who are putting on a false front. That's why it will do no good, and may do quite a bit of harm, to try and pass your child off as someone he or she is not.

On occasion, of course, a child will be trying out for a highly specialized role that requires the actor to speak in a particular accent, dress for a period piece, or blatantly resemble a real-life figure or fellow cast member. Such was the case when Jason Hervey had to leave his own personality behind in order to win the coveted role of the young Rodney Dangerfield in *Back to School*. This time the trick *was* to become someone else. Normally, though, naturalism wins every time.

The main personality traits all children should convey are politeness, attentiveness, and enthusiasm. The rest has to be up to each kid individually. But even if the audition comes that finds your child shy, unfocused, and sluggish (and believe me, I had a few of those myself), don't give up. It's all part of the learning and growing process.

As Garrison True sees it, parents should give serious thought to launching a show business career for their children, since the benefits are so substantial. "If there's even a bit of interest and ability, a child can earn enough money for college simply by doing one commercial," he says. "Most of all, I happen to feel very strongly that if one pursues the craft of acting at a young age, whether or not one stays in that field later on, it's going to be a plus. To be able to get up in front of people and present yourself with confidence, to speak properly, and to be aware of yourself—these are wonderful qualities. There are many terrific people I've met in my life who are heads of major companies today who studied acting while they were growing up. It's an invaluable training ground for life."

"It's true, it is a wonderful place for a child to learn self-confidence real fast," says Marsha Hervey. "When they have something to do, they have to be ready to do it themselves. They grow up knowing they have a responsibility to themselves and to other people. They learn that there's a time to work and a time to play. They are self-sufficient people, and they are the survivors in this world!"

The rewards *are* incomparable, but remember that the competition is stiff. Success may come gradually, not overnight.

But each step will bring you closer to the top of the ladder. Whether fame and fortune are reached tomorrow or a year from now, the very process of *trying* will guarantee that your child will become a more self-reliant and self-assured person.

Now that you've taken the time to sit down and read this book, it's time to stand up and get going. Don't look back ten years from now and say, "Why didn't we do something back then?" Simply make up your mind to move into high gear and explore this thrilling new horizon. Best of all, be assured that *whatever* happens, you'll experience an unforgettable adventure that will help your child develop into a well-rounded adult. On the child's part, he or she will learn about life, creativity, and responsibility. For your part, you'll enjoy a fulfillment you would never have experienced without taking that first important step.

It worked for me, and it could work for you.

Good luck!

GLOSSARY OF TERMS

A CAPPELLA
Singing with no musical accompaniment.

ACCOUNT EXECUTIVE
An advertising agency representative who serves as the point person between his or her office and the sponsor during the making of a commercial.

ACTRA
Alliance of Canadian Cinema, Television, and Radio Artists. This organization is the equivalent of SAG and AFTRA in the United States combined.

AD
Assistant director.

AD LIB
Dialogue or physical action improvised by a performer.

ADR
Additional dialogue replacement. The process by which an actor overlays fresh dialogue over a poor sound track. Also referred to as "looping."

AEA
Actors' Equity Association, or Equity, as it is commonly known.

AFL-CIO
The American Federation of Labor and Congress of Industrial Organizations. This is the parent body of the American labor unions.

AFTRA
The American Federation of Television and Radio Artists.

AGMA
The American Guild of Musical Artists.

AGVA
The American Guild of Variety Artists.

AIR DATE
The date on which a show or commercial is broadcast.

AUDITION

A performance in which an actor is evaluated for a role. Also known as a "tryout" or "call."

AVAIL

A situation in which an actor makes himself available to a producer even when there is no contract between them.

BACKGROUND

Extras.

BEST BOY

Assistant to the electrician on a film set.

BILLING

The size and placement of credits in advertisements for a theatrical, film, or video production.

BIO

A short biography or résumé.

BLOCKING

The planning of cast and camera positions and movements during a given scene in theater, film, or video.

BOOKING

A performing or modeling assignment.

BOOM

An extended pole to which an overhead microphone is attached. A camera boom is a crane used to extend the camera.

BREAKAWAY

A prop or set piece that is built so that it breaks easily or can shatter harmlessly.

BREAKDOWN

A cast list with brief descriptions of each role, used for casting purposes.

BUSINESS MANAGER

An expert in managing financial and tax-related matters for others.

CALL

(a) An audition or interview with casting personnel or produc-ers. (b) The specific time a performer is scheduled to be on the set or on location (e.g., "makeup call," "on-set call").

CALLBACK

An audition subsequent to the first, reflecting interest on the part of the powers that be.

CASTING DIRECTOR

The person who assembles all prospective cast members and helps to choose the actors for a given production.

CASTING NOTICE

Posted information about an upcoming audition, as printed in a trade paper or placed on a union bulletin board.

CATTLE CALL

Slang expression for an open call, when a large group of people arrive en masse to compete for one or more roles in a production.

CLIO AWARD

The most prestigious prize in the field of television commercials.

CLOSE-UP

Term denoting a tight camera angle, usually head and shoulders. In a script it may appear as CU or ECU (extreme CU).

COLD READING

The occasion when an actor is auditioned with a scene or other written material he or she has never seen before and has had little or no time to prepare.

COMMISSARY

The restaurant or cafeteria located on a motion picture studio lot.

COMMISSION

That percentage of an actor's (or model's) earnings that is retained by an agent or manager.

COMPOSITE

An 8 x 10" page with several different poses of the actor or model featured.

CONTACT SHEET
>A photographer's print of all the pictures taken during a session, the best of which are chosen for a head shot or composite.

CREDITS
>A compilation of one's professional and amateur experience.

CUE CARDS
>Cards with the performers' lines written on them.

DAY PLAYER
>A performer hired for a single day's work.

DEMO
>An audio- or videotape used for audition purposes or a commercial produced by an ad agency to test consumer reaction.

DOUBLE
>A person who takes the place of another performer in a scene for various reasons, as in "stunt double" or "hand double."

DRESSER
>The person who oversees cast costumes and helps performers make changes of wardrobe.

DRESSING
>Those elements in a scene other than the set itself, such as furniture, drapes, pictures, and the like.

DUBBING
>Recording sound to match the picture after principal photography. Voice dubbing is also known as "looping."

DUPE
>A duplicate copy of an audio, video, or film element.

ELECTRICIAN
>A member of a crew responsible for the lighting.

EMANCIPATED MINOR
>A young performer who has been given adult status and self-determination by a court.

EXCLUSIVITY
>A contractual condition by which a producer or advertiser has sole rights to a performer's work for a proscribed period of time.

EXT

In scripts, refers to an exterior setting, as opposed to an interior one.

EXTRA

Person who appears in the background without dialogue in a film, television show, or commercial.

FITTING

A session in which one's wardrobe is tried on.

FRAMING

The composition of a photograph as determined by its boundaries.

FRANCHISED AGENT

Talent agent approved by a union to represent its members.

FX

Special effects such as explosions or physical tricks used during filming or taping.

GAFFER

A person who places lighting devices on a film set.

GLOSSY

A photo with a smooth, shiny finish.

GOFER

On-set helper available to "go for" things (coffee and supplies) or help in other ways.

GRIP

One who moves set pieces or props on a film set.

HEAD SHEET

A booklet or poster featuring small photos of all the talent a particular agency or manager represents, designed to be circulated among casting personnel within the business.

HEAD SHOT

A photo of an actor's or model's face.

HOLDING CYCLE

A union-designated period of time during which a commercial contract has rights over a performer (21 months broken into seven 13-week holding cycles); during the holding cycle, a producer can choose to run the commercial or hold it. As used in series television, it denotes a period of time during which a producer may hold an actor for a contracted period.

HOLDING FEE

A fee paid to a performer for his or her exclusivity during a holding cycle.

INDUSTRIAL

Film, tape, or theatrical production, sometimes educational but more often created for the purpose of promoting a company or product.

INSERT

Close camera shots inserted into previously produced footage.

INT

In scripts, refers to an interior setting, as opposed to an exterior one.

INTERVIEW

(a) When a photographer first meets a prospective model and studies his or her book or portfolio. (b) When a producer, director, or casting director, before an actual audition, first meets a performer and evaluates him or her for a role. Also known as a "go-see."

IN THE CAN

A slang expression that means filming or taping is completed.

LIP SYNC

To record a voice so that it matches the lip movements of the same or another performer on camera. Lip synchronizing is the same as "looping," and the terms are used interchangeably.

LOCATION

The filming or taping site when it is not on a soundstage or studio lot.

LONG SHOT

In scripts, LS. Means just what it says: a camera angle that encompasses a broad scene or action.

LOOPING

The process of matching a voice to the lip movements of the same or another performer on camera.

MEAL PENALTY

A fee set by union contract that is paid when a performer is not given meals or meal breaks at the required times.

MONOLOGUE

A short scene for one actor drawn from published material or written specifically for the showcasing of an actor's abilities; customarily used for audition or training purposes.

MOS

A film or video sequence shot without sound. Derivation is traditionally attributed to a Middle European assistant director in the '30s who described such scenes as being "mitout sound!"

MOW

TV Movie of the Week.

NIGHT PREMIUM

A 10 percent surcharge paid to a SAG performer for work performed after 8:00 p.m.

OPEN CALL

The occasion when a large group of actors is invited to be interviewed for a role. Open calls are posted in trades and on bulletin boards, and no appointment is necessary.

OS

Off-scene. Dialogue delivered off-camera.

OUT CLAUSE

Stipulation in a contract that allows a performer or producer to terminate the agreement under certain conditions.

OUT TIME

The actual time a performer is permitted to leave a set or location and head home.

PA

Production assistant.

PER DIEM

Money provided to performers on location to cover daily basic expenses.

PERSONAL MANAGER

A person or firm hired to guide the career of a client by contacting and working with agents to set up auditions and interviews and offering a wide range of advice relative to career advancement. A personal manager receives a commission only when the client has been paid.

PHOTO DOUBLE

A performer hired to perform on camera in place of another.

PORTFOLIO

Usually an 11 x 14" zippered case containing one's photos and tear sheets of press reviews, ads, and films in which that person has appeared. Also known as a "book."

PRINCIPAL

The main performer in a television show, film, commercial, or play.

PRODUCER

That person(s) who supervises and is ultimately responsible for every element of a production, from the initial story, to expenditures and budget, to the completed film or tape.

PROP

Short for "property," referring to an object used in a scene.

READING

When an actor is called upon to act out a role while reading from the script, sometimes without benefit of rehearsal, as in a cold reading or audition. In the theater, the term refers to a preliminary read-through of the script by cast members without movement or blocking.

RELEASE

A written agreement signed by a performer, which grants the employer certain specific rights.

REPERTORY

A theatrical company that presents several plays in one season, alternating them regularly every few days or weeks.

RESIDUAL

A payment made to a performer for a repeat showing of a particular television show or commercial, or airing of a radio performance.

RÉSUMÉ

A summary of one's work history and other relevant personal interests and statistics.

RIGHT-TO-WORK STATE

A state in which a performer is not required to belong to a union in order to work in any industry.

RUNNING PART

A role that recurs in a television series.

SAG

Screen Actors Guild.

SCALE

Minimum payment due for services under the various union contracts.

SCALE + 10

Minimum payment due plus 10 percent to cover the agent's commission.

SEG

Screen Extras Guild. This is the union that represents all extras who perform on the screen.

SEGUE

In film or tape, a transition from one shot to another.

SFX

In scripts, refers to sound effects.

SIDES

The pages of a script that pertain to a given role. An actor is said to have his or her "sides" when given the pages to memorize and perform.

SILENT BIT

A performance that requires specific action or "special business" without lines; an extra is frequently upgraded to a silent bit and earns extra money for it.

SINGLE CARD
A credit in which only one performer's name appears.

SLATE
A small chalkboard and clapper device used to label the scene number, director, and production title to identify a given scene. Also known as "clapboard" and "clapper board."

SOUND TRACK
The audio portion of a film or tape production.

SPECIAL BUSINESS
Action requested of an extra by the director, which qualifies the extra as a "silent bit."

STABLE
Slang term for a group of clients represented by a theatrical or model agency.

STAND-INS
Extra players who take the place of principals prior to filming to help set lights and camera.

STORYBOARD
A rendering, frame by frame, of what a commercial (or other type of film) will look and sound like, usually in sketch form.

STUNT COORDINATOR
The expert who creates and coordinates difficult or dangerous action sequences on a film or tape set.

STUNT DOUBLE
The performer who undertakes action sequences on behalf of an actor.

SUBMISSION
An agent makes a submission when he or she suggests a performer for a role.

TAFT-HARTLEY ACT
The federal statute that allows 30 days after first employment before being required to join a union.

TEAR SHEET
A page from a newspaper or magazine showing an ad in which a person is featured, and then used by the person as a sample of past work.

TELEPROMPTER
The manufacturer's brand name for a crawl device that provides a performer with lines while looking directly into the camera.

THEATRICAL
A term that distinguishes films shown in theaters and legitimate theatrical productions from television and other forms of film and video.

TIGHT SHOT
An extreme close-up.

TRADE SHOWS
Productions by business or industry for the purpose of self-promotion and product awareness.

TRADES
Newspapers and periodicals that feature current events having to do with the entertainment business; e.g., the Hollywood Reporter.

TURNAROUND
The number of hours between dismissal from the set on one day and call time the next.

TWO-SHOT
A camera shot in which two performers appear simultaneously.

TYPE
A comparative term having to do with physical characteristics such as age, size, and coloration, and personal traits such as accent and ethnic background.

UNDERSTUDY

The performer who rehearses and is ready to step in for another performer when he or she is indisposed or otherwise unable to perform. (As earlier noted, the understudy role has been the gateway to stardom for a number of performers. The great operatic tenor Luciano Pavarotti understudied a principal tenor role in London and was called to perform. He was an instant success and his career took off from there!) Also referred to as "standby."

UPGRADE

Acknowledgment by a producer that a person hired as an extra has been given lines and performed as an actor and is thereby eligible for an actor's pay.

VO

In scripts, means voice-over.

WILD SPOT

Commercial designed to air on local stations as opposed to a network broadcast.

WILD TRACK

A sound track that is recorded to add atmospheric sound to a production; e.g., crowd, traffic, voices. It is picked up on the production site. Any other atmospheric sound is classified as "sound effects" and is drawn from sound-effects libraries.

WORK PERMIT

A document that allows a child to work, issued by state or local agencies.

WRAP

A slang word denoting the end of a production day or the conclusion of filming. "It's a wrap!" is a welcome call from the assistant director on any set. In this case, however, it signifies the end of the book. But only the beginning for you!

APPENDIX

ALABAMA

CASTING OFFICES

BIRMINGHAM
Shirley Fulton Crumley ....(205) 856-7382
Marie Prater ....(205) 822-8135
Janelle Cochrane Sims ....(205) 833-8882

FLORENCE
Tonya Suzanne Holly................................(205) 764-1434

MOBILE
Mary Gaffney...(334) 661-0599

MONTGOMERY
Bob Vardaman ....(334) 271-5300

RAINBOW CITY
Marian "Mitch" duPont ....(205) 413-0081

REGIONAL THEATER

ANNISTON
Anniston Community Theater ....(205) 236-8342

BIRMINGHAM
Birmingham Children's Theater................(205) 324-0470
Birmingham Festival Theater....................(205) 322-5259
Carnegie's ....(205) 822-6216
Terrific New Theater ....(205) 328-0868
Town & Gown Theater..............................(205) 934-5088

DECATUR
Backstage Theater Co..............................(205) 340-1783
Dreamweavers...(205) 350-6464

DOTHAN
Southeast Alabama Community Theater ....(334) 794-0400

FLORENCE
Zodiac Theater ....(205) 764-1700

GADSDEN
Theater of Gadsden.................................(205) 547-7469

HUNTSVILLE
Huntsville Little Theater ....(205) 533-6565
Twickenham Mobile Repertory Co. ....(205) 539-TWIK

MOBILE
Joe Jefferson Players Playhouse ....(334) 471-1534
Mobile Theater Guild ....(334) 433-7513
Playhouse in the Park ....(334) 344-1537
Saenger Theater ....(334) 438-5686

MONTGOMERY
Alabama Shakespeare Festival................(334) 271-5300
Davis Theater for the Performing Arts ....(334) 241-9567
Montgomery Little Theater......................(334) 263-4856

TUSCALOOSA
Bama Theater..(205) 758-5195
Theater Tuscaloosa ....(205) 345-3912

TALENT AND MODELING AGENCIES

ANNISTON
Images Unlimited ....(205) 236-0952
Macy's Modeling School & Agency ....(205) 236-3597

BIRMINGHAM
Kiddin' Around/Real People ....(205) 323-KIDS
E'lan Agency ....(205) 985-3001
Cathi Larson Agency................................(205) 951-2445

DECATUR
Hamilton Academy of
  Personal Development & Modeling ......(205) 351-8022
Star Quality ....(205) 350-6005

DOTHAN
Rare Quality Models & Talent ....(334) 671-2200

HUEYTOWN
ACT Productions......................................(205) 491-3205

MONTGOMERY
Beau Monde Productions Unlimited, Inc. ..(334) 286-3696
Cynthia's Studio Model & Talent Agency ..(334) 272-5555
Rare Quality Models & Talent ....(334) 244-4464
Stone Cole Talent ....(334) 277-1212

TUSCALOOSA
Alabama Talent & Model Management ......(205) 345-1199

ALABAMA FILM OFFICES

MONTGOMERY
Alabama Film Office ....(800) 633-5898

MOBILE
Mobile Film Office ....(334) 434-7304

ALASKA

CASTING OFFICES

ANCHORAGE
Alaska Models & Talent ....(907) 561-5739
Carlson's Company..................................(907) 258-2454
Northern Stars...(907) 688-1370

MODELING AGENCIES AND SCHOOLS

ANCHORAGE
Alaska Image Agency ....(907) 561-5739
Carlson's Company of Talent....................(907) 258-2454
Foto's by Frank ....(907) 274-8487
Model Perfect the Agency ....(907) 344-1132
Powers Finishing School
  & Modeling Agency ....(907) 344-2525
Simply Pilar School of Modeling ....(907) 344-1132
Stanley & Company ....(907) 561-6877 or 563-6160

ALASKA FILM OFFICE

ANCHORAGE
Alaska Film Office....................................(907) 269-8137

ARIZONA

CASTING OFFICES

PHOENIX
Casting Unlimited ....(602) 465-0315
Darlene Wyatt, CSA...............................(602) 263-8650
Leavey and Associates ....(602) 331-4945
Tondu Studios..(602) 252-5565

SCOTTSDALE
American Celebrity Brokers.....................(602) 481-2002
Christal Blue Casting ....(602) 994-1162
Gay Gilbert ....(602) 423-8722
Sunny Seibel...(602) 956-7700

TUCSON
Conklin Casting ....(520) 229-2699
Holly Hire Casting...................................(520) 586-3326
New Age Movies & Management ....(520) 883-4025

TALENT AND MODELING AGENCIES

PHOENIX
Dani's Agency ....(602) 263-1918
Leighton Agency ....(602) 224-9255
Signature Models & Talent ....(602) 996-1102

PRESCOTT
New Visions Modeling-Talent Agency........(520) 445-3382
Pine Mountain Talent Agency ....(520) 771-1380

SCOTTSDALE
American Celebrity Brokers, Inc...............(602) 481-2002
Cosmos Model & Talent, Inc. ....(602) 949-6004
Ford Robert Black Agency.......................(602) 966-2537
J & J International ....(602) 945-1005

TUCSON
ACT Theatrical & Modeling Agency ....(520) 885-3246
The Actor's Agency ....(520) 321-1973
Flair Parisienne Model & Talent Agency ....(520) 742-1090

ARIZONA FILM OFFICES

FLAGSTAFF
Flagstaff Film Office ....(520) 774-5118

GLOBE
Globe Miami Film Office.........................(520) 425-4495

PHOENIX
Arizona Film Office ....(800) 523-6695
Phoenix Film Office.................................(602) 262-4850

TUCSON
Tucson Film Office ....(520) 792-4400

ARKANSAS

TALENT AND MODELING AGENCIES

FAYETTEVILLE
Call-Casting International ....(800) 495-8540

JONESBORO
Lewis-Glaub Agency................................(501) 933-7400

LITTLE ROCK
The Agency ....(501) 374-6447
Excel School of Modeling........................(501) 227-4232
Ferguson Modeling & Talent....................(501) 375-3519
Mike Humphrey Casting ....(501) 375-9663
Solutions...(501) 664-2830

NORTH LITTLE ROCK
Entertainment, Etc. ....(501) 372-2772

THEATERS

LITTLE ROCK
Arkansas Actor's Lab...............................(501) 568-3456
Arkansas Arts Center Children's Theater ....(501) 372-4000
Arkansas Repertory Theater ....(501) 378-0405
Community Theater of Little Rock.............(501) 663-9494

ARKANSAS FILM OFFICES

EUREKA SPRINGS
Eureka Springs Film Office ....(501) 253-8737

LITTLE ROCK
Arkansas Film Office................................(501) 682-7676

CALIFORNIA

STUDIOS/NETWORKS (SOUTHERN REGION)

BURBANK
Burbank Media Center ....(818) 845-3531
Disney Studios ....(818) 560-1000
KNBC, Channel 4 ....(818) 840-4444
Warner Bros. Studios ....(818) 954-6000

CULVER CITY
Culver City Studios.................................(310) 202-1234
GMT Studios...(310) 649-3733
Sony Pictures Entertainment....................(310) 280-8000
Sony Pictures Studios..............................(310) 280-6926

GLENDALE
Glendale/Oakridge Studios ....(818) 502-5500

HOLLYWOOD
ABC Watermark Studios ....(213) 882-8330
CFI Stage ....(213) 960-7444
Embassy Television..................................(213) 460-7330
Fox Television ....(213) 856-1000
Hollywood Center Studios ....(213) 469-5000
Hollywood National Studios ....(213) 467-6272
KCAL-TV, Channel 9...............................(213) 467-9999
KCBS, Channel 2 ....(213) 460-3000
KCOP, Channel 13 ....(213) 851-1000
Paramount Pictures Corporation...............(213) 956-5000
Sunset-Gower Studios, Ltd. ....(213) 467-1001
World Television ....(213) 469-5638

LOS ANGELES
ABC Television Center Studios ....(310) 557-7777
Carthay Studios ....(213) 938-2101
CBS Television City ....(213) 852-2345
KABC, Channel 7 ....(310) 557-7777
KCET Studios ....(213) 953-5258

KCET, Channel 28 ....(213) 666-6500
Lacy Street Production Center ....(213) 222-8872
Raleigh Studios, Inc. ....(213) 466-3111
20th Century Fox ....(310) 277-2211
Warner Hollywood Studios ....(213) 850-2837
SANTA CLARITA
Santa Clarita Studios ....(805) 294-2000
STUDIO CITY
CBS Studio Center ....(818) 760-5000
UNIVERSAL CITY
Universal City Studios, Inc. ....(818) 777-1000

CASTING OFFICES (SOUTHERN REGION)
BEVERLY HILLS
Marilyn Granas ....(310) 278-3773
20th Century Fox Casting ....(310) 369-1824
Gerrie Wormser Casting ....(310) 277-3281
Joanne Zaluski Casting ....(310) 456-5160
BURBANK
Casting Works, LA ....(818) 556-6218
Central Casting ....(818) 569-5200
Marion Dougherty ....(818) 954-3021
Eddie Foy Casting ....(818) 841-3003
Katy & Company ....(818) 563-4121
Vivian McRae ....(818) 848-9590
Jeff Meschel ....(818) 840-4729
Steven O'Niell ....(818) 840-3835
Lori Openden ....(818) 840-3774
Treadwell & Associates Casting ....(818) 846-1666
The Voicecaster.......................................(818) 841-5300
CULVER CITY
Long/DiMatteo Casting............................(310) 841-4457
EL CENTRO
Imperial County Arts Council ....(619) 337-1777
Imperial Valley College Drama Club ....(619) 352-8220
ENCINO
Brien Scott ....(818) 343-3669
HOLLYWOOD
A Prime Casting ....(213) 962-0377
Casting Suite ....(213) 874-6139
Casting Underground ....(213) 465-9999
Annelise Collins Casting..........................(213) 962-9562
Elaine Craig Voice Casting ....(213) 469-8773
Creative Image Management. ....(213) 935-7655
Hollywood Casting ....(213) 856-9070
George Jay Agency ....(213) 466-6665
R. Smith Celebrity Look-Alikes ....(213) 467-3030
Star Group Services ....(213) 874-1239
Studio 3.1..(213) 962-3025
TLC Booth, Inc...(213) 464-2788
Jose Villaverde ....(213) 876-4477
Keith Wolfe Casting ....(213) 469-5995
INLAND EMPIRE
Cattle Call Productions............................(909) 371-2944
LA JOLLA
Ten Management......................................(619) 459-7502
LA MESA
Multi-Media Arts......................................(619) 589-9919

LOS ANGELES
A. C. Casting...(213) 782-9314
Sandy Allison ....(213) 874-3631
Anderson/McCook/White Casting............(310) 659-5535
Baker/Nisbet ....(310) 657-5687
BCI Casting..(213) 951-1010
Brown/West Casting ....(213) 938-2575
Caro Jones Casting..................................(213) 664-0460
Casting Company ....(213) 938-0700
Casting Society of America......................(213) 463-1925
CHN International Agency.........................(213) 874-8252
Christal Blue Casting ....(213) 654-7717
Margie Clark Casting ....(310) 859-2807
Lori Cobe Casting....................................(818) 757-3020
Eleanor Cooke..(213) 664-6384
Divisek Casting ....(213) 876-1554
Film Casting Associates ....(310) 657-8457
Flashcast Kids...(818) 760-7986
Megan Foley Casting ....(310) 659-4116
Lisa Frielberger ....(213) 852-2335
Jan Glaser..(310) 820-6733
Goldman & Associates ....(213) 463-1600
Aaron Griffith ....(310) 659-6412
Joe Guinan & Associates ....(213) 782-6968
Patti Hayes ....(213) 933-0116
Hispanic Talent Casting ....(213) 934-6465
Alan Kaminsky ....(213) 463-1600
Barbara Lauren-Ryan ....(213) 932-1113
Carol Lefko ....(310) 397-7790
Liberman/Hirschfield ....(213) 525-1381
Michael Lien Casting ....(213) 937-0411
Marci Liroff ....(213) 953-7203
Manning Casting ....(213) 852-1046
Marvel Enterprises ....(213) 650-0498
Helen Mossler..(213) 956-5578
Robin Nassif ....(310) 557-6423
New Age Casting......................................(213) 782-9313
Jill Newton ....(213) 852-2803
Pauline O'Con..(310) 557-6425
Paradoxe Casting ....(213) 655-3492
Bonnie Pietila ....(310) 369-3632
Principal Casting ....(213) 782-3966
Barbara Remsen & Associates ....(213) 464-7968
Lila Selik Casting ....(310) 556-2444
Bill Shepard ....(818) 789-4776
Tony Shephard ....(213) 965-5718
Stuart Stone Casting................................(310) 820-9200
Tepper/Gallegos ....(213) 469-3577
Teschner Casting ....(310) 557-5542
NORTH HOLLYWOOD
Chelsea Studios ....(818) 762-1900
Ruth Conforte Casting..............................(818) 760-8220
Debra Neathery ....(818) 506-5524
Rainbow Casting.......................................(818) 752-2052
PACIFIC PALISADES
Jessica Overwise......................................(310) 459-2686
RIDGECREST
High Desert Talent Agency ....(619) 384-1042
or (213) 621-2097

SAN DIEGO

California Casting Associates ....(619) 291-3700
Christina Productions ....(619) 484-2514
D. J. Sullivan Casting ....(619) 274-1731
David Glanzer Casting.............................(619) 479-1834
Iris's Casting ....(619) 685-7879
Nouveau Model Talent Management ....(619) 231-2583
Screen Arts ....(619) 296-9844
Barbara Shannon Casting Service............(619) 224-9555
Tina Real Casting ....(619) 298-0544
Samuel Warren & Associates ....(619) 264-4135

SANTA BARBARA

SB Location & Casting Services ....(805) 565-1562

SANTA MONICA

Elina de Santos Casting ....(310) 829-5958
James Idell Casting...............................(310) 393-9935
Judy Laudau Casting ....(310) 393-6886

SHERMAN OAKS

Cereghetti Casting ....(818) 789-2115

STUDIO CITY

Buck/Edelman Casting ....(818) 506-7328
First Action Casting ....(818) 754-0960
Alan C. Hochberg ....(818) 505-6600
Beth Holmes Casting ....(818) 752-8100
Kelly Casting.......................................(818) 762-0500
Molly Lopata..(818) 753-8086
Ava Shevitt ....(818) 509-9850
Melissa Skoff Casting ....(818) 760-2058
Susan Tyler ....(818) 506-0400

SUNLAND

Anna Miller Casting ....(213) 461-4075

UNIVERSAL CITY

Donna Dockstader..................................(818) 777-1961
Nancy Nayor ....(818) 777-3566
Dava Waite ....(818) 777-1114

VAN NUYS

R. C. Allison & Associates ....(818) 782-3676

WEST HILLS

Celebrity Endorsement Network ....(818) 704-6709

WEST HOLLYWOOD

Louie Goldstein Casting ....(310) 657-0630
Marvin Paige..(818) 760-3040
TBS Casting ....(310) 854-1955

MODELING AND TALENT AGENCIES
(SOUTHERN REGION)

BEVERLY HILLS

Ambrosio/Mortimer & Associates, Inc.......(310) 274-4274
Irvin Arthur Agency.................................(310) 278-5934
Artists' Management West.........................(310) 550-0028
Associated Talent International ....(310) 271-4662
Belson & Klass Associates ....(310) 274-9169
Broder/Kurland/Webb/Uffner.....................(310) 281-3400
Iris Burton Agency ....(310) 288-0121
Capital Artists ....(213) 658-8118
Century Artists ....(310) 273-4366
Creative Artists Agency ....(310) 288-4545
Edenetti & Associates ....(310) 281-5915
Elite Model Management ....(310) 274-9395

Carol Faith Agency ....(310) 274-0776
Gallin Morey Associates ....(310) 278-0808
Gersh Agency ....(310) 274-6611
Gilla Roos West ....(310) 274-9356
Henderson Hogan Agency, Inc...................(310) 274-7815
ICM...(310) 550-4000
Image Talent Agency ....(310) 277-4515
Karg/Weissenbach & Associates...............(310) 205-0425
Paul Kohner Agency ....(310) 550-1060
Lax Corporation ....(310) 286-6666
Lemack & Company Management ....(310) 659-6300
LW 1, Inc. ....(213) 653-5700
Major Clients Agency ....(310) 205-5000
Media Artists Group ....(213) 658-5050
Progressive Artists Agency ....(310) 553-8561
Roger Richman Agency Inc. ....(310) 276-7000
Irv Schechter Company...........................(310) 278-8070
Special Artists Agency ....(310) 859-9688
TGI ....(310) 273-1496
United Talent ....(310) 273-6700
Michael Wallach Management ....(310) 273-5563

BURBANK

William Carroll Agency............................(818) 848-9948
Cavaleri & Associates.............................(818) 955-9300
Gold/Marshak & Associates ....(818) 972-4300
Sarnoff Company, Inc..............................(818) 972-1779
Gerald Smith Associates ....(818) 849-5388

CARLSBAD

Elegance Talent Agency...........................(619) 434-3397

ENCINO

Bresler-Kelly & Associates ....(818) 905-1155
Preferred Artists ....(818) 990-0305
Camille Sorice Agency ....(818) 995-1775

HOLLYWOOD

Alfie Enterprises ....(213) 957-0233
Angel City Talent...................................(213) 463-1680
Bloom Atford...(213) 462-7274
BOPLA Talent Agency ....(213) 466-8667
CNTV Talent & Literary Agency.................(213) 463-5677
Creative Image Management.....................(213) 935-7655
Film Artists Associates ....(213) 463-1010
Gorfaine/Schwartz Agency ....(310) 969-1011
Kruglov & Associates ....(213) 957-9000
Lynne & Reilly Agency ....(213) 850-1984
Savage Agency ....(213) 461-8316
Don Schwartz & Associates ....(213) 464-4661
Showbiz Entertainment ....(213) 469-9931
Shumaker Artists Agency ....(213) 464-0745
Tannen & Associates, Inc., Herb ....(213) 466-6191

LA JOLLA

Beatrice Lilly Talent Agency ....(619) 454-3579

LOS ANGELES

Doug Apatow Agency ....(310) 478-0400
Abrams Rubaloff Lawrence Assoc. ....(213) 935-1700
The Agency ....(310) 551-3000
Agency for the Performing Arts.................(310) 273-0744
Allied Artists Management ....(310) 652-0122
Carlos Alvarado Agency ....(213) 655-7978
Amsel, Eisenstadt & Frazier, Inc...............(213) 939-1188

Apodaca Agency ....(310) 284-3484
The Artists Agency ....(310) 277-7779
The Artists Group ....(310) 552-1100
ASA Affordable Services ....(213) 662-9787
Associated Artists Management ....(213) 852-1972
Baldwin Talent, Inc. ....(310) 472-7919
Bauman Hiller & Associates ....(213) 857-6666
Sara Bennett Agency ....(213) 965-9666
J. Michael Bloom Ltd. ....(310) 275-6800
Camden Artists Ltd. ....(310) 289-2700
Carlyle Management ....(213) 469-3086
Castle-Hill Agency ....(213) 653-3535
Chasin Agency ....(310) 278-7505
Cooper Agency ....(310) 277-8422
Craig Agency ....(213) 655-0236
D. H. Talent Agency ....(213) 962-6643
Marv Dauer & Associates ....(310) 479-1224
Devroe Agency ....(213) 962-3040
Liana Fields Talent Agency ....(213) 292-8550
Innovative Artists Talent ....(310) 553-5200
It Model Agency ....(213) 962-9564
Kelman/Arletta ....(213) 851-8822
LA Model Agency ....(213) 656-3722
Robert Light Agency ....(213) 651-1777
Lyons/Sheldon Agency ....(213) 655-5100
Stone Manners ....(213) 654-7575
Metropolitan Talent Agency......................(213) 857-4500
Mirisch Agency ....(310) 282-9940
Nassif & Associates ....(310) 556-4343
Susan Nathe & Associates ....(213) 653-7573
Paradigm Talent Agency ....(310) 177-4400
Partos Company ....(213) 876-5500
Privilege Talent Agency ....(213) 658-8781
Gordon Rael Company ....(310) 285-9552
Sanders Agency Ltd. ....(310) 652-1119
Judy Schoen & Associates ....(213) 962-1950
Selected Artists Agency...........................(213) 368-1271
Shapiro-Lichtman, Inc. ....(310) 859-8877
Silver & Massetti Agency Ltd ....(310) 289-0909
Richard Sindel & Associates....................(213) 653-5051
Charles H. Stern Agency ....(310) 479-1788
Sutton Barth & Vennari ....(213) 938-6000
Talent Group, Inc. ....(213) 855-9559
Turnstall Management..............................(310) 474-6600
Ruth Webb Agency ....(213) 874-1700
Shirley Wilson & Associates.....................(213) 857-6977
Writers & Artists Agency..........................(310) 824-6300
Stella Zadeh & Associates ....(310) 207-4114
Mark Levin & Associates ....(310) 288-0421

MALIBU
Gundry Agency, Inc. GG ....(310) 456-5602

NORTH HOLLYWOOD
BDP & Associates...................................(818) 506-7615
Eileen Farrell Talent Agency ....(818) 765-0400
Film Music Associates ....(818) 761-4040
Mary Grady Agency ....(818) 766-4414
Jack Scagnetti Agency ....(818) 762-3871
Screen Artists Agency.............................(818) 755-0026

OCEANSIDE
Liana Fields Talent Agency ....(619) 433-6425

PALM SPRINGS
Cindy Romano Modeling Agency ....(619) 323-3333
Dorothy Shreve Agency............................(619) 327-5855

SAN DIEGO
A 2 Model & Talent Agency ....(619) 291-9556
Andy Anderson Agency............................(619) 294-4629
Artist Management Agency ....(619) 233-6655
Nina Blanchard Talent Agency..................(619) 462-7274
Shannon Freitas & Co. ....(619) 234-3043
Nouveau Model Talent Management.........(619) 231-2583
Janice Patterson Agency ....(619) 295-9477
Real Agency ....(619) 298-0544
San Diego Model Management..................(619) 296-1018

SANTA MONICA
Contemporary Artists Ltd. ....(310) 395-1800
Durkin Artists Agency ....(310) 458-5377
LA Artists ....(310) 202-0254
Steve Lovett Management ....(310) 451-2536

SHERMAN OAKS
Aimee Entertainment Associates ....(818) 783-9115
Artists & Jr. Artists Unltd. ....(818) 763-9000
Barbara Best ....(818) 501-7172
Hervey/Grimes Talent Agency ....(818) 981-0891
David Shapira & Associates ....(818) 906-0322
Twentieth Century Artists ....(818) 788-5516

STUDIO CITY
Beverly Hecht Agency ....(818) 505-1192
Booth Schut Company ....(818) 760-6669
Career Artists International ....(818) 980-1315
Production Agency ....(818) 752-8018
Turtle Agency ....(818) 506-6898

TOLUCA LAKE
Tyler Kjar Agency ....(818) 760-0321
Star Talent Agency ....(818) 509-1931

UNIVERSAL CITY
Brad Waisbren Management ....(818) 506-3000

WEST HILLS
Barbara Cameron & Associates ....(818) 888-6107

WEST HOLLYWOOD
Jane Bloom & Associates ....(213) 654-7181
Geddes Agency ....(213) 878-1144
Motion Artists ....(213) 851-7737
Players Talent Agency ....(310) 289-8777

WOODLAND HILLS
A Total Acting Experience ....(818) 340-9249

CASTING OFFICES (NORTHERN REGION)

CARMEL
Phyllis Decker..(408) 373-7195

GRANITE BAY
Media Casting...(916) 652-3312

LOS ALTOS
California Casting ....(415) 961-6546

MONTEREY
Central Coast Production Services ....(408) 646-9191

NAPA
Cal-North Media Services........................(707) 435-5397

OAKLAND
Vernon & Baldwin Casting ....(510) 530-6475
PALO ALTO
California Casting ....(415) 858-0747
PLACERVILLE
Tahoe Foothill Casting Company ....(916) 622-7110
RANCHO CORDOVA
California Image Associates ....(916) 638-8383
ROSEVILLE
Sandra Quen/Quen Casting.....................(916) 782-5033
SACRAMENTO
Kathryn Shallcross ....(916) 334-2739
SAN FRANCISCO
The Actors Guide ....(415) 673-1006
Background Casting ....(415) 931-4593
Casting Works ....(415) 922-6218
Steve Dobbins Casting ....(415) 441-6655
Laura Folger Casting..............................(415) 664-3072
Globus Casting Services.........................(415) 495-0915
Hayes & Van Horn Casting ....(415) 567-2278
International Talent Casting......................(415) 775-7349
Cecily Jordan Casting.............................(415) 383-5545
Kids on Camera ....(415) 882-9878
Annette Pirrone......................................(415) 221-4118
Scott Fortier/Beau Bonneau Casting ....(415) 777-1142
Martha Sherratt Casting ....(415) 457-5575
Suzanne Stack..(415) 861-0508
Susan & Friends Voice-Over Casting ....(415) 956-3878
Voiceover ....(415) 567-2278
SAN RAFAEL
Sammis Associates, Inc...............(415) 492-XTRA (9872)
SAUSALITO
Samantha Paris Casting ....(415) 331-7267
UP Image Company ....(415) 331-3246
STOCKTON
Talent Source Central ....(209) 464-1387
SUNNYVALE
Professional Dynamics ....(408) 733-8182

COACHES AND CONSULTANTS
MORAGA
Cynthia Brian's Starstyle Productions.......(510) 376-STAR
Barbara Simpson
    Blue Shadow Productions.................. (510) 376-7343
OAKLAND
Marlene Ryan ....(510) 547-3418
Vicki Saputo ....(510) 932-6335
Voice One ....(510) 886-0484
SAN FRANCISCO
Linda Clements......................................(415) 433-4711
Jerry Mark Take Flight Productions ....(415) 487-1258
Susan & Friends Voice-Over Workshops ..(415) 956-3878
Zephyr Entertainment ....(415) 441-6655
SAN JOSE
Lee Kopp...(408) 984-2320
SAUSALITO
Carolyn Crimley ....(415) 389-5914

MANAGERS
GREENBRAE
Suzanne Sammis ....(415) 461-0648

MODELING AND TALENT AGENCIES
(NORTHERN REGION)
KINGS BEACH
Michael McCue.......................................(916) 546-4355
LOS ALTOS
Actors Phantasy Company ....(415) 961-6546
MILL VALLEY
Super Talent Agency Resources ....(415) 479-STAR (7827)
NAPA
B. Dicks ....(707) 435-5397
OAKLAND
Vitalent Agency ....(510) 601-7701
PLACERVILLE
Gemini Talent Agency & Management ......(916) 622-2996
SACRAMENTO
Ambiance Model & Talent Management ....(916) 442-3488
Cast Images Talent Agency ....(916) 444-9720
Actors Exchange ....(415) 433-3920
Marla Dell Talent Agency ....(415) 563-9213
Generations Model & Talent Agency.........(415) 777-9099
Look Model Agency ....(415) 781-2822
Look Talent ....(415) 781-2841
Mitchell Talent Management.....................(415) 395-9291
Quinn-Tonry, Inc. ....(415) 543-3797
Jennifer Spalding & Associates ....(415) 346-6177
Stars, The Agency..................................(415) 421-6272
Top Models & Talent................................(415) 391-1800
SAN JOSE
Frazer Agency ....(408) 554-1055
Los Latinos Talent Agency ....(408) 296-2213
Mayes Talent Agency ....(408) 249-9737
Talent Plus Agency ....(408) 296-2213
SAN LEANDRO
T-Best Talent Agency..............................(510) 357-6865
SANTA CLARA
Integrity Talent Agency ....(408) 243-9466
SANTA ROSA
Covers Model & Talent Agency................(707) 539-9252
Entertainment Alliance ....(707) 526-1471
Panda Talent Agency..............................(707) 576-0711

THEATERS/WORKHOPS
BERKELEY
Verna Winters Studio for Performing Arts..(510) 524-1601
BLUELAKE
DellArte School of Physical Theater ....(707) 668-5663
MILL VALLEY
Shelly Michell's Method Acting ....(415) 389-6429
SAN FRANCISCO
Bedini Theatre Project.............................(415) 921-2769
Bruce Ducat's Young Actor's Workshop ....(415) 380-8024
Clark Suzanne Productions......................(415) 776-7911
Dolores San Miguel-Wagner....................(415) 433-2487
Full Circle Productions............................(415) 982-2024
Jean Shelton Acting School ....(415) 433-1226

Kids On Camera TV Acting & Modeling ....(415) 882-9878
Monroe Mark Productions ....(415) 951-0226
Osmond Cliff School for Creative Arts ......(415) 986-3435
Phoenix Theater Company ....(415) 621-4423
Rob Reece Actor's Workshop ....(415) 989-4228

CALIFORNIA FILM OFFICES

BERKELEY
Berkeley Film Office ....(510) 549-7040
CHICO
Butte County Film Commission ....(800) 852-8570
or (916) 891-5556
EL CENTRO
Imperial County Film Commission ....(619) 339-4290
EUREKA
Eureka-Humboldt County CVB ....(707) 443-5097
MONTEREY
Monterey County Film Commission ....(408) 646-0910
OAKLAND
Oakland Film Commission ....(410) 238-4734
PLACERVILLE
El Dorado/Tahoe Film Commission ....(916) 626-4400
SAN DIEGO
San Diego Film Office..............................(619) 234-3456

Siegel Represents, Inc. ....(303) 722-3456
GREELEY
Dulcie Camp Talent................................(970) 356-5445
Lakewood Sundance Talent Agency ....(303) 233-4949

COLORADO FILM OFFICES

BOULDER
Boulder County Film Commission ....(303) 442-1044
CANON CITY
Fremont/Custer Film Commission ....(719) 275-5149
COLORADO SPRINGS
Colorado Springs Film Commission ....(719) 578-6943
DENVER
Colorado Motion Picture
& TV Commission ....(303) 630-4500
Mayor's Office of Art, Culture & Film ....(303) 640-2686
FORT MORGAN
Fort Morgan Area Film Commission.........(303) 867-3001
GREELEY
Greeley/Weld County Film Commission ....(303) 352-3566
STEAMBOAT SPRINGS
Yampa Valley Film Board ....(303) 879-0882
TRINIDAD
Trinidad Film Commission ....(719) 846-9412

COLORADO

CASTING OFFICES
ASPEN
Aspen Production Services......................(970) 925-1031
DENVER
Big Fish Talent Representation ....(303) 744-7170
Celebrity Casting Company of Colorado....(303) 986-9274
Colorado Casting Associates ....(303) 355-5888
Kidskits, Inc. ....(303) 446-8200
Premier Talent Services...........................(303) 987-0777
LITTLETON
McNeil Film Enterprises ....(303) 973-6207
TELLURIDE
Didi Johnson Productions ....(970) 728-3794

TALENT AND MODELING AGENCIES
ASPEN
Lifestock Agency, Inc. ....(970) 920-6936
BOULDER
Silverman/Rubino Agency........................(303) 447-9222
COLORADO SPRINGS
Donna Baldwin Talent, Inc. ....(719) 635-4101
Jeanine's Modeling & Talent ....(719) 598-4507
DENVER
Donna Baldwin Talent Inc., ...(303) 320-0067
Big Fish, Talent Representation.................(303) 744-7170
Edge Talent Management ....(303) 685-4949
Kidskits, Inc. ....(303) 446-8200
Marbles Kids Management, Inc. ....(303) 322-5004
Maximum Talent ....(303) 691-2344

CONNECTICUT

CASTING OFFICES
EAST GLASTONBURY
Creative Talent Ltd. ....(203) 295-8546
MILFORD
The Actors Network Center ....(203) 877-8799
Lelas Talent Casting ....(203) 877-8355
NEW HAVEN
World Promotions, Inc.............................(203) 781-3427
PAWCATUCK
Andrea Star Carey ....(203) 599-5855
PRESTON
Loren Michaels Lichtenstein ....(203) 886-7782
WEST HARTFORD
Media Inc..(203) 523-4388
WESTON
Faces and Places, Inc. ....(203) 221-1400

TALENT AGENCIES
EAST GLASTONBURY
Creative Talent Ltd. ....(203) 295-1060
HARTFORD
Meezmeyer Productions ....(203) 951-0547
Patrick Media Productions, Inc. ....(203) 522-8118
MILFORD
The Actors Network Center ....(203) 877-8799
RIVERSIDE
Reflections Agency ....(203) 531-9000
ROWAYTON
Elan Agency ....(203) 855-1112

SOUTH NORWALK
Johnston Agency, Inc. ....(203) 838-6188
SOUTHBURY
TalentMart ....(203) 262-8032
STAMFORD
Barbizon School & Agency ....(203) 359-0427
WEST HAVEN
L.T. Modeling Talent Management ....(203) 933-1348
WILTON
Gregg Glaser..(203) 353-4634

CONNECTICUT FILM OFFICES
DANBURY
Danbury Film Office ....(203) 743-0546
ROCKY HILL
Connecticut Film Commission ....(203) 258-4301

DELAWARE

TALENT AND MODELING AGENCIES
BEAR
The May Studio...(302) 845-3048
WILMINGTON
Robert Taylor...(302) 217-3675
DOVER
Delaware Film Office ....(302) 739-4271

DISTRICT OF COLUMBIA

CASTING OFFICES
WASHINGTON, D.C.
BHK Arts Consultants, Inc. ....(202) 554-0131
Capital Casting ....(202) 797-8621
Central Casting ....(202) 547-6300
Doran ....(202) 333-6367
Stars Casting ....(202) 429-9494
T-H-E Artist Agency, Inc............................(202) 342-0933

DISTRICT OF COLUMBIA FILM OFFICE
WASHINGTON, D.C.
Mayor's Office of MP & TV ....(202) 727-6600

FLORIDA

CASTING OFFICES
FT. MEYERS
Lisa Connelly Casting...............................(813) 945-3033
HOLLYWOOD
Casting by McLean, Inc. ....(813) 351-0079

SARASOTA
Casting Crew ....(954) 927-2329
Beverly McDermott Casting ....(954) 625-5111
MIAMI
Ivonne Casas Casting ....(305) 858-0997
                                         or (305) 442-8029
Florida Casting Group...............................(305) 757-5030
MIAMI BEACH
DiPrima Casting ....(305) 672-9232
Ellen Jacoby Casting International ....(305) 531-5300
Unique Casting ....(305) 532-0226
MIRAMAR
Extras Casting Central of South Florida ....(954) 894-0757
NORTH MIAMI
Casting Directors ....(305) 895-0339
Hollywood Casting ....(305) 891-7225
NORTH MIAMI BEACH
Lori S. Wyman ....(305) 354-3901
OCALA
Model Centre ....(904) 237-1611
ORLANDO
CIS ....(407) 363-1396
Extras Only, Inc. ....(407) 240-5200
For Casting, Inc. ....(407) 240-5200
Herb Mandell Casting ....(407) 855-3400
Reality Group, Inc. ....(407) 345-9294
Stuart Turnabout Talent Agency................(407) 283-1449
TAMPA
Rosen Casting..(813) 968-9399

TALENT AND MODELING AGENCIES
CLEARWATER
Hamilton Hall Talent Agency.....................(813) 538-3838
Tampa Bay's Best ....(813) 726-5393
COCONUT GROVE
Coconut Grove Talent ....(305) 858-3002
CORAL GABLES
Elva's Talent Agency ....(305) 444-9071
CORAL SPRINGS
Style Entertainment ....(954) 752-1930
DEERFIELD BEACH
Boca Talent and Modeling Agency ....(954) 428-4677
FERN PARK
A-1 Peg's Talent and Modeling Agency......(407) 834-0406
FT. LAUDERDALE
Aaron Model & Talent Agency, Inc............(305) 772-8944
British Bureau Public Relations ....(305) 730-9646
Dawn Doyle Enterprises ....(954) 467-2838
Scott Harvey Talent Agency......................(954) 565-1211
Image Group ....(954) 763-3669
Marian Polan Talent Agency ....(954) 525-8351
FT. MEYERS
Robert Wood Productions, Inc. ....(813) 540-0001
HALLANDALE
Syd Martin Talent Agency ....(305) 932-4041
HEATHROW
Christensen Group ....(407) 333-2506
HOLLYWOOD
Famous Faces Entertainment Co. ....(954) 922-0700

JACKSONVILLE
Model & Talent Management, Inc. ....(904) 739-0619

LARGO
Book & Company ....(813) 538-2614

MIAMI
Beautyworks ....(305) 446-6892
Judity Gindy Talent Agency.....................(305) 666-3470
MTM, Model & Talent..............................(305) 279-0101
Talent Seekers ....(305) 233-5815

MIAMI BEACH
BMN Model & Talent Agency ....(305) 531-2700
Click Models Miami ....(305) 674-9900
Elite Model Management Miami ....(305) 674-9500
Ford Models ....(305) 534-7200
Green & Green Model & Talent Agency ....(305) 532-9880
Image Talent & Model Agency ....(305) 531-9096
International Artists Group ....(305) 538-6100
L'Agence Models.....................................(305) 672-0804
Debra Lewin Productions ....(305) 531-2234
Next Management Co...............................(305) 531-5100
Page Parkes-Models Rep ....(305) 672-4869
Michele Pommier Models........................(305) 672-9344
Stellar Talent Agency..............................(305) 672-2217
Top Talent/Splash Models.......................(305) 532-4285
World of Kids ....(305) 672-5437

MIAMI SPRINGS
Charmette Modeling Agency....................(305) 870-0509

NORTH MIAMI
Ada Gordon Talent Agency ....(305) 940-1311
Just for Kids ....(305) 940-1311
MarBea Talent and Modeling Agency ....(305) 949-0615

ORLANDO
Dimension III Modeling & Talent Agency ..(407) 851-2575
Sirkus Talents ....(407) 823-7854

ORMOND BEACH
Michele & Group ....(904) 676-1702

PLANTATION
Miami Body Partz ....(954) 472-1707
Miami Talent & Models............................(954) 472-1707

SAFETY HARBOR
Video Composite, Inc...............................(813) 725-3902

SARASOTA
Sea Stars Talent Agency, Inc. ....(813) 995-5341
Take 1 Employment Group ....(800) 226-9285

STUART
Entertainment Consultants ....(407) 287-2515

TALLAHASSEE
Set Five Models & Talent ....(904) 224-8500

TAMPA
Florida Sun Promotions ....(813) 969-1706

KENNETH CITY
Florida Talent & Model Management ....(813) 545-8686

TAMPA
Strictly Entertainment, Inc. ....(813) 879-1514

WINTER PARK
Casablancas Model & Talent Agency ....(407) 740-6697
Hunt Garver Talent ....(407) 740-5700

FLORIDA FILM OFFICES
BARTOW
Central Florida/Polk County Film Office ....(813) 534-4371
DAYTONA BEACH
Volusia County Film Office ....(904) 255-0415
FT. LAUDERDALE
Broward/Ft. Lauderdale Film & TV Office ..(305) 524-3113
FT. MEYERS
Southwest Florida Film Commission ....(800) 330-3161
FT. WALTON BEACH
Northwest Florida & Okaloosa
    Film Commission. ....(904) 651-7374
GAINESVILLE
Gainesville Chamber of Commerce...........(904) 334-7100
JACKSONVILLE
Jacksonville Film & TV Office...................(904) 630-2522
KEY WEST
Florida Keys & Key West
    Film Commission ....(305) 259-5988
MELBOURNE
Brevard County Film Commission ....(800) 936-2326
MIAMI
Miami/Dade Film Office ....(305) 375-3288
MIAMI BEACH
Florida Entertainment Commission...........(305) 673-7468
OCALA
Ocala/Marion County Film Office ....(904) 629-2926
ORLANDO
Metro Orlando Film & TV Office ....(407) 422-7159
ST. PETERSBURG
St. Petersburg Film Commission ....(813) 823-5831
TAMPA
Tampa Motion Picture & TV Film Office ....(813) 223-1111
WEST PALM BEACH
Palm Beach County Film
    & TV Commission ....(407) 233-1000

GEORGIA

CASTING OFFICES
ATLANTA
Atlanta Models & Talent Inc.....................(404) 261-9627
Borden & Associates, Ted ....(404) 266-0664
Chez Casting Agency ....(404) 873-1215
The Genesis Agency ....(404) 350-9212
L'Agence Models & Talent........................(404) 396-9015
People Store ....(404) 233-2278
Annette Stilwell Casting ....(404) 233-2278

GEORGIA FILM OFFICES
ATLANTA
Georgia Film & Videotape Office...............(404) 656-8570
SAVANNAH
Savannah Film Commission.....................(912) 651-3696

HAWAII

TALENT AND MODELING AGENCIES
HILO
Big Island Production Services ....(808) 961-0031
Zee of Hawaii International Modeling
  & Talent Agency ....(808) 935-7048
HONOLULU
A FeinRose Model & Talent Agency ....(808) 734-0456
ADR Model & Talent Agency......................(808) 524-4777
Robert Enrietto Agency ....(808) 943-0738
First Model Management Inc. ....(808) 599-5515
Amos Kotomori Agent Services ....(808) 955-6511
Kathy Muller Talent and Modeling Agency (808) 737-7917
Susan Page Model & Talent Agency ....(808) 955-2271
John Robert Powers ....(808) 596-2800
Prestige Model & Talent Management ......(808) 524-8881
Studio Center Stage ....(808) 487-1672
Ruth Woodhall Talent Agency ....(808) 947-3307
KAPAA
Island Faces Modeling Agency ....(808) 822-7263
KOLOA
Casting Kauai ....(808) 742-1506
KONA
Encore Talent Agency ....(808) 326-1636
MAUI
Chameleon Talent Agency, Ltd. ....(808) 879-7817
WAIMANALO
Central Island Agency, Inc. ....(808) 259-7914

CASTING OFFICES
HILO
Big Island Production Services ....(808) 981-0031
HONOLULU
Anna Fishburn Casting ....(808) 521-9100
Garrison True ....(808) 591-3956
Reel Services/Hawaii Inc.........................(808) 524-CAST
KAMUELA
Anne Johns..(808) 735-7877
KAPAA
Island Faces Modeling Agency ....(808) 822-7263
KAUAI
Island Faces ....(808) 822-7263
KOLOA
Casting Kauai ....(808) 742-1506
KOLOA
Linda Antipala Casting ....(808) 742-1506
WAILUKU
Ann Rae International Model Management ..(808) 244-0006

CHOREOGRAPHERS
HONOLULU
A FeinRose Model & Talent Agency ....(808) 734-0456
ADR Model & Talent Agency.....................(808) 524-4777
Express: A Contemporary Dance Co. ....(800) 680-7340
Pamela Los Banos/Big City Productions ..(808) 373-5175
Pamela Mei Ying Gasinski ....(808) 395-3603

NARRATORS/VOICE TALENT/VOICE-OVERS
HAIKU
Alaka'i Communications ....(808) 575-2207
HONOLULU
ADR Model & Talent Agency.....................(808) 524-4777
Brad Bate ....(808) 545-8055
KIHEI
Chameleon Talent Agency, Ltd. ....(808) 879-7817

ACTING STUDIOS/TRAINING/WORKSHOPS
HILO
Zee of Hawaii ....(800) 935-7048
HONOLULU
Evan Nelson Productions ....(808) 396-0765
Reel Services/Hawaii, Inc. ....(808) 524-CAST
KAILUA
Actors, Inc. ....(808) 263-0202
KIHEI
Chameleon Talent Agency, Ltd. ....(808) 879-7817

HAWAII FILM OFFICES
HILO
Big Island Film Office ....(808) 961-8366
HONOLULU
Hawaii Film Office...................................(808) 586-2570
Oahu Film Office.....................................(808) 527-6108
KAUAI
Kauai Film Commission ....(808) 241-6390
MAUI
Maui Film & TV Office ....(808) 243-7710

IDAHO

CASTING OFFICES
CENTRAL MOUNTAIN REGION
Gretchen Palmer......................................(208) 788-4501
EASTERN REGION
Terry Ryan...(208) 529-0976
NORTH REGION
Northwest Casting & Location Service ......(208) 263-3016
NORTH REGION
Carolyn Olson..(509) 467-6453
SOUTHWEST REGION
Reel McCoy ....(208) 343-5617
Tamara Lynne Thomson ....(208) 343-0038
OTHER AREAS
Sunny Anderson Casting ....(406) 933-8461
Cowboys & Indians/On Location ....(800) 784-5757
Helen S. Dollan..(406) 862-3308

TALENT AGENCIES
CENTRAL MOUNTAIN REGION
Palm Models & Prods. ....(208) 788-4501
EASTERN REGION
United Models & Talent ....(208) 529-3771

NORTH REGION
Northwest Casting & Location Services ....(208) 263-3016
SOUTHWEST REGION
The Artists Agency ....(208) 345-0038
Blanche B. Evans Agency ....(208) 344-5380

IDAHO FILM OFFICE
BOISE
Idaho Film Bureau ......(208) 334-2470 or (800) 942-8338

ILLINOIS

CASTING OFFICES
ALSIP
Marvel Enterprises ....(708) 848-5755
CHICAGO
Alderman Casting ....(312) 549-6464
Alert Casting ....(312) 944-7319
All-City Casting ....(312) 296-9268
Jane Brody Casting....................................(312) 527-0665
Chambliss Casting ....(312) 278-9123
Heitz Casting..(312) 664-0601
Holzer & Ridge Casting ....(312) 922-9860
Judith Jacobs Casting................................(312) 649-9585
Tracy Kaplan Casting ....(312) 222-1300
Kidz Casting ....(312) 943-9303
K.T.'s ....(312) 525-1126
Cherle Mann Casting ....(312) 751-2927
Karen Peake Casting..................................(312) 360-9266
Rabedeau Casting ....(312) 222-0181
Lawrence Santoro ....(312) 327-9377
Carol Verblen Casting................................(312) 348-0047
HIGHLAND PARK
Norman Schucart Enterprises ....(708) 433-1113

TALENT AGENCIES
CHICAGO
Aria Model & Talent Management.............(312) 243-9400
Cunningham, Escott, Dipene.....................(312) 280-5155
David & Lee ....(312) 670-4444
Elite Model Mgmt ....(312) 943-3226
ETA, Inc. ....(312) 752-2955
Geddes Agency ....(312) 348-3333
Shirley Hamilton ....(312) 787-4700
Harrise, Davidson & Associates ....(312) 782-4480
Jefferson & Associates ....(312) 337-1930
Lily's Talent Agency...................................(312) 792-1366
The Models Workshop ....(312) 527-2807
Salizar & Navas...(312) 751-3419
Sa-Rah Talent Agency ....(312) 733-2822
Karen Stavins Enterprises ....(312) 938-1140
Stewart Talent ....(312) 943-3131
Susanne's/A-Plus Talent ....(312) 943-8315
HIGHLAND PARK
Norman Schucart Enterprises ....(708) 433-1113

ILLINOIS FILM OFFICES
CHICAGO
Chicago Film Office ....(312) 744-6415
Illinois Film Office.....................................(312) 814-3600
ROCK ISLAND
Quad Cities Development Group/
    Film Coalition ....(309) 326-1005

INDIANA

CASTING OFFICES
INDIANAPOLIS
Artists Enterprises.....................................(317) 577-1717
Kim Cline ....(317) 571-1341

TALENT AND MODELING AGENCIES
CARMEL
Helen Wells Agency ....(317) 843-5363
FT. WAYNE
Charmaine School & Model Agency.........(317) 485-8421
INDIANAPOLIS
Act I Agency ....(317) 255-3100
Taylor Nichols, Inc. ....(317) 255-2996
WHITING
C. J. Mercury, Inc. ....(219) 659-2701

INDIANA FILM OFFICES
INDIANAPOLIS
Indiana Film Commission.........................(317) 232-8800
                            or (317) 232-8829

IOWA

CASTING OFFICES
CEDAR LAKE
Greg Schmidt ....(515) 357-5177
CEDAR RAPIDS
International Group ....(319) 369-0639
DES MOINES
Actor's Workshop ....(515) 277-0770
Avant Studios ....(515) 255-0297
Complete Casting Services ....(515) 276-0170
Copeland Creative Talent ....(515) 271-5970
Talent/Iowa ....(515) 285-1209
Winning Combinations ....(515) 287-2100
DUBUQUE
Sue Riedel ....(319) 556-4367
FairfieldHedquist Productions, Inc...........(515) 472-6708
Kansas CityWright/Laird Casting ....(816) 531-0331
ROCK ISLAND
Dennis Hitchcock ....(309) 786-4119
WEST DES MOINES
Performance Film, Video
    & Stage Productions.............................(515) 221-2514

TALENT AND MODELING AGENCIES
DES MOINES
Actor's Workshop ....(515) 277-0770
Avant Studios ....(515) 255-0297
Copeland Creative Talent ....(515) 271-5970
Talent/Iowa ....(515) 285-1209
Winning Combinations...............................(515) 287-2100

ACTING CLASSES/WORKSHOPS
DES MOINES
Actor's Workshop ....(515) 277-0770
The Talent Source ....(515) 221-2517
WEST DES MOINES
Talent Factory ....(515) 267-8515

IOWA FILM OFFICES
CEDAR RAPIDS
Cedar Rapids Area Film Commission ....(319) 398-5009
DES MOINES
Greater Des Moines Film Commission ......(515) 286-4960
Iowa Film Office ....(515) 242-4726

KANSAS

CASTING OFFICES
INDEPENDENCE
Lorraine Young-Yocum ....(816) 833-2272
KANSAS CITY
Wright/Laird Casting...................................(816) 531-0331
LAKE LOLAWANA
All Star Casting Company.........................(913) 831-9953
LENEXA
Linda Baska ....(913) 888-5370
SHAWNEE
Scott Zipp ....(913) 631-0906
WICHITA
Actor's Lab ....(316) 265-2323

TALENT AND MODELING AGENCIES
KANSAS CITY
Agency Models & Talent...........................(913) 342-8382
Career Images Model & Talent Agency ......(913) 334-2200
MTC: Model, Talent, Charm, Ltd. ....(816) 531-3223
Talent Unlimited ....(816) 561-9040
OVERLAND PARK
Hoffman International Agency ....(913) 642-9212
Jackson Artists Corp. ....(913) 384-6688
WICHITA
Crown Uptown Theatre ....(316) 681-1566
Focus Model Management ....(316) 264-3100
The Gregory Agency ....(316) 687-5666
J. W. Productions ....(316) 686-5336

KANSAS FILM OFFICES
LAWRENCE
Lawrence, Overland Park & Topeka
Film Office ....(913) 865-4411

MANHATTAN
Manhattan Film Commission ....(913) 776-8829
TOPEKA
Kansas Film Commission ....(913) 296-4927
WICHITA
Wichita Convention & Visitors Bureau ......(316) 265-2800

KENTUCKY

CASTING OFFICES
BOWLING GREEN
Fountain Square Players...........................(502) 842-8844
DANVILLE
Eben Henson...(606) 236-2747
FT. WRIGHT
Jennifer Carroll ....(606) 261-8750
LEXINGTON
Tillie Moore ....(606) 266-0789
Vogue of Lexington, Inc. ....(606) 254-4582
LOUISVILLE
Actors Theatre of Louisville ....(502) 584-1265
Alix Adams Agency ....(502) 587-0765
Mary Aklin ....(502) 595-4636
Mina Davis ....(502) 451-7923
Scott Davis ....(502) 459-6478
Lorraine Doss ....(502) 896-1394
M. J. Kaufman..(502) 585-4152
Stage One Children's Theatre ....(502) 589-5946
Walden Theatre ....(502) 454-8355
Youth Performing Arts High School ....(502) 454-8355
PADUCAH
Vanir Productions ....(502) 442-4463

TALENT AND MODELING AGENCIES
JEFFERSONVILLE
Alix Adams Modeling School & Agency ....(502) 266-6990
LEXINGTON
Images ....(606) 273-2301
LOUISVILLE
Cosmo Model & Talent Agency ....(502) 425-8000
MJK Studio/Talent Unlimited ....(502) 585-4152
PADUCAH
Vickrey School of Modeling ....(502) 554-4225

KENTUCKY FILM OFFICE
FRANKFORT
Kentucky Film Commission ....(502) 564-3456

LOUISIANA

CASTING OFFICES
NEW IBERIA
Gail Boudreaux...........(318) 365-1198 or (318) 367-1003

NEW ORLEANS

Claudia Baumgarten ....(504) 948-3416 or (504) 899-6485
Stephanie Brett Samuel..............................(504) 895-5666
Rick Landry Casting ....(504) 454-8000
Dave LeBlanc ....(504) 282-2221
Tommy Staub Casting...............................(504) 866-2175

TALENT AND MODELING AGENCIES

BATON ROUGE
Model & Talent Management ....(504) 295-3999
METAIRIE
Models & Talent Plus..(504) 831-8000 or (800) 506-6335
Talented Teens, Etc....................................(504) 887-2239
Victor's International Model & Talent ....(504) 885-3841
NEW ORLEANS
Faces Model & Talent Management ....(504) 522-3030
del Corral Model & Talent Agency ....(504) 288-8963
Ellis in Wonderland...................................(504) 525-0000
Fame Model & Talent Agency ....(504) 522-2001
New Orleans Model & Talent Agency ....(504) 525-0100
Premiere Events ....(504) 391-9120
Rockit Talent ....(504) 282-2221

LOUISIANA FILM OFFICES

BATON ROUGE
Louisiana Film Commission ....(504) 342-8150
JENNINGS
Parish Film Commission ....(318) 821-5534
NEW ORLEANS
New Orleans Film & Video Commission ..(504) 565-8104
SHREVEPORT
Shreveport-Bossier Film Commission ......(318) 222-9391

MAINE

CASTING OFFICES

BELGRADE
Mid Maine Models & Talent Casting ....(207) 495-2143
CAPE ELIZABETH
C.S. Casting ....(207) 799-4924
KENNEBUNK
Laura Butterwork Read ....(207) 985-9729
SACO
Skip Peacock ....(207) 283-8578
Karen True Casting ....(207) 286-3299
SCARBOROUGH
Portland Models Group & Talent ....(207) 286-3299
THOMASTON
Entertainment Resources...........................(207) 354-8928

MAINE FILM OFFICE

AUGUSTA
Maine Film Office ....(207) 287-5705

MARYLAND

CASTING OFFICES

BALTIMORE
Central Casting...........(410) 889-3200 or (202) 547-6300
Taylor Royall Casting, Inc. ....(410) 466-5959
Call All Kids ....(301) 970-2170
EDGEWOOD
Accurate Casting & Talent.........................(410) 679-2116
Severna Park
Steele Casting...(410) 544-8444
SILVER SPRING
Camera Ready Kids ....(301) 589-4864 or (301) 270-1640
Young Professionals ....(301) 567-0831

MODELING AND TALENT AGENCIES

BETHESDA
Clowning Around ....(301) 365-7455
EDGEWOOD
Accurate Casting & Talent.........................(410) 679-2116
OWINGS MILLS
Inlingua Translations................................(410) 356-8877
WHEATON
Sashay Agency ....(310) 942-1361

MARYLAND FILM OFFICES

BALTIMORE
Maryland Film Office ....(410) 767-6340
LANDOVER
Media/Film Office ....(301) 386-3456

MASSACHUSETTS

CASTING OFFICES

BEDFORD
Rose Agency ....(617) 275-9084
BOSTON
Boston Casting ....(617) 864-9749
BostonModel Club Kids ....(617) 247-9020
BROOKLINE
John McGee Casting.................................(617) 964-2607
Outcasting..(617) 738-6322
CAMBRIDGE
Collinge-Pickman Casting, Inc. ....(617) 492-4212
Nadette Stasa Casting ....(617) 864-1344
REHOBOTH
Studio I Gallery of Models ....(508) 336-8247
                                              or (617) 986-5755
SAUGUS
Peter Bezernes Casting ....(617) 231-3202
STONEHAM
M. J. Eagle Casting ....(800) 942-9304 or (617) 438-2643

ACTING SCHOOLS/WORKSHOPS

BOSTON
Actors Workshop ....(617) 423-7313

MASSACHUSETTS FILM OFFICE
BOSTON
Massachusetts Film Office ....(617) 973-8800

MICHIGAN

CASTING OFFICES
ADA
Fahey-Dreher Casting ....(616) 676-1005
ANN ARBOR
Catherine M. Thomas ....(313) 995-4030
DEARBORN
Alicia Wells...(313) 724-0140
DETROIT
Hollywood Stars Talent Management ....(313) 818-4357
Mary Locker Casting.................................(313) 366-4942
GARDEN CITY
Elizabeth Grayson Models & Talent ....(313) 421-9009
HUNTINGTON WOODS
Action Casting ....(810) 398-3027

TALENT AND MODELING AGENCIES
BERKLEY
Ta-Dah! Productions................................(810) 548-2324
BIRMINGHAM
The Talent Shop ....(810) 644-4877
CLINTON TOWNSHIP
Hot Spots Entertainment ....(810) 228-1717
DETROIT
Hollywood Stars Talent Management ....(313) 818-4357
Mary Locker Casting.................................(313) 366-4942
GARDEN CITY
Elizabeth Grayson Models & Talent ....(313) 421-9009
GRAND RAPIDS
Pastiche Models & Talent, Inc. ....(616) 451-2181
Pro Talent Agency ....(616) 458-2513
HASLETT
Class Modeling & Talent Agency ....(517) 339-2777
LATHRUP VILLAGE
The i Group Model & Talent Management (810) 552-8842
SOUTHFIELD
Signet Creative, Inc. ....(810) 443-2446
TROY
Affiliated Talent Agency............................(810) 244-8770
WEST BLOOMFIELD
Silver Star Entertainment..........................(810) 334-7733

MICHIGAN FILM OFFICES
DETROIT
Mayor's Office of Film/TV ....(313) 224-3430
LANSING
Michigan Film Office................................(800) 477-3456

MINNESOTA

CASTING OFFICES
DULUTH
Midwest Connections Inc..........................(218) 727-0997
HOPKINS
Kelly Foster...(612) 938-5241
Akerlind Steele Gersh Casting ....(612) 339-6141
Bab's Casting ....(612) 332-6858
Lynn Blumenthal Casting ....(612) 338-0369
Jason Cooper Hall ....(612) 874-9977
Jodi Josephson..(612) 551-0663
JR Casting ....(612) 288-0505
Shannon McNeely.....................................(612) 431-1214
M'Liz Totten ....(612) 374-2860
SHAKOPEE
Lori Ness ....(612) 496-1663

TALENT AND MODELING AGENCIES
BROOKLYN PARK
Crewlink ....(612) 560-3858
GOLDEN VALLEY
Jan Hilton ....(612) 544-9450
MINNEAPOLIS
Creative Casting Talent & Model ....(612) 375-0525
Kimberly Franson Talent & Model ....(612) 338-1605
Nancy Kremer ....(612) 338-7525
Lipservice ....(612) 338-5477
Eleanor Moore Agency, Inc. ....(612) 827-3823
Portfolio I Models & Talents ....(612) 338-5800
Richter Casting ....(612) 338-8223
Wehmann Models & Talent, Inc................(612) 333-6393
ST. PAUL
Meredith Model & Talent Agency ....(612) 298-9555
WHITE BEAR LAKE
Actors Plus/Voice Plus ....(612) 426-9400

MINNESOTA FILM OFFICE
MINNEAPOLIS
Minnesota Film Board...............................(612) 332-6493

MISSISSIPPI

CASTING OFFICES
BRANDON
Lacey Lee Ashley ....(601) 825-5190
CANTON
Stephanie Gordon ....(601) 859-6243
Heartland Casting ....(601) 864-5193
JACKSON
Dawn Buck ....(601) 981-1360
Connections Casting.................................(601) 354-3642
Misty Wakeland Monroe ....(601) 362-2381
Alice Theresa Stamps ....(602) 373-5055
Jack Stevens ....(601) 355-7535

NATCHEZ
Angie Druetta ....(601) 446-7799
OCEAN SPRINGS
Evelyn Dorn ....(601) 875-2040
TUPELO
Debbie Edge ....(601) 365-8873
UNIVERSITY
Denise Wax..(601) 234-7461

TALENT AND MODELING AGENCIES
CLARKSDALE
Delta Talent ....(601) 624-6956

MISSISSIPPI FILM OFFICES
CANTON
Canton Film Office ......(601) 859-1307 or (601) 859-3369
COLUMBUS
Columbus Film Commission ....(800) 327-2686
or (601) 329-1191
CORINTH
Corinth Film Office......(800) 748-9048 or (601) 287-5269
GREENVILLE
Greenville Film Office ....(800) 467-3582
or (601) 334-2711
GREENWOOD
Greenwood Convention & Visitors Bureau (601) 453-9197
GULFPORT
Gulf Coast Film Office...............................(601) 863-3807
HATTIESBURG
Hattiesburg Film Office ....(800) 638-6877
or (601) 268-3220
HOLLY SPRINGS
Holly Springs Film Office ....(601) 252-1924
JACKSON
Mississippi Film Office............................(601) 359-3297
MERIDIAN
Meridian Film Office....(800) 748-9970 or (601) 693-1306
NATCHEZ
Natchez Film Commission ....(601) 446-6345
OXFORD
Oxford Film Commission ....(601) 234-4680
STARKVILLE
Starkville Film Office ..(800) 649-8687 or (601) 323-3322
TUPELO
Tupelo Film Commission ....(800) 533-0611
or (601) 841-6521
VICKSBURG / WARREN COUNTY
Vicksburg Film Commission.....................(601) 636-9421
YAZOO CITY
Yazoo City Film Office (800) 381-0662 or (601) 746-1815

MISSOURI

CASTING OFFICES
BRANSON
Catrine McGregor ....(417) 272-6056

INDEPENDENCE
Lorraine Young Yocum ....(816) 833-2272
KANSAS CITY
Wendy Gray ....(816) 931-5828
Wright-Laird Casting ....(816) 531-0331
KIMBERLING CITY
Colleen Tucker ....(417) 739-5502
ST. LOUIS
Carrie Houk...(314) 862-1236

TALENT AND MODELING AGENCIES
KANSAS CITY
MTC ....(816) 531-FACE
Patricia Stevens Model Agency.................(816) 221-1188
Talent Unlimited ....(816) 561-9040
Voices, Inc...(816) 753-8255
SPRINGFIELD
Austin Talent International.........................(417) 886-5633
Louie Michael Management ....(417) 887-8955
ST. LOUIS
Talent Plus, Inc. ....(314) 367-5588
Top of the Line ....(314) 241-7791

THEATER GROUPS/WORKSHOPS
KANSAS CITY
The Coterie Theatre..................................(816) 474-6785
Martin City Melodrama.............................(816) 942-7576
Missouri Repertory Theatre......................(816) 235-2727
Music Hall ....(816) 871-3745

MISSOURI FILM OFFICES
JEFFERSON CITY
Missouri Film Office ....(314) 751-9050
KANSAS CITY
Kansas City Film Office.............................(816) 221-0636
ST. LOUIS
St. Louis Film Office ....(314) 259-3409

MONTANA

TALENT AND MODELING AGENCIES
BILLINGS
Creative World, Inc. ....(406) 259-9540
BOZEMAN
Montana Mystique Talent Agency ....(406) 586-6099
CLANCY
Maxie's Agency ....(406) 933-8461
HELENA
Adams/O'Connell Talent Agency ....(406) 443-7547

MONTANA FILM OFFICES
GREAT FALLS
Great Falls Film Liaison ....(800) 735-8535
HELENA
Montana Film Office ....(406) 444-1800

NEBRASKA

CASTING OFFICES

BEATRICE
Earthbound ....(402) 645-8214
LINCOLN
Imagine..(402) 464-4821
Koor Entertainment ....(402) 477-8722
OMAHA
Actor's Etc. ....(402) 391-3153
Helen Blume ....(402) 556-1359
Manya Nogg ....(402) 391-3153
Omaha Theater Company ....(402) 345-4852
Talent Pool, Inc. ....(402) 455-3000
B. J. Tobin..(402) 342-2944

NEBRASKA FILM OFFICES

LINCOLN
Nebraska Film Office.................................(800) 228-4307
OMAHA
Omaha Film Commission ....(402) 444-7737

NEVADA

CASTING OFFICES

LAS VEGAS
Baskow Agency...(702) 733-7818
Bass Creative Bookings ....(702) 898-2277
Creative Casting & Acting.........................(702) 737-0611
Lear Casting ....(702) 459-2090

TALENT AND MODELING AGENCIES

LAS VEGAS
Baskow Agency...(702) 733-7818
Bass Creative Bookings ....(702) 898-2277
Classic Models & Talent...........................(702) 367-1444
Creative Casting & Acting.........................(702) 737-0611
Creative Concepts......................................(702) 792-4111
Lenz Talent Agency ....(702) 733-6888
Premiere Models..(702) 369-2003

TALENT WORKSHOPS

LAS VEGAS
Joe Behar's Community Drama Workshop..(702) 457-0234
Center for Creative Professional Performer ..(702) 399-4680
Creative Casting & Acting.........................(702) 737-0611
Gerald Gordon Enterprises ....(702) 648-8716
Nevada Education Society.........................(702) 221-3234
Screen Actors Guild Conservatory ....(702) 226-5620
Young Actors Film Workshop ....(702) 223-1232

NEVADA FILM OFFICES

CARSON CITY
Reno/Tahoe Office ......(800) 336-1600 or (702) 687-4325

INCLINE VILLAGE
Incline Village Visitor Authority ....(702) 831-3993
LAS VEGAS
Nevada Motion Picture Division ....(702) 486-2711

NEW HAMPSHIRE

PERFORMING ARTS CENTERS/WORKSHOPS

CONCORD
Concord Community Music School ....(603) 228-1196
DEERFIELD
New Hampshire Shakespeare Festival.......(603) 666-9088
DERRY
Southern New Hampshire Community
  School of the Arts ....(603) 432-3623
DURHAM
Department of Theater & Dance ....(603) 862-3038
EXETER
Exeter Players ....(603) 772-9035
FRANCONIA
North Country Chamber Players...............(603) 869-3154
KEENE
Colonial Theater ....(603) 357-2936
Keene State College ....(603) 358-2168
LINCOLN
North County Center for the Arts ....(603) 745-6032
LONDON
New London Playhouse ....(603) 526-4631
NASHUA
Nashua Center for the Arts ....(603) 880-7538
NEWPORT
Newport Opera House................................(603) 863-2412
NORTH CONWAY
Mt. Washington Valley Theater Co............(603) 356-5776
PETERBOROUGH
Peterborough Players ....(603) 924-7585
PLYMOUTH
Arts Alliance of Northern New Hampshire..(603) 536-2279
PORTSMOUTH
Ballet New England ....(603) 430-9309
New Hampshire Theater Project ....(603) 431-6644
Pontine Movement Theater ....(603) 436-6660
Portsmouth Academy of Performing Arts ..(603) 433-7272
Seacoast Repertory Theater......................(603) 433-4472
TAMWORTH
Barnstormers Summer Theater ....(603) 323-8500
WHITEFIELD
Weathervane Theater Players ....(603) 837-9010
WILTON
Andy's Summer Playhouse ....(603) 654-5970
WOLFEBORO
Village Players Community Theater ....(603) 569-1396

NEW HAMPSHIRE FILM OFFICE

CONCORD
New Hampshire Film & TV Bureau ....(603) 271-2598

NEW JERSEY

CASTING OFFICES

ATLANTIC CITY
Weist/Barron/Ryan ....(609) 347-0074
Wickline Casting.......................................(609) 347-0074
BERKELEY HEIGHTS
Shirley Hoe Enterprises.............................(908) 464-2844
EDISON
Robert Donatelli Agency ....(201) 908-5169
LINDENWOLD
Robert Taylor Talent ....(609) 346-1763
MARGATE
McCullough's Agency ....(609) 822-2222
MERCHANTVILLE
Kayden Productions, Inc. ....(609) 665-6634
MOORESTOWN
Curt Crane Productions ....(609) 273-8886
NEWARK
Swann & Associates ....(201) 621-7331
PERRINEVILLE
Barbara A. Hanes Casting ....(908) 792-1118
RED BANK
Prime Time Casting Associates.................(908) 219-0422
RIVER EDGE
Cover Girl Studio ....(201) 261-2042
SEWELL
The Dell Center.......................................(609) 589-4099
TOTOWA
Meredith Agency......................................(201) 812-0122
UPPER MONTCLAIR
Adine Duron ....(201) 744-5698
VERONA
Blanche Zeller...(201) 239-1545

TALENT AND MODELING AGENCIES

BERNARDSVILLE
Classic Beauties, Inc. ....(908) 766-6663
BRICKTOWN
New Talent Management ....(908) 477-3355
CLEMENTON
Tiffany Talent Agency ....(609) 784-2256
CLIFTON
Talent Marketing ....(201) 779-0700
HACKENSACK
Big Look Management ....(201) 488-1111
LINDENWOLD
Robert Taylor Talent ....(609) 346-1763
MADISON
Model Works, Inc.....................................(201) 377-1140
NORTH HALEDON
Giraldo Modeling & Talent Agency ....(201) 423-5115
OAKLYN
Miss GeorgeAnn's Modeling School..........(609) 854-2710
OCEAN
DM Management ....(908) 493-6407
RED BANK
Special Artists Management, Inc. ....(908) 758-9393

RIDGEWOOD
ParkWest Model & Talent Agency ....(201) 447-3335
TEANECK
Shirley Grant Management ....(201) 692-1653
TENAFLY
Adams & Phillips Talent ....(201) 569-5033
VOORHEES
Cathy Parker Management, Inc. ....(609) 354-2020

NEW JERSEY FILM OFFICE

NEWARK
New Jersey Motion Picture & TV Office ....(201) 648-6279

NEW MEXICO

CASTING OFFICES

ALBUQUERQUE
Kathryn Brink ....(505) 266-6211
The Phoenix Agency ....(505) 260-0467
Alan D. Swain IV.....................................(505) 265-0098
ARROYO HONDO
Jo Edna Boldin ....(505) 776-8062
ESPANOLA
Outlaw Extras ....(505) 891-2274
LAS CRUCES
Desiree Acting & Modeling.......................(888) 385-8000
SANTA FE
Ellen Blake Casting.................................(505) 262-9733
Casting House ....(505) 988-3624
Ronnie Hollis Casting..............................(505) 983-3628
Huddleston Productions, Inc. ....(505) 983-0600
Sally Jackson Casting..............................(505) 982-3886
MDF Extras ....(505) 988-4838
Musica Mundial Production ....(505) 983-6237
New Mexico Casting ....(505) 982-1061
Perez Investments ....(800) 977-3989
Rainbow Casting Service ....(505) 268-9315
Emre Sonmez ....(505) 989-1719
TAOS
Aspen Productions de Taos.......................(505) 758-2280

TALENT AND MODELING AGENCIES

ALBUQUERQUE
Am. India Heritage Fnd. ....(505) 268-3701
Applause Talent Agency ....(505) 262-9733
Aspire Modeling & Talent Agency..............(505) 898-6980
BF Photographics ....(505) 246-1973
Cimarron Talent Agency ....(505) 292-2314
Eaton Agency, Inc....................................(505) 344-3149
Mannequin Agency ....(505) 266-6823
Phoenix Agency ....(505) 881-1209
South of Santa Fe Talent Guild ....(505) 880-8550
Sunshine Generation................................(505) 294-5200
ALMAOGORDO
Hooser World Enterprises ....(505) 437-2669

LAS CRUCES
Desiree Acting & Modeling......................(888) 385-8000
SANTA FE
Aesthetic's Talent Management.................(505) 982-5883
Characters...(505) 982-9729
MDF Extras...(505) 988-4838
Musica Mundial Productions....................(505) 983-6237
Santa Fe Model & Talent Resource..........(505) 455-2690
TAOS
Wildfire Productions...............................(505) 758-1873

NEW MEXICO FILM OFFICES
ALBUQUERQUE
Albuquerque TV & Film Office..................(505) 842-9918
LAS CRUCES
Las Cruces Film Commission....................(505) 524-8521
LOS ALAMOS
Los Alamos County Film Office...............(505) 662-8401
SANTA FE
New Mexico Film Office...........................(505) 827-7365

NEW YORK

CASTING OFFICES
BREWSTER
Eileen Powers Casting.............................(914) 279-5106
BROCKPORT
Sandra Collister......................................(716) 637-5561
LAURELTON
Bad Girl Casting......................................(718) 712-0887
NEW YORK CITY
Amerifilm Casting, Inc.............................(212) 334-3382
Baby Wranglers Casting, Inc....................(212) 736-0060
Bass/Visgilio Casting...............................(212) 598-9032
Jerry Beaver & Associates.......................(212) 979-0909
Breanne Benjamin Casting.......................(212) 977-5377
Jay Binder Casting...................................(212) 586-6777
Boricua Casting.......................................(212) 627-1789
Jane Brinker Casting................................(212) 924-3322
Kit Carter Casting....................................(212) 864-3147
Donald Case Casting, Inc........................(212) 889-6555
Cast-Away! Casting Service.....................(212) 755-0960
Bob Collier Casting..................................(212) 246-5989
Jodi Collins Casting.................................(212) 982-1086
Contemporary Casting, Ltd......................(212) 838-1818
Sue Crystal Casting.................................(212) 877-0737
CTP Casting...(212) 696-1100
Moni Damevski Casting...........................(212) 684-0477
Donna De Seta Casting............................(212) 274-9696
Merry L. Delmonte Casting......................(212) 279-2000
DiGiaimo Associates, Ltd.........................(212) 713-1884
Leonard Finger..(212) 944-8611
Maureen Fremont Casting........................(212) 302-1215
Godlove, Serow & Sindlinger Casting......(212) 627-7300
Maria Greco Casting................................(212) 247-2011
Carol Hanzel Casting...............................(212) 242-6113
Hedges Hoffman May Casting..................(212) 304-8500

Judy Henderson & Associates.................(212) 877-0225
Herman & Lipson Casting, Inc.................(212) 807-7706
Hispanicast...(212) 691-7366
Stuart Howard Associates, Ltd................(212) 725-7770
Hughes/Moss Casting, Ltd.......................(212) 307-6690
Hyde-Hamlet Casting...............................(718) 783-9634
Johnson-Liff Casting...............................(212) 391-2680
Rosalie Joseph Casting............................(212) 921-5781
KEE Casting...(212) 995-0794
Judy Keller Casting..................................(212) 463-7676
Jodi Kipperman Casting...........................(212) 228-5551
Lynn Kressell Casting..............................(212) 605-9122
Andrea Kurzman Casting..........................(212) 684-0710
Liz Lewis Casting Partners......................(212) 645-1500
Ellen Lewis...(212) 245-4635
Vince Liebhart Casting............................(212) 757-4350
Joan Lynn Casting...................................(212) 675-5595
John S Lyons...(212) 333-4552
MC2 Casting..(212) 369-6291
McCorkie Casting, Ltd..............................(212) 840-0992
Abigail McGrath, Inc...............................(212) 768-3277
Philip Wm. McKinley................................(212) 333-4552
Beth Melsky Casting................................(212) 505-5000
Navarro/Bertoni & Associates..................(212) 736-9272
Ellen Novack Casting...............................(212) 431-3939
Scott Powers Productions, Inc.................(212) 242-4700
Riccy Reed Casting..................................(212) 691-7366
Richin Casting...(212) 243-4448
Mike Roscoe Casting, Ltd........................(212) 725-0014
Caroline Sinclair Casting........................(212) 675-4094
Stage Door Enterprises, Inc.....................(212) 865-3966
Elsie Stark Casting..................................(212) 366-1903
Irene Stockton Casting............................(212) 964-9445
Strickman-Ripps, Inc...............................(212) 966-3211
VideoActive Talent...................................(212) 541-8106
Grant Wilfley Casting...............................(212) 685-3537
Marji Camner Wollin & Associates...........(212) 472-2528
ROCHESTER
Alvarez...(716) 273-9058
Anders Productions.................................(716) 442-8227
B-HIVE...(716) 853-0553
Yvonne Conte..(716) 256-2916
Focus International..................................(716) 442-5511
Foxwood Talent Payment, Inc..................(716) 223-1635
Goodlein-Donaldson.................................(716) 544-4649
Nexus Personal Management, Inc............(716) 425-1306
Rochester Community Players...................(716) 385-5580
Pat Urban..(716) 442-3384

TALENT AND MODELING AGENCIES
BUFFALO
Darlene Pickering Hummert.......................(716) 883-7942
June 2 Modeling School............................(716) 883-0700
Studio Arena Theatre School...................(716) 856-8025
CHEEKTOWAGA
Wright Modeling Agency..........................(716) 632-4391
FAIRPORT
Foxwood Talent Payment, Inc...................(716) 223-1635
Nexus Personal Management, Inc............(716) 426-1306

HICKSVILLE
Omnipop, Inc. ....(516) 937-6011
MACEDON
Pierce, Virginia Hayden..........................(315) 986-5628
NEW YORK CITY
Abrams Artists & Associates....................(212) 935-8980
The Actors Group Agency ....(212) 245-2930
Bret Adams Limited..................................(212) 765-5630
Agency for Collaborative Arts ....(212) 713-1635
Agency for Performing Arts......................(212) 582-1500
Agents for the Arts, Inc. ....(212) 229-2562
Alliance Talent, Inc. ....(212) 840-6868
Michael Amato Agency ....(212) 247-4456
Ambrosio/Mortimer & Associates............(212) 719-1677
American International Talent ....(212) 245-8888
Beverly Anderson Agency ....(212) 944-7773
Andreadis Talent Agency, Inc. ....(212) 315-0303
Artist Group East.....................................(212) 586-1452
Associated Booking Corporation..............(212) 874-2400
Richard Astor Agency ....(212) 581-1970
Avenue Talent Group................................(212) 628-1380
Carol Baker Agency..................................(212) 719-4013
Barry, Haft, Brown Artists Agency ....(212) 869-9310
Bauman, Hiller & Associates ....(212) 757-0098
Peter Bellin Agency, Inc. ....(212) 949-9119
Berman, Boals & Flynn, Inc. ....(212) 966-0389
The Bethel Agency ....(212) 664-0455
Big Duke Six Artists, Inc. ....(212) 989-6927
J. Michael Bloom & Associates ....(212) 529-6500
Bookers, Inc..(212) 645-9706
Don Buchwald & Associates....................(212) 867-1070
Carry Company/Carry Kids Talent Reps.....(212) 768-2793
The Carson Organization, Ltd. ....(212) 221-1517
Carson-Adler Agency, Inc. ....(212) 307-1882
Richard Cataldi Agency............................(212) 741-7450
Coleman-Rosenberg ....(212) 838-0734
Columbia Artists Management ....(212) 397-6900
Cunningham-Escott-Dipene & Associates (212) 477-1666
Duva-Flack Associates, Inc. ....(212) 957-9600
Ginger Dicce Talent..................................(212) 974-7455
Douglas, Gorman, Rothacker
    & Wilhelm, Inc. ....(212) 382-2000
Eastwood Talent Group, Ltd. ....(212) 645-2500
Dulcina Elsen Associates ....(212) 355-6617
Epstein/Wyckoff & Associates..................(212) 586-9110
Flick East-West Talents, Inc. ....(212) 307-1850
Frontier Booking International...................(212) 221-0220
The Gage Group, Inc. ....(212) 541-5250
Garber Talent Agency ....(212) 292-4910
Gersh Agency N.Y., Inc. ....(212) 997-1818
Gilchrist Talent Group, Inc. ....(212) 692-9166
Grant, A Theatrical & Literary Agency.......(212) 626-6730
H.W.A. Talent Representatives, Ltd............(212) 529-4555
Peggy Hadley ....(212) 246-2166
Harden-Curtis Associates ....(212) 977-8502
Michael Hartig Agency, Ltd. ....(212) 929-1772
Henderson/Hogan Agency, Inc..................(212) 765-5190
Ingber & Associates ....(212) 889-9450
Innovative Artists Talent & Literary ....(212) 315-4455

Integrity Talent, Inc..................................(212) 575-5756
International Creative Management, Inc.....(212) 556-5600
Jam Theatrical Agency, Inc. ....(212) 376-6330
Jan J. Agency, Inc. ....(212) 967-5265
Jordan, Gill & Dornbaum Talent Agency....(212) 463-8455
Jerry Kahn, Inc..(212) 245-7317
Kerin-Goldberg & Associates ....(212) 838-7373
Archer King, Ltd..(212) 765-3103
Roseanne Kirk Artists ....(212) 315-3487
KMA Associates ....(212) 581-4610
The Krasny Office, Inc. ....(212) 730-8160
L.B.H. Associates ....(212) 501-8936
Lally Talent Agency ....(212) 974-8718
Lionel Larner Ltd. ....(212) 246-3105
Bruce Levy Agency ....(212) 563-7079
Bernard Liebhaber Agency ....(212) 631-7561
Lure International Talent Group.................(212) 260-9300
Madison Talent Group...............................(212) 922-9600
Marge McDermott Enterprises ....(212) 889-1583
McDonald Richards, Inc............................(212) 627-3100
William Morris Agency ....(212) 586-5100
Nouvelle Talent Management ....(212) 645-0940
Fifi Oscard Agency, Inc. ....(212) 764-1100
Harry Packwood Talent, Ltd. ....(212) 586-8900
Dorothy Palmer Talent Agency ....(212) 765-4280
Paradigm Talent & Literary Agency...........(212) 246-1030
Professional Artists Unlimited...................(212) 247-8770
Rachel's Talent Agency ....(212) 967-0665
Radioactive Talent, inc. ....(212) 315-1919
Norman Reich Agency...............................(212) 399-2881
Gilla Roos, Ltd..(212) 727-7820
Sames & Rollnick Associates ....(212) 315-4434
Sanders Agency, Ltd. ....(212) 779-3737
Schiffman, Ekman, Morrison & Marx ....(212) 627-5500
William Schill Agency, Inc. ....(212) 315-5919
Schuller Talent, Inc. ....(212) 532-6005
Sheplin Artists & Associates....................(212) 647-1311
Silver-Massetti & Associates ....(212) 391-4545
Special Artists Agency, Inc.......................(212) 420-0200
Spotlight Entertainment Services, Inc. .....(212) 956-4557
Stewart Artists Corp.................................(212) 744-2272
Strain & Associates, Inc...........................(212) 391-0380
Talent Representatives, Inc.......................(212) 752-1835
The Tantleff Office, Inc. ....(212) 752-1835
Michael Thomas Agency, Inc. ....(212) 867-0303
Tranum, Robertson & Hughes, Inc............(212) 371-7500
Trawick Artists Management ....(212) 874-2482
Van der Veer People, Inc. ....(212) 688-2880
Waters & Nicolosi Talent Representatives..(212) 302-8787
Hanns Wolters Theatreatical Agency.........(212) 714-0100
Ann Wright Representatives, Inc. ....(212) 764-6770
Writers & Artists Agency..........................(212) 391-1112
Babs Zimmerman Agency ....(212) 348-7203
Zoli Management, Inc. ....(212) 242-7490
PENFIELD
Chauncey Street ....(716) 387-0788
PITTSFORD
David Dwayne Clark ....(716) 461-2300
Robert Nolan...(716) 248-2477

ROCHESTER

And Much, Much More Entertainment ......(716) 256-0627
Azetah Model & Talent Management.........(716) 387-0930
Cameleon Productions ....(716) 886-6300
Dawn Carmell ....(716) 234-4419
Marlene Casamento ....(716) 227-4137
Mike Casella ....(716) 987-1322
Michael Ciccone ....(716) 227-8720
Yvonne Conte ....(716) 256-2916
Conwell Model Management ....(716) 631-0251
Kevin Corstange ....(716) 442-3198
Kevin Gillan ....(716) 292-6316
Gold Apple Communications ....(716) 342-8590
Innerloop Productions ....(716) 254-6256
Michael Koldan..(716) 242-9063
Frances Ann McKenzie ....(716) 271-2698
Karen Pailler ....(716) 461-2551
Fortunato Pessimente ....(716) 451-3869
Larry Richardson......................................(716) 244-6394
Rochester Community Players ....(716) 385-5580
Stewart T. Roth ....(716) 663-1038
Raymond Salah..(716) 529-5714
Summer Productions ....(716) 442-1631
US Model/Talent Management ....(716) 244-0592
Danny Vee Modeling Experience..............(716) 328-0776

SCOTTSVILLE

Diane St. Cyr...(716) 889-9031

WILLIAMSVILLE

Faces: A Modeling Agency ....(716) 634-5634

THEATER GROUPS

ROCHESTER

Blackfriars, Inc. ....(716) 473-6760
Downstairs Cabaret Theater ....(716) 325-4370
GeVA Theatre ....(716) 232-1366
Innerloop Productions ....(716) 254-6256
Rochester Association of Performing Arts..(716) 442-0190
Rochester Community Players ....(716) 385-5580
Rochester Philharmonic ....(716) 454-2620
School of the Arts....................................(716) 256-6580

NEW YORK FILM OFFICES

BUFFALO

Greater Buffalo Film Office ....(716) 852-0511

NEW YORK CITY

New York State Governor's Office ....(212) 803-2330
NYC Mayor's Office...................................(212) 489-6710

POUGHKEEPSIE

Hudson Valley Film Office.........................(914) 473-0318

ROCHESTER

Rochester/Finger Lakes Film Office ....(716) 546-5490

NORTH CAROLINA

CASTING OFFICES

ASHEVILLE

RBA Studios ....(704) 253-1634

CHARLOTTE

Carolina Winds ....(704) 338-1141
Jay Howard Production.............................(704) 525-7804
Indigo Productions, Inc. ....(704) 541-3411

DURHAM

Starbroker...(919) 493-4054
Universal Productions, Inc.......................(919) 598-4003

GREENSBORO

Ragland & Associates..............................(910) 547-0871

KERNERSVILLE

Triad Casting...(910) 993-1387

WEAVORVILLE

Beverly McDermott Casting ....(704) 645-3404

WILMINGTON

Action Casting of the Southeast ....(910) 231-3929
Casting, Inc./Film Connection ....(910) 395-1917
DeCoursey, Francine................................(910) 763-0288
Fincannon & Associates ....(910) 251-1500
Music City Casting Co..............................(910) 251-0110

WRIGHTSVILLE BEACH

Tracy Kilpatrick ....(910) 763-2778

TALENT AND MODELING AGENCIES

ASHEVILLE

Artisans Agency ....(704) 253-3771
Talent Trek Agency ....(704) 251-0173

CAPE CAMERET

Talent Associates International ....(919) 393-2728

CARY

Capital Artists, Inc. ....(919) 467-8682

CHARLOTTE

Classique Models & Talent ....(704) 536-8185
JTA, Inc. ....(704) 377-5987
Marco Productions ....(704) 875-8000
Model & Talent Management ....(704) 523-6966
William Petitt Agency ....(704) 343-4922
Taylor'd Arrangements.............................(704) 527-3820

DURHAM

Conroy Audio ....(919) 489-0251
Barbara Helen Dickson ....(919) 660-3356
Ninth Street Dance Coop ....(919) 286-6011

GREENSBORO

Directions USA ....(910) 292-2800
Marilyn's, Inc. ....(910) 292-5950

MONROE

Amron School of Fine Arts & Agency........(704) 283-4290

RALEIGH

Actors Unlimited ....(919) 878-4342
The Barbizon Agency ....(910) 876-8201
Knight Talent Management ....(919) 834-3688

SNOW HILL

Touch of Class Models & Talent ....(919) 747-8861

SUMMERFIELD
Artists Resource Agency ....(910) 349-6167
WAXHAW
Watson Agency, Inc., Nancy ....(704) 843-1219
WILMINGTON
Agent's Modeling ....(910) 256-3130
Bontalent ....(910) 343-0445 or (910) 270-9413
Cape Fear Film & Theatre Conservatory ....(910) 350-1904
C.M.A. Talent ....(910) 251-2185
Cornucopia Agency, Inc., The ....(910) 350-1904
Delia Model Management ....(910) 343-1753
Harry's Niche Talent Agency ....(910) 251-1411
Maultsby Model & Talent ....(910) 256-9662
MJM Talent Representative ....(910) 251-3734
William Pettit Agency ....(910) 762-1933
Show People Talent.................................(910) 313-0083
                                            or (910) 815-0131
WINSTON-SALEM
Johnson West Talent................................(910) 722-9099

NORTH CAROLINA FILM OFFICES
ARDEN
Western North Carolina
   Film Commission ....(704) 687-7234
DURHAM
Durham Convention & Visitors Bureau......(919) 687-0288
RALEIGH
North Carolina Film Office ....(919) 733-9900
WILMINGTON
Greater Wilmington Film Office.................(919) 762-2611
WINSTON-SALEM
Winston-Salem Piedmont Triad Film ....(910) 777-3787

NORTH DAKOTA

CASTING/TALENT AGENCIES
FARGO
Academic Modeling & Talent Agency ....(701) 235-8132
The Acting Studio ....(701) 232-7313
Fargo-Moorhead Community Theater........(701) 235-1901
Plain People Entertainment......................(701) 232-1646
Larry Ruth...(701) 237-9893
WEST FARGO
International Talent Search
   & Model Directory ....(701) 282-2556

NORTH DAKOTA FILM OFFICE
BISMARCK
North Dakota Film Commission ....(800) 328-2871

OHIO

CASTING OFFICES
AKRON
Anita Ferris-Sears...................................(216) 665-3001
Jim Walser ....(216) 923-7682
CINCINNATI
Anita Daugherty ....(800) 509-1055 or (513) 681-5767
D. Lynn Meyers.......................................(513) 574-8301
CLEVELAND
Sharon Dane ....(216) 331-5051
Stacy Herman ....(216) 779-6630
Perry Lively...(216) 561-4714
Julie Matthews ....(216) 932-7995
Gayle Wilson...(216) 838-4825
COLUMBUS
Mary S. Evans...(614) 261-6459
M. A. Henry ....(614) 486-1643
Betty McCormick-Aggas ....(614) 294-5726
Angela Palazzolo ....(614) 451-0216
Nancy Paul ....(614) 471-2991
Casyle Wise ....(614) 888-3497
YOUNGSTOWN
Linda Weaver ....(216) 758-4417

TALENT AND MODELING AGENCIES
AKRON
Protocol Models & Talent Agency.............(216) 666-6066
BOARDMAN
Lemodeln, Inc. ....(216) 758-4417
CINCINNATI
Creative Talent Company ....(513) 241-7827
Focus International Modeling
   & Talent Agency ....(513) 530-8105
Heyman Halper Talent.............................(513) 533-3113
CLEVELAND
David And Lee..(216) 522-1300
Sierra Vista Entertainment
   & Lacey Agency ....(216) 575-0848
Stone Productions Model
   & Talent Agency ....(216) 642-5445
CLEVELAND HEIGHTS
American Performing Arts Network............(216) 932-7995
COLUMBUS
CAM Talent ....(614) 488-1122
Creative Talent Company ....(614) 294-7827
Goenner Talent ....(614) 459-3582
John Robert Powers ....(614) 846-1046
Mac Worthington Studio..........................(614) 294-0100
SWANTON
Send Me Talent Casting ....(800) 375-1023
YOUNGSTOWN
LJF Talent Agency...................................(216) 759-1442

OHIO FILM OFFICES
CINCINNATI
Greater Cincinnati Film Commission ....(513) 784-1744

CLEVELAND
City of Cleveland Film Office ....(216) 664-3660
COLUMBUS
Ohio Film Commission.............................(800) 230-3523
DAYTON
Greater Dayton Film Commission..............(513) 277-8090

UNIONS
CINCINNATI
AFTRA ....(513) 579-8668 or (800) 541-8668
CLEVELAND
AFTRA/SAG ....(216) 781-2255
COLUMBUS
Ohio's Child Labor Laws...........................(800) 230-3523

OKLAHOMA

CASTING OFFICES
OKLAHOMA CITY
American Indian Casting...........................(405) 789-4300
Headshot Promotions ....(405) 632-4269
Ricki G. Masler ....(405) 848-4839
TULSA
A'mazin, Inc. ....(918) 254-4190
Broken Arrow Community Playhouse ....(918) 258-0077
Karri Hartman ....(918) 743-0079
Lisa LaFortune ....(918) 254-2379
Linda Layman Agency, Ltd........................(918) 744-0888
David McCally ....(918) 224-4451
Model & Talent Management, Inc. ....(918) 622-2593
Patrycia Moore Agency ....(918) 682-1221
Terri Nimerick ....(918) 234-9342
Oklahoma Performing Arts ....(918) 455-0285
Gloria Pasternak ....(918) 747-8276
Mary Simons ....(918) 744-6828

TALENT AND MODELING AGENCIES
OKLAHOMA CITY
A'mazin, Inc. ....(405) 843-5583
John Casablancas Model & Talent ....(405) 842-0000
Hammon & Associates ....(405) 329-8111
Harrison Gers Model & Talent Agency ......(405) 840-4515
Headshot Promotions ....(405) 632-4269
Modeling & Casting of Oklahoma..............(405) 341-4413
Oklahoma Talent & Models Association ....(405) 732-2212
Starblaze Entertainment & Marketing ....(405) 947-0080
TULSA
Modeling & Casting Agency......................(405) 848-4839
Linda Layman Agency, Ltd........................(918) 744-0888
McCally's Talent Agency ....(918) 224-4451
M/L Talent & Management, Inc. ....(918) 584-4645
Model & Talent Management, Inc. ....(918) 622-2593
Native American Registry ....(918) 458-5199
Tulsa Talent Agency ....(918) 747-9246

OKLAHOMA FILM OFFICES
GUTHRIE
Logan County Film Commission ....(405) 282-0060
TULSA
Oklahoma Film Office ....(800) 766-3456

OREGON

CASTING OFFICES
BEAVERTON
Penguin Talent Agency ....(503) 848-9644
EUGENE
Multicultural Media...................................(541) 485-6647
Talent Management Associates ....(541) 345-1524
PORTLAND
A&M Casting ....(503) 249-1945
ABC Kids-N-Teens Talent ....(503) 249-2945
Actors Only ....(503) 233-5073
Artists & Xtras...(503) 227-4119
Barbara Balsz Casting ....(503) 245-6343
Janet Barrett ....(503) 285-0708
Douglas Byers..(503) 239-0714
Central Xtras Casting ....(503) 243-2468
Creative Artists Management, Inc. ....(503) 241-2855
Cusick's Talent Agency ....(503) 274-8555
The Extras Group ....(503) 227-3132
Extras Only ....(503) 227-6055
Pam Gilles Casting ....(503) 227-2656
Carol Lukens Casting ....(503) 255-3785
Pacific Talent, Inc.....................................(503) 228-3620
Megann Ratzow..(503) 251-9050
Reel Kids, Inc...(503) 248-4565
Ryan Artists, Inc.......................................(503) 274-1005
LaVerne Springer ....(503) 281-8875
Jessica Stuart ....(503) 629-2078
Nannette Troutman Casting......................(503) 241-4233
REDMOND
High Desert Locations..............................(541) 923-5970
or (800) 484-2301

TALENT AND MODELING AGENCIES
BEAVERTON
Ice Breakers ....(503) 644-7337
EUGENE
Multicultural Media...................................(541) 485-6647
Talent Management Associates ....(541) 345-1525
Unlimited Model & Talent Agency, Inc.......(541) 683-9323
GRANTS PASS
Total Look Talent ....(503) 476-9098
PORTLAND
ABC Kids-N-Teens
   Talent Management, Inc. ....(503) 249-2945
Actors Only ....(503) 233-5073
Creative Artists Management ....(503) 241-2855
Cusick's Talent Agency ....(503) 274-8555
New Faces..(503) 277-4757

Pacific Talent, Inc. ....(503) 228-3620
Rose City Talent ....(503) 274-1005
Wilson Entertainment, Inc. ....(503) 243-6362

OREGON FILM OFFICE
PORTLAND
Oregon Film & Video Office ....(503) 229-5832

PENNSYLVANIA

CASTING/TALENT/MODELING AGENCIES
BALA CYNWYD
Hot Foot Agency ....(215) 564-0820
BUTLER
Kane Model/Talent Management..............(412) 287-0576
HARRISBURG
Constance Rankin Arter............................(717) 233-4882
Corey Productions ....(717) 387-1146
Cynmar Talent Locators ....(717) 234-2994
HERSHEY
Fashion Mystique Modeling ....(717) 534-2750
NEW CUMBERLAND
MiShar Productions ....(717) 774-4315
PHILADELPHIA
The John Barth Agency.............................(215) 238-0800
Nick Cofone ....(800) 868-3007
Wayne Harcum ....(215) 639-7296
Inlingua Translations................................(215) 735-7646
Mike Lemon Casting.................................(215) 627-8927
Hedges May Casting.................................(800) 331-7840
Philadelphia Casting Company, Inc. ....(215) 592-7575
Reinhard Model & Talent Agency ....(215) 567-2008
SIERRA CENTER
Models & Talent ....(215) 953-8410
PITTSBURGH
Donna Belajac & Company.......................(412) 391-1005
Rik Billock...(412) 567-6316
Docherty Casting ....(412) 765-1400
Nina Jack ....(412) 963-8159
Canice Kennedy Casting..........................(412) 441-3579
Mina-Wihe Consultants ....(412) 431-9050
Models Unlimited ....(412) 343-7700
Nancy Mosser..(412) 381-1694
Sister Mania Productions, Inc. ....(412) 226-2964
The Talent Group......................................(412) 471-8011
READING
Donatelli Model, Casting & Talent Agency (610) 921-0777
Greer Langes Associates, Inc...................(610) 647-5515
The Sentry Post ....(610) 520-1283

PENNSYLVANIA FILM OFFICES
HARRISBURG
Pennsylvania Film Bureau.........................(717) 783-3456
PHILADELPHIA
Greater Philadelphia Film Office ....(215) 686-2668

PITTSBURGH
Pittsburgh Film Office..............................(412) 261-2744

PUERTO RICO

CASTING OFFICES
SAN JUAN
Rosa del Mar Acosta................................(787) 758-3917
Mildred Alvarez..(787) 767-1871
Wanda Berrios ....(787) 725-5246
Mayte Flores ....(787) 753-8074
Ivette Gonzalez ....(787) 767-6630
Sonia Landivar ....(787) 761-5349
Tere Lopez..(787) 783-8693
Zoraida Sanjurjo ....(787) 732-6749
Johana Santiago Soto ....(787) 786-6316

TALENT AND MODELING AGENCIES
SAN JUAN
D'Rose International ....(787) 722-5580
Eminh Child Modeling Agency ....(787) 765-0737
Fontecha Model & Talent Management......(787) 723-8193
Miramar Talent Agency ....(787) 722-3556
New Faces Talent Agency ....(787) 728-1818
Petite Kingdom Agency.............................(787) 723-3270
Protocol Institute......................................(787) 780-2955
Unica...(787) 756-7834
Vargas International Productions, Inc. ......(787) 723-2705

PUERTO RICO FILM OFFICE
SAN JUAN
Puerto Rico Film Commission ....(787) 758-4747
or (787) 754-7110

SOUTH CAROLINA

CASTING AND TALENT AGENCIES
ANDERSON
Wendy Cooper Earley ....(864) 261-7088
CAMDEN
Athena Beleos ....(803) 432-5234
CHARLESTON
Jean Arthur ....(803) 795-0806
Cheryl Bourgeois......................................(803) 974-7561
Maggie Burbank ....(803) 207-8108
Brenda Cook..(803) 722-6720
Richard Futch ....(803) 853-8738
Suzanne Manseau.....................................(803) 571-7781
Margaret Mullins ....(803) 853-8738
Chris Limehouse White.............................(803) 881-2877
CHESTER
Donna Lynn Ehrlich ....(803) 581-2278

COLUMBIA
Florette Morgan Broadwater ....(803) 738-9003
Christopher Cline ....(803) 787-7777
Tana B. Dahlquist ....(803) 732-7590
Sheila Dixon ....(803) 782-7338
Gail Groomster ....(803) 865-0204
Ernest Mitchell ....(803) 252-6575
Jenny Trussell ....(803) 796-1715
CONWAY
Beverly McDermott ....(803) 248-5867
GOOSE CREEK
Sandra M. Ballard...............................(803) 873-6119
Karen D. Keyes ....(803) 764-0248
GREENVILLE
George Corell ....(864) 299-1101
HILTON HEAD
Sallie Jane Gibble...............................(803) 689-6551
Marcia Weissman ....(803) 681-8023
JOHNS ISLAND
Marcia Chandler Rhea..........................(803) 559-1028
LITCHFIELD BEACH
Lisa Casselman..................................(800) 465-7282
MT. PLEASANT
William Walton ....(803) 856-0496
NORTH CHARLESTON
Dane T. Culp ....(803) 552-1272
NORTH MYRTLE BEACH
Bill Drake ....(803) 451-3764
ROCK HILL
Maxann Crotts ....(803) 328-2173
SUMMERVILLE
Boots E. Crowder ....(803) 871-4335
Joan Johnson ....(803) 871-0952

SOUTH CAROLINA FILM OFFICE
COLUMBIA
South Carolina Film Office ....(803) 737-0490
GREENVILLE
Upstate South Carolina Film
   & Video Association ....(803) 239-3712

SOUTH DAKOTA

CASTING/THEATER GROUPS/ARTS COUNCILS
ABERDEEN
Aberdeen Area Arts Council ....(605) 226-1557
Aberdeen Community Theater..................(605) 225-2228
BROOKINGS
Brookings Arts Council..........................(605) 692-4177
Prairie Repertory Theater ....(605) 688-4151
South Dakota Art Museum ....(605) 688-5423
CHAMBERLAIN
Missouri Valley Arts Council ....(605) 734-6298
CUSTER
Custer Area Arts Council ....(605) 673-4226
Max Merchan ....(605) 673-2652

Sun Dog Films ....(605) 673-4065
DEADWOOD
Historic Deadwood Arts Council...............(605) 578-1016
South Dakotans for the Arts ....(605) 578-1783
HOT SPRINGS
Hot Springs Area Arts Council ....(605) 745-6696
HURON
Huron Area Arts Council........................(605) 352-3173
MADISON
Madison Area Arts Council.....................(605) 256-9732
PIERRE
Pierre Players: Studio 109 ....(605) 224-6593
South Dakota Arts Council ....(605) 773-3131
RAPID CITY
Black Hills Community Theater................(605) 394-1787
Black Hills Playhouse ....(605) 394-7797
Black Hills Pow-Wow Association ....(605) 341-0925
Company "H" 7th Cavalry.......................(605) 341-0620
Dakota Artists Guild ....(605) 394-4108
Rapid City Area Arts Council ....(605) 394-4101
SIOUX FALLS
Civic Fine Arts Center..........................(605) 336-1167
Lawrence & Schiller ....(605) 338-8000
Sioux Empire Arts Council ....(605) 332-6510
Sioux Falls Community Playhouse ....(605) 336-7418
SPEARFISH
Spearfish Area Arts Council ....(605) 642-7973
STURGIS
Sturgis Area Arts Council ....(605) 347-4359
VERMILLION
Discovery Mime Theater ....(605) 624-6718
Vermillion Area Arts Council....................(605) 624-4342
WATERTOWN
Town Players......................................(605) 882-4804
Watertown Area Arts Council ....(605) 882-2076
WINNER
Winner Area Arts Council ....(605) 842-2067
WORTHING
Old Towne Theater Company ....(605) 372-4653
YANKTON
Lewis & Clark Playhouse ....(605) 665-4711
Yankton Area Arts Association ....(605) 665-9754

TALENT AND MODELING AGENCIES
RAPID CITY
Black Hills Talent & Booking ....(605) 341-5940
Inter-Mountain Entertainment Co..............(605) 348-7777
SIOUX FALLS
Bernice Johnson School of Modeling........(605) 338-3918
Professional Image by Rosemary ....(605) 334-0619

SOUTH DAKOTA FILM OFFICES
KADOKA
Badlands Film Commission ....(605) 837-2229
PIERRE
South Dakota Film Office ....(605) 773-3301
   or (800) 952-3625

TENNESSEE

CASTING OFFICES

ALCOA
George Roberts ....(423) 983-3302
ANTIOCH
MCM Casting ....(615) 361-5342
GATINBURG
Sisters Casting Services ....(615) 436-9254
KNOXVILLE
Bruce Ribble ....(423) 588-3166
Sisters Casting Services ....(423) 637-3634
MEMPHIS
Christopher Gray.......................................(901) 795-9659
Novella Smith ....(901) 526-6265
Theatrics, Etc. ....(901) 278-7454
NASHVILLE
The Casting Net ....(615) 297-0339
Chez Casting...(615) 320-6500
Jo Doster ....(615) 365-3850
Catherine Fleming.....................................(615) 269-6029
Diane Gayden ....(615) 377-3816
Jimmy Kup Casting....................................(615) 327-0181
Music City Casting ....(615) 320-9594
Kim Petrosky...(615) 226-2772
Pure Talent Casting...................................(615) 242-3811
Dorian F. Rogers ....(615) 329-2226
The Talent Connection ....(615) 831-0039
PLEASANT VIEW
Tom Webb Castings, Inc. ....(615) 780-3514

TALENT AND MODELING AGENCIES

BARTLETT
Actors & Others ....(901) 377-5527
CHATTANOOGA
Carol Daughtrey ....(423) 867-1228
FRANKLIN
Jennifer R. Corey ....(615) 794-8360
GERMANTOWN
Carvel Model & Talent Agency ....(901) 324-1122
KNOXVILLE
Stage One Productions ....(423) 693-6388
Juanell Walker ....(423) 977-8735
MEMPHIS
Colors Talent Agency, Inc..........................(901) 523-9900
Creative Communities...............................(901) 458-3900
Donna Groff Agency ....(901) 854-5561
Jackie Jason ....(901) 458-2918
Model & Talent Management, Inc. ....(901) 685-0079
People of Color Talent Agency ....(901) 372-3733
Robbins Models & Talent ....(901) 761-0211
SRO Entertainment ....(901) 680-9540
NASHVILLE
Robert D. Daugherty ....(615) 352-3172
Makin' Pictures ....(615) 269-6770
Mariena McClure ....(615) 269-8981
The Talent Connection ....(615) 831-0039

TENNESSEE FILM OFFICES

MEMPHIS
Memphis & Shelby Film Office.................(901) 527-8300
NASHVILLE
Nashville Film Office.................................(615) 259-4777
Tennessee Film Office ....(615) 741-3456
or (800) 251-8594

TEXAS

CASTING OFFICES

ALPINE
Kelly Frazier & Associates ....(800) 592-6738
AUSTIN
Kitty Blair Casting....................................(512) 708-9953
Jo Edna Boldin ....(512) 472-4247
Barbara Brinkley & Associates ....(512) 927-2299
Lone Star Casting ....(512) 339-9290
Jacqueline Powell ....(512) 477-4823
Tracy Roswell ....(512) 458-4769
Third Coast Casting ....(512) 472-4247
BRACKETVILLE
Alamo Village, Inc. ....(210) 563-2580
CARROLTON
Danette Goss Alberts................................(214) 242-1094
CORPUS CHRISTI
Pat Harrison Peraino.................................(512) 852-3203
DALLAS
Shirley Abrams ....(214) 484-6774
Lynn Ambrose...(214) 823-8702
Barbara Blanchette ....(214) 348-5190
Dallas Casting Company............................(214) 416-4455
Rody Kent ....(214) 837-3418
Screen Actors Guild/AFTRA ....(214) 363-8300
Ethel Stephens ....(214) 343-2100
EL PASO
The Talent House ....(915) 533-1945
ELMENDORF
Grace C. Hines ....(210) 621-0698
FORT WORTH
International Theater School/
Kids Who Care ....(817) 737-5437
HOUSTON
Caryn Gorme...(713) 953-7825
Lucille Graham ....(713) 522-6703
Rona Lamont...(713) 785-0465
LANCASTER
Carla James ....(214) 218-6639
SAN ANTONIO
BETH Casting ....(210) 690-1844
Marge Moody ....(210) 492-9688
Kathy Leigh Pryor ....(210) 692-3664
Republic Casting.......................................(210) 826-3615
SPRING
Ada Lang..(713) 370-8452

TALENT AND MODELING AGENCIES

AMARILLO
Anderson Agency ....(806) 374-1159

AUSTIN
Acclaim Partners Talent Agency ....(512) 323-5566
Actors Clearinghouse ....(512) 476-3412
BLVD Company, Inc......................(512) 458-BLVD (2583)
CIAO! Talents ....(512) 918-2426
db Talent ....(512) 292-1030
K Hall Agency ....(512) 476-7523
Starcraft..(512) 243-1630

CORPUS CHRISTI
Corpus Christi Reflections, Inc. ....(512) 857-5414

DALLAS
Mary Collins Agency ....(214) 360-0900
Kim Dawson Agency ....(214) 630-5161
Marquee Talent ....(214) 257-0355
Screen Actors Guild/AFTRA ....(214) 363-8300

EL PASO
The Talent House ....(915) 533-1945

FORT WORTH
Spotlight Enterprises, Inc..........................(817) 334-0800

GARLAND
The Daniel-Horne Agency ....(214) 613-7827

HOUSTON
Actors, Etc., Inc. ....(713) 785-4495
Pastorini-Bosby Talent, Inc. ....(713) 266-4488
Sherry Young/Mad Hatter Model & Talent ..(713) 266-5800

HUMBLE
Calligan's Talent Agency ....(713) 447-7572

SAN ANTONIO
Calliope Talent and Modeling Agency........(210) 804-1055
Condra/Artista Talent & Model ....(210) 492-9947
Sinclair Talent International......................(210) 614-2281

SOUTHLAKE
W. Hetzer Theatrical Productions ....(817) 481-6298

TEXAS FILM OFFICES

AMARILLO
Amarillo Film Office ....(806) 374-1497

AUSTIN
City of Austin ....(512) 499-2404
Texas Film Commission ....(512) 463-9200

DALLAS/FORT WORTH
Dallas/Fort Worth Film Commission..........(214) 621-0400

EL PASO
El Paso Film Commission ....(915) 534-0698

HOUSTON
Houston Film Commission ....(800) 365-7575
or (713) 227-3100

IRVING
Irving Texas Film Commission ....(214) 869-0303

SAN ANTONIO
San Antonio Film Commission.................(800) 447-3372

U.S. VIRGIN ISLANDS

CASTING OFFICE

ST. THOMAS
Linda Colon Casting................................(809) 772-6138

REGIONAL THEATER

ST. CROIX
Island Center Group ....(809) 778-5272

ST. THOMAS
Little Theater of the University ....(809) 776-9200

VIRGIN ISLANDS FILM OFFICE

ST. THOMAS
Virgin Islands Film Office ....(809) 774-8784
or (809) 775-1444

UTAH

CASTING OFFICES

HOLLIDAY
D.G. Casting ....(801) 485-7399

LAYTON
Galaxy Talent Agency ....(801) 544-4682

LEHI
Professional Atmosphere ....(801) 768-4016

MOAB
Griffith Production Services ....(801) 259-7937

OREM
High Angie Technologies, Inc. ....(801) 226-7498
Lasting Impressions ....(801) 224-1837

SALT LAKE CITY
ACT-1 ....(801) 277-9127
Barbizon Models......................................(801) 487-7591
The Casting Company..............................(801) 467-7544
Casting Talent Agency.............................(801) 272-9543
Central Casting ....(801) 467-4443
Cheeky Productions ....(801) 486-6386
Eastman Agency ....(801) 364-8434
Elite Media Model Talent Management ......(801) 539-1740
Hailie Talent Agency, Inc. ....(801) 532-6961
Hotshotz Talent Promotion ....(801) 355-7468
KLC Talent, Inc..(801) 364-7447
McCarty Agency ....(801) 581-9292
Models International ....(801) 942-8485
Premiere Media Artists Agency.................(801) 355-2308
Silver Screen Casting ....(801) 485-9319
Take One! Casting ....(801) 461-5843
Utah Civil War Association ....(801) 467-4209
Walker Talent Agency, Inc. ....(801) 363-6411

SOUTH JORDAN
Call Back Casting ....(801) 254-1847

ST. GEORGE
Network Casting ....(801) 628-0484

TABIONA
Gary D. Stringham ....(801) 848-5667

TALENT AND MODELING AGENCIES

LAYTON
Galaxy Talent Agency ....(801) 544-4682
OREM
Lasting Impressions ....(801) 224-1837
PROVO
Ethnic Extras ....(801) 377-3339
SALT LAKE CITY
Barbizon Models......................................(801) 487-7591
Cheeky Productions ....(801) 486-6386
Cover Agency ....(801) 364-9706
Eastman Agency/Model & Film
  Management ....(801) 364-8434
Elite Media Model Talent Management ......(801) 539-1740
Hotshotz Talent Promotion ....(801) 355-7468
KLC Talent, Inc...(801) 364-7447
McCarty Agency ....(801) 581-9292
Premiere Media Artists Agency.................(801) 355-2308
Utah Talent Find ....(801) 277-5533
Walker Talent Agency, Inc. ....(801) 363-6411
ST. GEORGE
Terry Talent & Production Services............(801) 634-9114

ACTING SCHOOLS

OREM
Lasting Impressions ....(801) 224-1837
PROVO
Brigham Young University
  Theater Department...............................(801) 378-6648
SALT LAKE CITY
Aardvark's Cabaret ....(801) 533-0927
ACT 1 ....(801) 277-9127
Deep Creek Productions ....(801) 359-0556
Eastman Agency ....(801) 364-8434
Elite Media Model Talent Management ......(801) 539-1740
Pioneer Theater ....(801) 581-6961
Premiere Media Artists Agency.................(801) 355-2308
Salt Lake Acting Company ....(801) 363-0526
Lynn Van Dam...(801) 583-0946
Walker Talent Agency, Inc. ....(801) 363-6411

REGIONAL THEATER

MOAB
Moab Community Theater...........................(801) 259-7263
PROVO
Brigham Young University
  Theater Department...............................(801) 378-6648
SALT LAKE CITY
Pioneer Theater ....(801) 581-6961
Salt Lake Acting Company ....(801) 363-0526

UTAH FILM OFFICES

KANAB
Kanab/Kane County Film Commission ......(801) 644-5033
MOAB
Moab/Monument Valley Film Commission..(801) 259-6388
OGDEN
Ogden Film Liaison...................................(801) 629-8242

PARK CITY
Park City Film Commission ....(801) 649-6100
PROVO
Central Utah Film Commission.................(801) 370-8390
SALT LAKE CITY
Utah Film Commission.............................(801) 538-8740
ST. GEORGE
Utah's Southwest Film Commission ....(801) 638-4171

VIRGINIA

CASTING AND TALENT AGENCIES

ARLINGTON
Capital Casting ....(202) 797-8621
AYLETT
A. Kay Ensing ....(804) 769-1592
BRISTOL
Karen Turner ....(540) 466-0962
CHARLOTTESVILLE
Studio for the Performing Arts ....(804) 295-5678
CHESTER
Illiya K. Clark ....(804) 768-8666
Page Sr. Brown Productions ....(804) 778-7595
CHESTERFIELD
Tracey M. Cole ....(804) 376-3660
COLONIAL HEIGHTS
Talent Group Virginia ....(804) 590-9344
FALLS CHURCH
Fox Enterprises, Inc. ....(703) 506-0335
MCLEAN
The Erickson Agency................................(703) 356-0040
MIDLOTHIAN
Marilyn's: Professional Model & Talent ....(804) 379-1946
NEWPORT NEWS
Spacer Corp...(804) 888-6229
Wright Agency/Talent and Modeling ....(804) 886-5884
NORFOLK
Talent Connection, Inc. ....(804) 624-1975
Chris Taylor Casting....................(804) 625-CAST (2278)
POWHATAN
The Type Casting ....(804) 794-5929
RICHMOND
Applause Unlimited..................................(804) 264-0299
Sherri L. Goodwin....................................(804) 321-2684
KLP Casting ....(800) 480-8031
Living History Associates, Ltd. ....(804) 265-9451
Liz Marks Casting ....(804) 740-0329
The Model Shoppe ....(804) 278-8743
Modelogic, Inc..(804) 644-1000
Monumental Talents Co. ....(804) 257-5961
Personality Plus Talent & Modeling Agency..(804) 226-2728
Richmond Modeling Registry
  & Finishing School...............................(804) 359-1331
The Stuart Agency, Inc. ....(804) 359-0999
Theatre IV ....(804) 783-1688
Uptown Talent, Inc. ....(804) 740-0307

ROANOKE
S. R. Eubank & Company ....(540) 562-4315
The Source ....(540) 342-0903
SANDSTON
Lisa Anne Brown.......................................(804) 737-0890
STAFFORD
Winning Image Models
& Talent Management ....(540) 720-4643
VIRGINIA BEACH
The Charm Associates ....(804) 490-8340
William Dean ....(804) 495-3607
Glamour Modeling & Talent Ltd...............(804) 363-8844
Evie Mansfield Modeling & Talent ....(804) 490-5990
Barbara LaFlov Simpson Unlimited ....(804) 486-6705
Norton Steinhart ....(804) 422-8535
X-TRA Talent..(804) 425-7220
WAYNESBORO
Shenandoah School of Modeling ....(540) 949-4867
WILLIAMSBURG
Talent Link, Inc..(804) 249-2232

DANCE COACHING
RICHMOND
Gwendolyn Glenn ....(804) 358-9345
Sharon Kinney ....(804) 358-6671
Arthur Murray Dance Center.....................(804) 288-3097

VIRGINIA FILM OFFICES
RICHMOND
Metro Richmond Film Office......................(804) 782-2777
Virginia Film Office...................................(804) 371-8204

WASHINGTON

CASTING OFFICES
BELLINGHAM
NorthCoast Casting...................................(206) 734-7968
LYNNWOOD
Producciones Pino ....(206) 774-7772
PORTLAND
Artists & Extras..(503) 227-4757
Extra Ones..(503) 227-4119
Pam Gilles Casting ....(503) 227-2656
L&M Ratzow Casting ....(503) 251-9050
Nannette Troutman Casting.......................(503) 235-9787
The Voices in Your Head...........................(503) 284-4565
POULSBO
Fred Saas Extra Casting ....(503) 437-FRED
SEATTLE
Casting by Walker & Company...................(206) 622-9646
Casting Real People ....(206) 322-5855
Complete Casting ....(206) 441-5058
Kalles/Levine Casting ....(206) 447-9318
On Location Casting, Inc. ....(206) 292-7010
Jodi Rothfield Casting Associates.............(206) 448-0927
Terry Terry Extras Casting ....(206) 546-4376
Heather Terzieff ....(206) 789-4417

SPOKANE
Glass International Talent Studio...............(509) 324-2862
VANCOUVER
Wendy O'Brien Casting Works ....(800) 996-5499

TALENT AND MODELING AGENCIES
BELLEVUE
Kid Biz Talent Agency ....(206) 455-8800
EDMONDS
Entco International ....(206) 670-0888
EUGENE
Talent Management Associates.................(800) 442-6505
LAKE STEVENS
S.A.M. Productions....................................(206) 355-5535
REDMOND
MDF Extras..(206) 885-5967
SEATTLE
ABC Kids, Inc..(206) 646-5440
The Actors Group ....(206) 624-9465
Kim Brooke Group Model
& Talent Management ....(206) 329-1111
Classic Promotions, Inc............................(206) 285-1901
Dramatic Artists Agency ....(206) 442-9190
Emerald City Model & Talent ....(206) 742-7340
Lola Hallowell Talent Agency ....(206) 281-4646
Heffner Talent Agency ....(206) 622-2211
Carol James Talent Agency.......................(206) 447-9191
Eileen Seals International ....(206) 448-2040
Topo Swope Talent Agency ....(206) 443-2021
Terry Terry Talent Management ....(206) 546-4376
Thompson Media Talent ....(206) 363-5555
Young Performers Studio ....(206) 989-9080
SPOKANE
Glass International Talent Studio...............(509) 324-2862

ACTING STUDIOS/TRAINING/WORKSHOPS
BELLEVUE
Kid Biz Talent Agency ....(206) 455-8800
PORTLAND
Nannette Troutman Casting.......................(503) 235-9787
SEATTLE
ABC Kids, Inc..(206) 646-5440
Brooke Group, Kim ....(206) 329-1111
Casting by Walker & Co. ....(206) 622-9646
Kalles Levine Casting ....(206) 447-9318
Thompson Media Talent ....(206) 363-5555
United Stuntman's Association ....(206) 542-1649
VoiceTech ....(206) 448-0787

WASHINGTON FILM OFFICES
SEATTLE
Seattle/Mayor's Office of Film & Video ......(206) 684-5030
Washington State Film & Video Office ......(206) 464-7148
SPOKANE
Spokane Film Office ....(509) 624-1341
TACOMA
Tacoma Film Office ....(206) 627-2836
VANCOUVER
Vancouver/Clark County Film Office.........(206) 693-1313

WEST VIRGINIA

CASTING OFFICES
CHARLESTON
Kanawha Players, Inc. ....(304) 925-5051
McHugh Management Co. ....(304) 776-6768
David Wohl ....(304) 766-3186
MORGANTOWN
Lakeview Theater......................................(304) 598-0144
SOUTH CHARLESTON
Image Associates ....(304) 345-4429
WHEELING
Kellas-Grindley Productions ....(304) 242-5201

WEST VIRGINIA FILM OFFICE
CHARLESTON
West Virginia Film Office ....(304) 558-2234
                                                    or (800) 982-3386

WISCONSIN

CASTING AND TALENT AGENCIES
DE PERE
Barbara Brebner Production Services ....(414) 336-3748
GREEN BAY
First Choice Talent and Modeling Agency..(414) 865-7916
GREENFIELD
Lori Lins Ltd. ....(414) 282-3500
MADISON
Cameron Casting ....(608) 251-3907
Dylan Scott Talent & Model Casting ....(608) 274-4944
Gered International ....(608) 238-6372
MILWAUKEE
Images International Model Management ....(414) 476-5980
Jennifer's Talent Unlimited, Inc. ....(414) 277-9440
Kandi International, Inc. ....(414) 264-8931
Arlene Wilson Management ....(414) 778-3838
RHINELANDER
Independent Contractor.............................(715) 369-1614

WISCONSIN FILM OFFICES
MADISON
Wisconsin Film Office..(608) 267-3456 or (800) 345-6947
MILWAUKEE
City of Milwaukee Film Liaison.................(414) 286-5700

WYOMING

CASTING OFFICES
CHEYENNE
Hamilton Casting ....(307) 637-5771

JACKSON
Hughes Productin Company ....(307) 733-6505
LARAMIE
University of Wyoming Theater & Dance ..(307) 766-3287
MOOSE
Extreme Locations & Real People Casting..(307) 733-8857
Suzanne Jordan ....(307) 733-8857
WILSON
Lisa Samford..(307) 733-3613

TALENT AND MODELING AGENCIES
CASPER
Casper Artist Guild ....(307) 265-2655
Casper Events Center ....(307) 235-8441
Stage III Theater Group ....(307) 234-0946
Wyoming Talent and Modeling Agency......(307) 266-6427
CHEYENNE
Aspen of the Arts ....(307) 638-9228
GILLETTE
Gillette Community Theater.......................(307) 682-1976
JACKSON
Dirty Jack's Wild West Musical Theater ....(307) 733-4775
Jackson Hole Playhouse ....(307) 733-6994
Jackson Hole Theater Company ....(307) 733-1753
Lighthouse Theater ....(307) 733-3670
LANDER
Lander Valley Arts Council ....(307) 332-4183
POWELL
Northwest College.....................................(307) 754-6306
SHERIDAN
Sheridan Civic Theater Guild ....(307) 672-9886

WYOMING FILM OFFICES
CASPER
Casper Film Group ....(307) 265-2266
CHEYENNE
Wyoming Film Commission ....(307) 777-7777
JACKSON
Jackson Hole Film Commission ....(307) 733-3316
SHERIDAN
Sheridan County Film Promotion ....(307) 672-2481

CANADA

CASTING OFFICES
ANJOU
Frap-Tek Cinema & Communication.........(514) 354-9940
BURNABY
Best Side Casting ....(604) 731-5681
Ruby Fleming ....(604) 298-0755
Principal Casting Company ....(604) 252-5988
Trish Robinson ....(604) 583-3883
CALGARY
Casting Line Canada, Inc.........................(403) 284-3799
Kymberley Kershaw Casting ....(403) 233-2278
Kroeker Casting ....(403) 285-0119
Planet Productions, Inc. ....(403) 233-2278

Leslie Swan Casting ....(403) 245-6335

CARAQUET
Renee Blanchar ....(506) 727-3900

CHARLOTTETOWN
Matsue Anderson ....(902) 583-3430
Jack MacAndrew.....................................(902) 892-4173

DAWSON CITY
Charles McLeod ....(403) 993-6352

EDMONTON
Other Agency Casting, Ltd. ....(403) 433-2700

GRAND BAY
Janet L. Clarke ....(506) 738-3693 or (506) 455-5733

HALIFAX
ACTRA Performers Guild ....(902) 420-1404
Dunsworth...(902) 423-7375
Murray James Agency..............................(902) 497-4334

KAMLOOPS
Jeff Irwin..(604) 573-3282

KELOWNA
Vivian Hughes Talent, Inc........................(604) 769-5101

MONTREAL
Agences de Mannequins.........................(514) 270-8236
Beauties ....(514) 527-8484
Ginette D'Amico Casting ....(514) 939-1442
Elite Productions....................................(514) 282-1631
Andrea Kenyon Casting Services ....(514) 948-2000
Murielle La Ferriere Casting ....(514) 272-8870
Productions Envers.................................(514) 281-7997
Lucie Robitaille, Inc. ....(514) 270-1036
Shooting PR ....(514) 527-8484

NORTH VANCOUVER
Carol Kelsay ....(604) 263-1105

NORTH YORK
Dierdre Bowen Casting, Inc. ....(416) 445-9848
Scott Mansfield Casting ....(416) 633-8790

QUEBEC
Agence Carmelli, Inc. ..(418) 694-1498 or (514) 944-9990
Casting Cauffope Enr. ....(418) 525-8497

REGINA
ACTRA ....(306) 757-0885
Beau Talent Agency................................(306) 781-8455
The Edge Models ....(306) 789-2403
Brenda McCormick Production Services ..(306) 525-0388

SASKATOON
C & E Talent & Company ....(306) 244-0443
International Casting Services ....(306) 955-2558

SURREY
Suzanne McLellan...................................(604) 535-4844

SYDNEY
Ronald Keough ....(902) 562-8839

TORONTO
Craig Alexander Casting, Inc. ....(416) 406-0811
Alliance Communications, Inc. ....(416) 927-1601
Allsorts Casting, Inc................................(416) 866-8339
Canadian Broadcasting Corp. ....(416) 205-7190
Marsha Chesley Casting...........................(416) 531-9906
Ross Clydesdale Casting ....(416) 972-6397
Comerford Casting ....(416) 691-2999
Dupere Casting......................................(416) 928-6783

Film Extras ....(416) 787-4305
Susan Forrest Casting.............................(416) 588-6696
Tina Gerussi Casting...............................(416) 534-0374
Karen Goora Casting...............................(416) 518-0660
Karen Hazzard Limited ....(416) 593-5194
Brian Levy Casting ....(416) 927-7511
Jeff Marshall & Associates ....(416) 925-8580
Masala Blue Casting ....(416) 533-6368
Media Casting..(416) 656-8893
Power House Casting ....(416) 777-0033
Nelleke Privett.......................................(416) 920-6573
Quinn Casting..(416) 631-8886
Marissa Richmond Casting......................(416) 480-1663
Rick Ruggaber Casting ....(416) 966-2030
Anne Sketchley Casting ....(416) 769-6308
Anne Tait Casting ....(416) 961-7179
Tracy Productions, Ltd. ....(416) 923-1292
Voicecasters ....(416) 777-9258
Clare Walker Casting ....(416) 929-0541
Actors Working Academy ....(604) 683-9290
Stuart Aikens Casting, Inc. ....(604) 682-1432
Michelle Allen Casting, Inc. ....(604) 732-0367

VANCOUVER
Anne Anderson's Casting, Inc. ....(604) 731-5681
Susan Brouse ....(604) 254-2008
The Casting House ....(604) 683-4300
Sandra Couldwell ....(604) 224-8920
Creative Image Casting ....(604) 684-7049
D & D Casting ....(604) 448-1691
Murdine Hirsch......................................(604) 224-1431
Sid Kozak ....(604) 987-1092
Coreen Mayrs Casting, Inc. ....(604) 682-1554
Wendy O'Brien ....(604) 686-5212
Carmen Ruiz-Laza...................................(604) 682-8295
Shoreline Studios, Inc. ....(604) 874-9979
Sue's Casting Company, Ltd. ....(604) 685-4733
Maria Skeys Taipale ....(604) 875-8871

WESTMOUNT
Ginette Goulet Casting ....(514) 932-8911

WHITEHORSE
Arlin McFarlane ....(403) 668-3735
Tina Sebert ....(403) 668-3310

WINNIPEG
Kathy Driscoll ....(204) 477-0120

YARMOUTH
David Olie...(902) 742-8150

TALENT AND MODELING AGENCIES

BEDFORD
Aspect Talent Agency ....(902) 835-1199

BURNABY
Momentum Talent Agency........................(604) 684-8831
Success Talent Management....................(604) 252-5988
Tristar Talent Company of the Stars ....(604) 252-5988

CALGARY
Dagaz Talent ....(403) 225-2536
Details Model & Talent Agency.................(403) 245-9078
Features Talent & Model Management ......(403) 251-2848
Oaks Modeling & Talent Agency..............(403) 263-1173

Patti Falconer Agencies.............................(403) 249-8222
Power Film Extras...................................(403) 245-5900
Sendos Talent ....(403) 228-6953

CONCORD
Latin Talent Agency................................(905) 738-5323

COQUITLAM
Colleen's Talent Agency ....(604) 937-5725

EDMONTON
Focus International Model & Talent ....(403) 448-4411
Mork & Ebbels Talent Agency..................(403) 455-4215
Twenty/20 Talent ....(403) 944-0095

HALIFAX
Brand Enterprises, Ltd. ....(902) 455-2681
Cassidy Group ....(902) 492-4410

KAMLOOPS
Majestic Models International...................(604) 372-1941
Shaw Talent Management ....(604) 851-0989
Charles Stuart Shea Internatinal Models....(604) 828-6774

LANGLEY
Dance Trance Dance & Talent Agency........(604) 530-6878

MAPLE RIDGE
Reel Kids Talent Agency ....(604) 465-8144

MONTREAL
Acteurs Associes.....................................(514) 525-4735
Agence Agenda.......................................(514) 866-1830
Agence Artistique Lyne Lemieux...............(514) 273-3411
Agence Artistique Micheline Saint-Laurent(514) 383-8378
Agence Constance Brown/Sybille Sasse...(514) 934-0396
Agence D'Artistes Louise Dergeron...........(514) 351-0507
Agence Gascon Wallers ....(514) 274-4607
Agence Girafe ....(514) 866-1830
Agence Marie Dupont..............................(514) 523-4970
Agence Le Petit Monde Des Artists, Inc.....(514) 845-6495
Agence Artistique Nathalie Plourde...........(514) 273-6805
Deslandes, Dickinson ....(514) 395-2411
Mungo Park, Inc. ....(514) 848-6664
Premier Role, Inc. ....(514) 844-7653

NOVA SCOTIA
Acadia Theater Department......................(902) 542-5157
Annapolis Royal Theater Co.....................(902) 532-5416
Astor Theater..(902) 354-5981

OAKVILLE
Nexus Personal Management ....(905) 847-9560

OHSWEKEN
All Nations ....(519) 445-4737

OTTAWA
A.K.A. Artists Management, Ltd. ....(613) 594-3474
Four Winds Talent Group ....(613) 234-7773
Mensour Agency, Ltd...............................(613) 241-1677

OUTREMONT
Agence Gineete Achim, Inc. ....(514) 271-3737

QUEBEC
Agence Carmelli, Inc. ....(418) 648-8040

REGINA
Liane's Model Agency..............................(306) 565-2299
Stages Model Agency..............................(306) 757-8370

RICHMOND
Reel Talent ....(604) 279-0818

SASKATOON
Pizzazz School of Personal Development ..(306) 653-3830
Portfolio Model & Talent Management ......(306) 652-6664
She Modeling Agency...............................(306) 652-7484

ST. ALBERT
Prime Talent, Inc. ....(403) 458-2676

SURREY
Kid's Only ....(604) 589-7270
Lloyd Talent ....(604) 589-7559

TORONTO
ACI Talent, Inc. ....(416) 363-7414
Armstrong Talent.....................................(416) 483-6951
Asian Action Talent ....(416) 366-8678
Christopher Banks & Associates...............(416) 530-4002
Butler Ruston Bell Talent.........................(416) 964-6660
Bookings Talent Management ....(416) 861-0655
Caldwell & Company ....(516) 465-6168
Characters Talent Agency, Ltd. ....(516) 964-8522
Core Group, The ....(416) 603-0819
Edward G. Agency Ltd. ....(416) 960-8683
Faces & Places Talent Agency ....(416) 593-5482
Fallis-McGuin Management ....(416) 920-6884
Fanian Model & Talent Management ....(416) 968-7870
Goddard & Associates Ltd., Gary ....(416) 928-0299
Great North Artists Management, Inc........(416) 925-2051
Hollywood North, Inc...............................(416) 481-1000
Jordan & Associates................................(416) 515-2028
Just for Kids ....(416) 922-3878
K.G. Talent ....(416) 368-4866
Karnick Management, David ....(416) 968-2003
Kidd-Taylor Inc. ....(416) 484-4144
Messinger Agency ....(416) 960-1000
Morris Talent Management ....(416) 929-2131
Noble Talent Management, Inc..................(416) 482-6556
Oscar & Abrams Association, Inc. ....(416) 860-1790
Phoenix Artists Management, Ltd. ....(416) 964-6464
Premiere Artists Management, Ltd............(416) 461-6868
Sherrida Personal Management ....(416) 928-2323
Sloan Agency, Inc. ....(416) 929-1915
Star Tracks ....(416) 868-6568
Starfleet Model & Talent Agency..............(416) 968-1010
Zoe Stotland Productions, Inc. ....(416) 656-0640
The Talent Group.....................................(416) 961-3304
Talent House ....(416) 960-9686
Talent Showcase ....(416) 960-6088
Talk of the Town ....(416) 482-9776
Trainco Limited ....(416) 923-2884

VANCOUVER
Anastas Talent Management ....(604) 689-9449
Baby Face Talent.....................................(604) 602-0692
Blanche's Model & Talent Management ....(604) 685-0347
John Casablancas Talent Management ......(604) 688-0261
Chameleon Talent ....(604) 688-0605
Characters..(604) 733-9800
The Commercial Connection.....................(604) 685-2443
CS Talent Agency ....(604) 683-4080
John Davies Talent ....(604) 685-2788
Echelon Talent Management ....(604) 689-3639
ETM Talent Agency ....(604) 683-6737

Excel Talent, Inc. ....(604) 683-3688
Extra's Solution Group ....(604) 669-1002
Hodgson & Company
   Artist Management, Inc. ....(604) 687-7676
Hollywood North Extras ....(604) 430-3035
International Artists Management, Ltd. ......(604) 684-3392
Just Kids Talent Agency ....(604) 683-6100
King Talent ....(604) 681-4001
LJR Talent, Inc. ....(604) 662-3393
Lucas Talent, Inc. ....(604) 685-0345
M.A. Entertainment Management ....(604) 688-6955
Moo-Vie Kidz Talent Agency ....(604) 684-9872
New Faces Talent ....(604) 689-9466
Northern Exposure
   Talent Management Group ....(604) 682-8070
Premiere Talent Agency, Inc. ....(604) 737-8068
Prime Talent ....(604) 879-6883
Richard's Agency....................................(604) 683-6484
Screen Actors Talent Agency....................(604) 669-4559
Tarlington Talent, Inc. ....(604) 688-4077
Twenty First Century Artists, Inc. ....(604) 736-8786
Universal Extras ....(604) 689-9056
Van Gogh Talent ....(604) 988-1654

VICTORIA
Coultish Talent
   and Modeling Management ....(604) 744-2388
Jager Talent Agency ....(604) 388-0511
L.D.I. Film Talent....................................(604) 361-3838
Look Model Talent ....(604) 383-3678

WILLOWDALE
Susan Charness Talent ....(416) 661-6060

WINNIPEG
Academy of Modeling
   & Self Improvement ....(204) 943-2158
BDM Talent ....(204) 488-9343
Elizabeth Diamond International ....(204) 667-7227
Marquee Entertainment & Media Comm. ..(204) 956-0535

DANCERS/CHOREOGRAPHERS
COURTICE
Theater Dance Company...........................(905) 435-0762
LANGLEY
Suzanne Zelmer ....(604) 530-6878
Sandi Croft ....(604) 899-2255
Trudi Forrest ....(604) 685-0345
Rosanne Hopkins ....(604) 929-4924
Shelly Stewart Hunt.................................(604) 683-7724
Carlos Loyola ....(604) 876-9061
Judith Marcuse ....(604) 921-8436

UNIONS AND GUILDS
MONTREAL
ACTRA ....(514) 844-3318
Alliance of Canadian Cinema TV
   & Radio Artists ....(514) 844-3318

CANADA FILM OFFICES
BURNABY
Burnaby Film Office ....(604) 294-7231

CALGARY
Calgary Film Office ....(403) 268-2771
CHARLOTTETOWN
Prince Edward Island Film Office ....(902) 368-6329
EDMONTON
Alberta Film Commission ....(403) 427-2005
Edmonton Motion Picture & TV Bureau ....(403) 424-9191
FREDERICTON
Film New Brunswick ....(506) 453-2553
HALIFAX
Nova Scotia Film Commission ....(902) 424-7185
KAMLOOPS
Thompson-Nicola Film Commission ....(604) 372-9336
KELOWNA
Okanagan-Similkameen Film Commission ..(604) 769-1834
MONTREAL
Montreal Film & TV Commission ....(514) 872-2883
Province of Quebec Film Office.................(514) 873-7768
QUEBEC CITY
Quebec City Film Bureau ....(418) 692-5338
REGINA
City of Regina Film Office ....(306) 777-7486
Locations Saskatchewan ....(306) 347-3456
TORONTO
Ontario Film Commission........................(416) 314-6858
Toronto Film Office ....(416) 392-7570
VANCOUVER
British Columbia Film Commission ....(604) 660-2732
VICTORIA
Victoria/Vancouver Island
   Film Commission ....(604) 386-3976
WHITEHORSE
Yukon Film Commission ....(403) 667-5400
WINNIPEG
Manitoba Film & Sound Development ......(204) 947-2040
YARMOUTH
South West Shore Film Commission ....(902) 742-3210
YELLOWKNIFE
Yellowknife Film Commission..................(403) 873-5772

EDUCATIONAL TOOLS

SERVICES AND PUBLICATIONS

ACADEMY PLAYERS DIRECTORY
8949 Wilshire Boulevard, Beverly Hills, CA 90211-1972. *A quarterly publication, a sourcebook of actors' photos and contacts, including a volume of child actors.*

AFTRA-SAG YOUNG PERFORMERS HANDBOOK
Info on AFTRA/SAG benefits, government regulations. Available through AFTRA/SAG offices.

BACK STAGE
P.O. Box 5017, Brentwood, TN 37024.

DANCE MAGAZINE
33 West 60th St., New York, NY 10023.

DRAMA-LOGUE
P.O. Box 480800, Hollywood, CA 90038-0771

HOLLYWOOD REPORTER
P.O. Box 480800, Hollywood, CA 90048.

ROSS REPORTS
40-29 27th Street, Long Island City, NY 11101. *Publishes comprehensive listings of advertising agencies, casting directors, talent agents, and various other offices in the United States with the emphasis on television activity.*

SAMUEL FRENCH, INC.
7623 Sunset Boulevard, Hollywood, CA 90046; (213) 876-0570
45 West 25th St., New York, NY 10001; (212) 206-8990. *Foremost publisher of plays and related materials; retail outlets carry an extensive line of reading material on all aspects of theatre, dance, film, and television.*

VARIETY (WEEKLY AND DAILY)
5700 Wilshire Boulevard, Los Angeles, CA 90036; (213) 857-6600

WORKING ACTORS GUIDE/ LA
Meni/Flattery Publications, 3006 Brookdale Road, Studio City, CA 91604. *Comprehensive directory of resources, with listing of children's acting classes and a summary of the current children's working regulations.*

SCENES AND MONOLOGUES

WINNING MONOLOGUES FOR YOUNG ACTORS
by Peg Kehret.

ENCORE! MORE WINNING MONOLOGUES FOR YOUNG ACTORS
by Peg Kehret. Meriwether Publishing Ltd., Box 7710, Colorado Springs, CO 80933.

MONOLOGUES FOR KIDS
by Ruth Mae Roddy. (Samuel French, Inc.)

SCENES FOR STUDENT ACTORS (VOLUMES I–VI).
Edited by Frances Cosgrove. (Samuel French, Inc.)

SCENES FOR TEENAGERS
by Roger Karshner. (Samuel French, Inc.)

HIGH SCHOOL MONOLOGUES THEY HAVEN'T HEARD
by Roger Karshner. (Samuel French, Inc.)

TEEN TALK, 16 CHARACTER SKETCHES FOR TEENAGE GIRLS AND BOYS
by Joyce R. Ingalls. (Samuel French, Inc.)

HITS FOR THE MISSES, 13 MONOLOGUES FOR TEENAGE GIRLS
by Joyce R. Ingalls. (Samuel French, Inc.)

PLAYS FOR CHILDREN, VOLUMES 1 AND 2
by Blanche Marvin. (Samuel French, Inc.)

SHORT PLAYS FOR YOUNG ACTORS
by Smith and Kraus, P.O. Box 127, Lyme, NH 03768.

KIDS' STUFF: AUDITION PIECES FOR CHILDREN
by Ruth Mae Roddy. (Samuel French, Inc.)

MONOLOGUES FOR KIDS
by Ruth Mae Roddy. (Samuel French, Inc.)

METHUEN BOOK OF DUOLOGUES FOR YOUNG ACTORS
(Samuel French, Inc.)

MULTICULTURAL MONOLOGUES FOR YOUNG ACTORS AND MULTICULTURAL

SCENES FOR YOUNG ACTORS
by Smith and Kraus, P.O. Box 127, Lyme, NH 03768.

RED LICORICE, MONOLOGUES FOR YOUNG PEOPLE
by Carole Tippit. (Samuel French, Inc.)

FITTING IN: MONOLOGUES FOR BOYS AND GIRLS
by Raf Mauro. (Samuel French, Inc.)

50 GREAT MONOLOGUES FOR STUDENT ACTORS
by Bill Majeski. P.O. Box 7710, Colorado Springs, CO 80933.

ALL NEW SCENES FOR THE YOUNG ACTOR
by Jill Donnellan. (Samuel French, Inc.)

CHILDSPLAY: SCENES AND MONOLOGUES
(Samuel French, Inc.)

GREAT SCENES AND MONOLOGUES FOR CHILDREN AGES 7–14.
(Samuel French, Inc.)

SAG AND AFTRA OFFICES

ATLANTA
AFTRA/SAG, 455 East Paces Ferry Road NE #334; (404) 239-0131

CHICAGO
SAG, 75 East Wacker Drive, 14th Floor; (312) 372-8081

HOLLYWOOD
AFTRA (West Coast), 6955 Hollywood Boulevard; (213) 461-8111

LAS VEGAS
SAG, 3305 West Spring Mountain Road, #60; (702) 367-8217
SAG, 2505 Mason Avenue; (702) 878-5530

LOS ANGELES
SAG, 5757 Wilshire Boulevard; (213) 954-1600

NEW YORK
AFTRA (National), 260 Madison Avenue; (212) 532-0800
SAG, 1515 Broadway, 44th Floor; (212) 944-1030

PHOENIX
AFTRA/SAG, 1616 E. Indian School Road #330; (602) 265-2712

SAN DIEGO
SAG, 7828 Convoy Court #400;
(619) 297-0201

AGENCIES THAT DEAL WITH THE RULES, REGULATIONS, AND LAWS GOVERNING EMPLOYMENT OF MINORS AS PERFORMERS

ALABAMA
Department of Industrial Relations;
Montgomery; (205) 242-8265

ALASKA
Labor Standards and Safety
Division; Anchorage;
(907) 264-2435

ARIZONA
State Labor Department; Phoenix;
(602) 255-4515

ARKANSAS
Department of Labor; Little Rock;
(501) 682-4505

CALIFORNIA
Division of Labor Standards;
Van Nuys; (818) 901-5312

CANADA
ACTRA; Calgary; (403) 228-3123

COLORADO
Department of Labor and Industry;
Denver; (303) 894-7541

CONNECTICUT
Department of Labor; Wethersford;
(203) 566-4550

DELAWARE
Department of Education; Dover;
(302) 736-4645

DISTRICT OF COLUMBIA
D.C. Film Office; Washington;
(202) 727-6600

FLORIDA
Division of Labor; Tallahassee;
(904) 488-8396

GEORGIA
Department of Labor; Atlanta;
(404) 656-3017

HAWAII
Department of Labor Relations;
Honolulu; (808) 548-4071

IDAHO
Department of Labor; Boise;
(209) 334-2327

ILLINOIS
Department of Labor; Chicago;
(312) 793-2800

INDIANA
Bureau of Child Labor;
Indianapolis; (317) 232-2675

IOWA
Division of Labor; Des Moines;
(515) 281-3606

KANSAS
Kansas Film Commission; Topeka;
(913) 296-4927

KENTUCKY
Kentucky Film Commission;
Frankfort; (502) 564-3456

LOUISIANA
Office of Labor; Baton Rouge;
(504) 342-7804

MAINE
Bureau of Labor Standards;
Augusta; (207) 289-3331

MARYLAND
Department of Licensing and
Regulation; Baltimore;
(301) 659-2261

MASSACHUSETTS
Department of Labor; Boston;
(617) 727-3478

MICHIGAN
Department of Labor; Lansing;
(517) 322-1825

MINNESOTA
Department of Labor and Industry;
St. Paul; (612) 296-2282

MISSISSIPPI
Miss. Film Office; Jackson;
(601) 359-3297

MISSOURI
Department of Labor; Jefferson
City; (505) 827-6875

MONTANA
Department of Labor; Helena;
(406) 444-5600

NEBRASKA
Department of Labor; Omaha;
(402) 554-3997

NEVADA
Department of Labor; Carson City;
(702) 885-4850

NEW HAMPSHIRE
Department of Labor; Manchester;
(603) 271-3176

NEW JERSEY
Department of Labor; Trenton;
(609) 292-2337

NEW MEXICO
State Labor Commission; Santa Fe
(505) 827-9870

NEW YORK
Human Resources Department;
New York; (212) 553-5681

NORTH CAROLINA
Department of Labor; Raleigh;
(919) 733-2152

NORTH DAKOTA
Department of Labor; Bismarck;
(701) 224-2660

OHIO
Department of Industrial Relations;
Columbus; (614) 466-3271

OKLAHOMA
Department of Labor; Oklahoma
City; (405) 528-1500

OREGON
Bureau of Labor and Industry;
Portland; (503) 731-4074

PENNSYLVANIA
Bureau of Labor Standards;
Harrisburg; (717) 787-4670

RHODE ISLAND
Department of Labor; Providence;
(401) 457-1800

SOUTH CAROLINA
Department of Labor; Columbia;
(803) 734-9612

SOUTH DAKOTA
Department of Labor; Pierre;
(605) 773-3681

TENNESSEE
Department of Labor; Nashville;
(615) 741-2582

TEXAS
Department of Labor Standards;
Austin; (512) 475-7003

U.S. VIRGIN ISLANDS
Department of Labor; St. Thomas;
(809) 776-3700

UTAH
Utah Industrial Commission; Salt
Lake City; (801) 533-5874

VERMONT
Department of Labor; Montpelier;
(802) 828-2157

VIRGINIA
Department of Labor; Richmond;
(804) 780-2386

WASHINGTON
Department of Labor; Olympia;
(206) 956-5311

WEST VIRGINIA
Department of Labor; Charleston;
(304) 348-7890

WISCONSIN
Department of Labor; Madison;
(608) 266-6860

WYOMING
Labor Commission; Cheyenne;
(307) 777-7262

TALENT AGENCY SERVICES CONTRACT

GENTLEMEN:

1. I hereby employ you as my sole and exclusive representative, agent, and manager throughout the world for a term of years commencing with the date hereof.

2. Your duties hereunder shall be as follows: to use all reasonable efforts to procure employment of my services as a writer, composer, editor, author, lyricist, musician, artist, performer, designer, consultant, cameraman, technician, director, producer, associate producer, supervisor, or executive and in any other capacity in the entertainment, literary, and related fields, to advise, counsel, or direct me in the development of my professional career. The aforesaid duties outside of the continental United States may, at your election, be performed by anyone else appointed by you.

3. You hereby accept this employment and agree to perform the services specified herein. You shall have the right to render your services to other persons, firms, and corporations, either in a capacity in which you are hereby employed by me or otherwise. However, I agree not to employ any other person, firm, or corporation to act for me in the capacity for which I have engaged you. I hereby represent and warrant that I am free to enter into this agreement and I do not have and will not have any contract or obligation which will conflict with it.

4. I agree to pay you as and when received by me, a sum equal to ten percent (10%) (fifteen percent [15%] with respect to any and all employment or contracts for "one-nighter" engagements or in the concert field) of the gross compensation as hereinafter defined, earned, or received by me, whether during the term hereof or thereafter, while I am employed or compensation is received as aforesaid upon any contracts or employment, now in existence or entered into or negotiated for during the term hereof, even though payments thereon may become due or payable after the expiration of the term hereof, and upon modifications, renewals, additions, substitutions, supplements, or extensions of or to such contracts or employment, whether negotiated for during or after the term hereof. You shall be obligated to continue to serve me and perform obligations after the expiration or termination of the term hereof with respect to any employment contract and to modifications, renewals, additions, substitutions, supplements, and extensions thereof and to any employment requiring my services on which such compensation is based. "Gross compensation" is defined to include all forms of compensation, money, things of value, and income (including salaries, earnings, fees, royalties, bonuses, gifts, monetary and nonmonetary consideration, securities, and shares of profits) directly or indirectly earned or received by me, or any other person, firm, or corporation in my behalf, or in which I have an interest, from my services or employment or both, and irrespective of whether the term of any such contract or employment shall be effective or continue before, during, or after the term hereof and whether or not such contract or employment was procured by you or by anyone else, and also shall include all forms of compensation, money, things of value, and income, directly or indirectly earned or received from any form of advertising or commercial tie-ups using my name, likeness, or voice. The sums due you hereunder shall be payable to you immediately upon the payment of any gross compensation to me.

5. No breach of the agreement by you or failure by you to perform the terms hereof, which breach or failure to perform would otherwise be deemed a material breach of this agreement, shall be considered a material breach of this agreement, unless within ten (10) days after I acquire knowledge of such breach or failure to perform or of facts sufficient to put me upon notice of any such breach or failure to perform I serve written notice upon you of such breach or failure to perform and you do not cure said breach or failure to perform within a further period of ten (10) days after receipt of said written notice by you.

6. If I fail to obtain a bona fide offer of employment from a responsible employer in the fields of endeavor above specified during a period in excess of four (4) consecutive months during the term hereof, during all of which time I am ready, able, and willing to accept employment, either party hereto shall have the right to terminate this contract by a notice in writing to such effect sent to the other party by registered mail, to the last known address of such party, provided, however, that such right shall be deemed waived by me and any exercise thereof by me shall be ineffective if after the expiration of any such four (4)-month period and prior to the time I exercise such right, I have received a bona fide offer of employment from a responsible employer, and provided further that such termination shall not affect your rights or my obligations under paragraph 4 of this contract with respect to contracts or employment in existence or entered into or negotiated for prior to the effective date of such termination.

7. Insofar as this agreement refers to any employment in California, controversies arising between us under the Labor Code of the State of California, and the rules and regulations for the enforcement thereof, shall be referred to the Labor Commissioner of the State of California, as provided in Section 1700.44 of said Labor Code, save and except to the extent that the laws of the State of California now or hereafter in force may permit the reference of any such controversy to any other person or group of persons.

8. This instrument sets forth the entire agreement between us. It shall not become effective until accepted and executed by you. As an inducement to you to execute this agreement, I hereby represent and warrant that no statement, promise, representation, or inducement except as herein set forth has been made on your behalf, or by any of your employers or representatives, and I acknowledge that I have been informed that your acceptance and execution hereof shall be in reliance on the representation and warranty made herein. This agreement may not be changed, modified, waived, or discharged in whole or in part except by an instrument in writing signed by you and myself. This agreement shall inure to the benefit of and be binding upon you and myself and your and my respective heirs, distributees, executors, administrators, and assigns, and you shall have the right to assign this agreement to any parent, subsidiary, affiliate, or successor entity or, pursuant to any reorganization, consolidation, combination, or merger, to any corporation, partnership, or other form. Should any provision of this agreement be void or unenforceable, such provision shall be deemed omitted and this agreement with such provision omitted shall remain in full force and effect.

9. Wherever the context so requires, the masculine gender shall include and apply to all genders, and the singular shall apply to and include, as well, the plural.

Very truly yours,

AGREED AND ACCEPTED: _____(Name)

TALENT AGENCY: _____(Address)

By_____

EXCLUSIVE PERSONAL MANAGEMENT AGREEMENT

GENTLEMEN:

I desire to obtain your advice, counsel, and direction in the development and enhancement of my artistic and theatrical career. The nature and extent of the success or failure of my career cannot be predetermined and it is therefore my desire that your compensation be determined in such manner as will permit you to accept the risk of failure and likewise benefit to the extent of my success.

In view of the foregoing, we have agreed as follows:

1. Term. I do hereby engage you as my sole and exclusive worldwide personal manager in all areas of the entertainment industry for an initial period of   year(s), commencing on the date hereof. The initial period, as it may be hereafter extended for any reason, is hereinafter referred to as "the term."

2. Services. As and when requested by me during and throughout the term hereof, you agree to advise and counsel me (a) in the selection of literary, artistic, and musical material; (b) concerning publicity, public relations, and advertising; (c) with respect to the adoption of proper format for presentation of my artistic talents and in the determination of proper style, mood, setting, and characterization in keeping with my talents; (d) in the selection of artistic talent to assist, accompany, or embellish my artistic presentation; (e) with regard to general practices in the entertainment and amusement industry; and (f) with respect to matters of which you may have knowledge concerning compensation and privileges extended for similar artistic values.

3. Authority. During the term of this contract and any extensions, renewals, substitutions, or modifications thereof, you are irrevocably authorized and empowered by me to act on my behalf as my attorney-in-fact, in your discretion, to do the following: (a) approve and permit any and all publicity and advertising; (b) approve and permit the use of my name, photograph, likeness, voice, sound effects, caricatures, and literary, artistic, and musical materials for purposes of advertising and publicity and in the promotion and advertising of any and all products and services; (c) execute for me in my name and/or on my behalf any and all agreements, documents, and contracts for my services, talents, and/or artistic, literary, and musical materials, and exercise, on my behalf, any rights to examine and/or audit books and records which I have in connection therewith; (d) collect and receive any and all compensation or other income or payments, as well as endorse my name upon and cash any and all checks, payable to me for my services, talents, and literary and artistic materials, and retain therefrom all sums owing to you; (e) engage as well as discharge and/or direct for me, and in my name, accountants, public relations firms, and lawyers, as well as other persons, firms, and corporations who may be retained in connection with my artistic business and financial affairs.

I shall perform all agreements and contracts entered into by you for the rendition of my services (as herein specified) pursuant to your authority hereunder. I shall also execute all documents and/or do such acts as are necessary and appropriate to effectuate the intent of this contract.

4. Loans and Advances. You are not required to make any loans or advances to me for my account, but in the event you do so, I shall repay them promptly, and I hereby authorize you to deduct the amount of any such loans or advances from any sums you may receive for my account under this contract or any other agreements between me and you or your affiliates.

5. Artist's Career. I agree at all times to devote myself to my career and to do all things necessary and desirable to promote my career and earnings therefrom. I shall at all times utilize proper theatrical or other employment agencies to obtain engagements and employment for me. I shall not sign any agreements concerning my services or my business affairs without first consulting you for your advice. I shall instruct any theatrical agency engaged by me, any record company with which I may hereafter sign, and all other persons, firms, or corporations utilizing my services to remit to you all monies that may become due me.

6. Not an Employment Agent. You have advised me that you are not an "artists' manager," but active solely as a personal manager; that you are not licensed as an "artists' manager" under the Labor Code of the State of California, as an employment agent under the Business and Professions Code of the State of California, or as a theatrical employment agency under the General Business Law of the State of New York; you have at all times advised me that you are not licensed to seek or obtain employment or engagements for me and that you do not agree to do so; and you have made no representations to me, either oral or written, to the contrary. Notwithstanding the foregoing, however, if you become an artist's manager or a theatrical employment agent at any time during the term of this contract, this contract shall, at your option, be superseded and supplemented by an artist's manager agreement or a theatrical employment agency agreement between you and me, upon the same terms and conditions as herein set forth, plus any additional rights accorded, subject to any additional obligations and limitations imposed on an artist's manager or a theatrical employment agent pursuant to either the California Labor Code or the General Business Law of New York, as the case may be, and the decisional and statutory law of the States of California and New York, as the case may be, as they shall be from time to time amended or revised.

7. Scope. This contract shall not be construed to create a partnership between us. I understand that you are acting hereunder as an independent contractor and you may appoint or engage any and all other persons, firms, and corporations throughout the world in your discretion to perform any or all of the services which you have agreed to perform hereunder. Your services hereunder are not exclusive. You may at all times render the same or similar services for others, and you may engage in any and all other business activities. You shall only be required to render reasonable services which are called for by this contract as and when reasonably requested by me, and in no event shall you be deemed to be in default hereunder unless and until

(a) I shall have given to you a written notice by certified mail, describing the exact service which I require on your part, and

(b) you shall thereafter fail, for a period of fifteen (15) consecutive business days from the date of your receipt of such notice, to commence the rendition of the particular service required and which is called for by this contract; provided, however, that if such default cannot, by its nature, be completely cured in fifteen (15) days, you shall only be required to initiate such steps within said fifteen (15)-day period as are necessary to remedy such default; provided such default is remedied in due course thereafter. In the event that you do not cure such default as described herein, then my sole and exclusive remedy shall be to terminate this contract by written notice to you, which must be sent within thirty (30) days after the expiration of said fifteen (15)-day period, and you shall have no further liability to me.

You shall not be required to travel or to meet with me at any particular place or places except in your discretion and following arrangements for costs and expenses of such travel as hereinafter set forth.

8. Compensation. I agree to pay to you, as and when received by me or on my behalf, and during and throughout the term hereof, a sum equal to _____ percent (___%) of any and all gross monies or other considerations which I may earn, receive, acquire, or become entitled to, directly or indirectly, as a result of my activities in and throughout the worldwide entertainment industries, including such activities pursuant to engagements, employments, and agreements now in existence. I likewise agree to pay you a similar sum following the expiration of the term hereof upon and with respect to any and all engagements, contracts, and agreements entered into or negotiated for prior to or during the term hereof relating to any of the foregoing, and upon any and all extensions, modifications, amendments, renewals, and substitutions thereof, and upon any resumptions of such engagements, contracts, and agreements which may have been discontinued and resumed within one (1) year after discontinuance. Agreements entered into within six (6) months after the term hereof on terms similar or reasonably comparable to any offer made during the term hereof, from or through the same offeror or any person, firm, or corporation directly or indirectly connected with such offeror, shall be deemed to have been entered into during the term hereof.

As used herein, the term "entertainment industries" shall include, without limitation, any and all aspects of the entertainment, amusement, music, recording, publishing, television, motion picture, nightclub, concert, radio, literary, and theatrical industries, and shall also include any and all forms of advertising, endorsements, merchandising, or other exploitations using my name, photograph, voice, sound effects, likeness, caricatures, talents, or materials. The term "activities" shall include, without limitation, my activities in any capacity whatsoever in the entertainment industries, whether as a live performer, recording artist, musician, singer, composer, writer, publisher, arranger, packager, owner of entertainment packages, actor, producer, author, director, cameraman, technician, consultant, or otherwise, and shall also include the use of my name, voice, likeness, etc., as aforesaid. The term "gross monies or other considerations" shall include, without limitation, salaries, earnings, fees, royalties, residuals, repeat and/or rerun fees, gifts, bonuses, shares of profit, shares of stock, partnership interests, percentages, and the total amount paid for a package television or radio program (live or recorded), motion picture, or other entertainment package, any and all sums resulting from my activities in the entertainment industries, and uses of the results and proceeds thereof, payments for termination of my activities, payments to refrain from any such activities, and payments in connection with the settlement or other disposition of any dispute concerning said activities, which are earned or received directly or indirectly by me or my heirs, executors, administrators, or assigns, or by any other person, firm, or corporation on my behalf, without deduction of any nature or sort. As to the proceeds of any motion picture, phonograph record, film, tape, wire, transcription, recording, or other reproduction or result of my activities in the entertainment industries that is created in whole or in part prior to or during the term hereof (or thereafter pursuant to an engagement, contract, or agreement subject to commission hereunder), your commission shall continue for so long as any of same are used, sold, leased, or otherwise exploited, whether during or after the term hereof. In the event I receive, as all or part of my compensation for activities hereunder, stock or the right to buy stock in any corporation, or I become the packager or owner of all or part of or rights in an entertainment property, whether as individual proprietor, stockholder, partner, joint venturer, or otherwise, your percentage shall apply to my said stock, right to buy stock, individual proprietorship, partnership, joint venture, or other form of interest, and you shall be entitled to your percentage share thereof. Should I be required to make any payment for such interest, you will pay your percentage share of such payment, unless you do not want your percentage share thereof.

9.   Expenses. All expenses other than your normal office operating expenses, actually incurred by you, including, without limitation, long-distance telephone calls, messenger fees, travel expenses, and other disbursements attributable to me and promotion and publicity expenses, shall be paid by me. In the event your presence is required outside of the metropolitan area of the City of Los Angeles, I agree that I will pay for the expenses incurred by you; such expenses will consist of first-class traveling expenses, and first-class living accommodations and requirements. All such expenses incurred on behalf of me are to be paid immediately by me upon the presentation of an itemized expense sheet or deducted by you from my gross monies or other considerations earned hereunder.

10. Life Insurance. You shall have the right during the term hereof to obtain life insurance on my life at your sole cost and expense, with you being the sole beneficiary thereof. I agree to fully cooperate in connection with the obtaining of same and to submit to a physical examination and complete any and all documents necessary or desirable in respect thereof. I hereby acknowledge that neither I nor my estate shall have any right to claim the benefits of any such policy obtained by you.

11. Publicity. You shall have the right to advertise and publicize yourself as my personal manager and representative.

12. Agency Coupled With an Interest. I understand and agree that the interest and compensation that you shall have and receive hereunder shall be a continuing interest and shall not be revocable at my pleasure; that this contract, being both a management contract and power of attorney, is intended to create an agency coupled with an interest, and therefore is irrevocable during the term hereof, and your appointment and engagement as personal representatives and manager and your right to receive the compensation as provided for by this contract are the inducements for you to enter into this contract and to render the services hereunder.

13. Conflicting Interest—Waiver of Commission When Employed By You.

(a) From time to time during the term of this contract, you or other persons or entities owned and/or controlled, directly or indirectly, by you, or your partners, shareholders, officers, directors, and employees, whether acting alone or in association with others, may package an entertainment program in which I am employed as an artist, or may act as the entrepreneur or promoter of an entertainment program in which I am employed as an artist, or may employ me in connection with the production of phonograph records, or as a songwriter, composer, arranger, or otherwise in connection with the creation of literary or musical works. Such activity on your or their part shall not be or be deemed to be a breach of this contract or of your fiduciary obligations and duties to me, and shall not in any way affect your right to commissions hereunder in all instances not covered by the following exceptions. However, you shall not be entitled to commissions from me in connection with any gross monies or other considerations derived by me (i) from any employment or agreement whereunder I am employed by you or by any person, firm, or corporation owned or controlled by you or by any of your partners, shareholders, officers, directors, or employees, whether you (or such person, firm, or corporation or such partner, shareholder, officer, director, or employee) are acting as (A) the package agent for the entertainment program in which I am so employed, (B) my music or literary publisher, (C) my record company, or otherwise, or (ii) from the sale, license, or grant of any literary or musical rights to you or any person, firm, or corporation owned or controlled by you; provided, however, that in any circumstance where you are not entitled to a management commission hereunder by reason of your being the "packager" or packaging agent of any entertainment program or project, you shall be entitled, in lieu thereof, to a packaging commission equal to ten percent (10%) of any gross monies or other consideration paid as a license fee or otherwise in respect of said entertainment program or project. Further, you shall not render nor shall you be obligated to render the personal management services contemplated in this contract with respect to the aforesaid noncommissionable employment, agreements, sales, licenses, and grants, in connection with which I shall have the right to seek and retain independent management advice.

(b) Nothing contained in paragraph 13(a) hereof shall be construed to excuse me from the payment of commissions upon gross monies or other considerations derived by me from my employment or any sale, license, or grant of rights in connection with any entertainment program, phonograph record, or other matter merely because you or any of your partners, shareholders, officers, directors, or employees are also employed in connection therewith as a producer, director, conductor; or in some other management or supervisorial capacity, but not as my employer, grantee, or licensee.

14. Suspension. You shall have the right, at your election, to suspend the operation of this contract if for any reason whatsoever I am unable or unwilling to render my services in the entertainment industries. Such suspension shall commence upon written notice to me and shall last for the duration of any such unavailability or unwillingness to render services.

At your election, a period of time equal to the duration of such suspension shall be added to the term of this contract. In addition, if I fail to render my services in the entertainment industries as aforesaid, then you may, in addition to other remedies provided for herein, terminate this contract upon written notice to me.

15. Arbitration. In the event of any dispute under or relating to the terms of this contract, or the breach, validity, or legality thereof, it is agreed that the same shall be submitted to arbitration, and judgment upon the award rendered by the arbitrator(s) may be entered in any court having jurisdiction thereof. In the event of litigation or arbitration the prevailing party shall be entitled to recover any and all reasonable attorney's fees and other costs incurred in the enforcement of the terms of this contract or for the breach thereof. This arbitration provision shall remain in full force and effect notwithstanding the nature of any claim or defense hereunder.

16. Assignment. You shall have the right to assign this Agreement to an individual who is a stockholder, or to a partnership at least one of whose partners is you or a stockholder of yours, or to a corporation owned or controlled by you or to another corporation which acquires all or substantially all of your stock or assets. However, this Agreement shall be personal to me and I shall not have the right to assign it to any other person.

17. Other Entities. I shall cause any corporation, partnership, trust, or other business entity which I now own or control or may hereafter own or control or in which I have a direct or indirect interest of any nature or sort, or which is directly or indirectly controlled by me or under the common control of me and others (hereinafter "firm") and which firm has a right to my services, to enter into an agreement with you on the same terms and conditions as contained in this agreement, and I agree that all gross monies or other considerations directly or indirectly earned or received by such firm in connection with my activities in the entertainment industries shall be subject to your commission hereunder. Any agreement with such firm shall provide that such firm has a right to furnish my services on the terms and conditions set forth in this contract and the firm shall become a party to this contract. I shall personally guarantee the obligation of any such firm.

18. Warranties and Representations. I represent and warrant that I am wholly free to enter into this contract and to grant the rights herein granted to you and that I am not a party to any agreements, and that I do not have any obligations, which conflict with any of the provisions hereof. I shall indemnify and hold you harmless from any and all claims, judgments, costs, expenses, damages, and liabilities (including reasonable attorney's and accountant's fees) resulting from the breach by me of any of the agreements, warranties, and/or representations made by me hereunder or the failure by me to perform agreements entered into pursuant to the provisions hereof.

19. Right to Legal Counsel. I represent and warrant that I have been advised of my right to seek legal counsel of my own choosing in connection with the negotiation and execution of this contract.

20. Applicable Law. This contract shall be deemed to be executed in the State of

Washington and shall be construed in accordance with the laws of said State. In the event any provision hereof shall for any reason be invalid, illegal, or unenforceable, then such provision shall be deemed amended only to the extent necessary to eliminate such invalidity, illegality, or unenforceability and in any such event, the same shall not affect the validity of the remaining portion and provisions hereof; however, if any such invalidity, illegality, or unenforceability materially affects your right to compensation hereunder, you may at any time thereafter terminate the term of this contract. In the event this entire contract is for any reason deemed to be invalid, illegal, or unenforceable, you shall be entitled to the reasonable value of your services and to retain all compensation paid to you hereunder as the reasonable value of said services.

21. Group Provisions. If I am executing this contract together with others as members of a group, this contract shall nevertheless be deemed between you, on the one hand, and me, individually, as well as each of the undersigned, collectively, and each of us shall be jointly and severally liable for the performance of each and all of our separate and collective obligations hereunder. All provisions hereof shall apply to each of the undersigned, individually and collectively, as if each of the undersigned has executed separate contracts with you, and regardless of the name or names under which any or all of the undersigned may perform. If this contract is terminated for any reason whatsoever as to any of the undersigned, it is agreed that this contract shall remain in full force and effect as to each of the undersigned with whom this contract is not terminated.

22. Notices. All notices hereunder shall be sent by prepaid telegram or cablegram, or by certified or registered mail, return receipt requested, postage prepaid, and if to you, shall be sent to the address above with a copy to   , and if to me, shall be sent to the address below, unless we notify each other as provided herein that notices shall be sent to a different address.

23. Miscellaneous. This contract constitutes the entire agreement between you and me relating to the subject matter hereof, all previous understandings, whether oral or written, having been merged herein. The headings of the paragraphs hereof are for convenience only and shall not be deemed to limit or in any way affect the scope, meaning, or intent of this contract or any portion hereof. This contract may not be changed or modified, or any covenant or provision hereof waived, except by an agreement in writing, signed by the party against whom enforcement of the change, modification, or waiver is sought.

If the foregoing meets with your approval, please indicate your acceptance and agreement by signing in the space herein below provided.

Very truly yours,

———————————————
(Addressee)

ACCEPTED AND AGREED TO:

———————————
(Company)

By———————————

INDEX

A

Aames, Willie, 15-16
acting, training for, 38-40
  workshops, 37
Actors' Equity Association, 161
advertising agency producers, 99
African-Americans, 123
agents. See also modeling agencies
  breakdowns sent to, 75-76
  casting directors and, 75-76
  checking out, 55
  contracts with, 60-61
  do's and don'ts of working with,
    63-64
  fees, 53
  first meeting with, 56
  functions of, 53
  getting, 55-58
  getting interviews with, 55-58
  need for, 55
  photos sent to, 55-56
  qualifications of, 53
  venting gripes through, 97
age of child, and child's size, 22
Alliance of Canadian Cinema,
  Television, and Radio Artists
  (ACTRA), 37
ambition, parents'. See motivation, of
  parents
American Federation of Television and
  Radio Artists (AFTRA), 36,
    161, 162
  benefits of membership in, 163-164
  jurisdiction, 163
American Guild of Musical Artists
  (AGMA), 161
answering machines, 74
Arngrim, Alison, 169-176
  interview with, 170-176
Associated Actors and Artists of
  America, 161
attorneys, 61
audiences, experience in front of, 37

auditions, 60
  attitude toward, 84-85
  ballet, 113
  callbacks, 77
  for commercials, 77, 78-80
  final calls, 78
  for musicals, 81-82
  process, 75-77
  readiness for, 74
  sense of perspective about, 84-85,
    89-90
  stage, 81-83
  what to expect at, 76-77

B

babies, 125-130
  in commercials, 127
  filming, 127-128
  legal workday, 166-167
  nurses required for, 167
  twins, 128-129
Back Stage, 36
ballet, 111-115
  auditions, 113
  decline of interest in, 111-112
  ideal body for, 112
  marketing child's talent, 113-115
  opportunities in, 112
  training for, 112-113, 113-114
ballet companies, acceptance by,
  113-114
Beery, Wallace, 142-143
Berle, Milton, 13
Bernstein, Arthur L. and Lillian,
  141-143
Brady Bunch, The, 96
Brando, Marlon, 14
breakdowns, 75-76
business managers, 132-138
  choosing, 134-136
  fees, 136
  functions of, 133-134
  interview with, 135-136
  why needed, 132-134